ISIS

ISIS

INSIDE THE ARMY OF TERROR

MICHAEL WEISS
HASSAN HASSAN

Regan Arts.

NEW YORK

Regan Arts.

Regan Arts
65 Bleecker Street
New York, NY 10012

First Regan Arts paperback edition, February 2015.

Library of Congress Control Number: 2015930621

ISBN 978-1-941393-57-4

Cover art © Abaca

Printed in the United States of America

10 9 8 7 6 5 4

CONTENTS

INTRODUCTION   ix

1 FOUNDING FATHER   1
ABU MUSAB AL-ZARQAWI'S JIHAD

2 SHEIKH OF THE SLAUGHTERERS   20
AL-ZARQAWI AND AL-QAEDA IN IRAQ

3 THE MANAGEMENT OF SAVAGERY   40
BIRTH OF THE ISLAMIC STATE OF IRAQ

4 AGENTS OF CHAOS   48
IRAN AND AL-QAEDA

5 THE AWAKENING   68
IRAQIS TURN ON ISI

6 WITHDRAWAL SYMPTOMS   82
ISI AND MALIKI WAIT OUT
THE UNITED STATES

7 ASSAD'S PROXY   99
SYRIA AND AL-QAEDA

8 REBIRTH   114
ISI UNDER ABU BAKR AL-BAGHDADI

9 REVOLUTION BETRAYED 131
JIHAD COMES TO SYRIA

10 CONVERTS AND
"FIVE-STAR JIHADISTS" 153
PROFILES OF ISIS FIGHTERS

11 FROM TWITTER TO *DABIQ* 170
RECRUITING THE NEW MUJAHIDIN

12 DIVORCE 179
AL-QAEDA SPLITS FROM ISIS

13 SHAKEDOWN OF THE SHEIKHS 200
ISIS CO-OPTS THE TRIBES

14 AL-DAWLA 210
THE ISLAMIC "STATE"

EPILOGUE 236

NOTES 243

ACKNOWLEDGMENTS 269

For Amy and Ola,
who have put up with ISIS
(and us)
more than any spouses
ever ought to

INTRODUCTION

In late 2011, Abdelaziz Kuwan approached his Syrian uncle to connect him to Riad al-Asaad, a colonel in the Syrian Air Force and one of the earliest military defectors from the dictatorship of Bashar al-Assad. Abdelaziz, a sixteen-year-old teenager from Bahrain, wanted to join the armed rebellion in Syria, but his parents forbade him from going. So he defied them.

In early 2012, he flew first to Istanbul and then, as so many other foreign fighters have done, took a thirteen-hour bus ride to the southern Turkish border town of Reyhanli. From there, he crossed into the Syrian province of Aleppo, the northern countryside that had by then completely fallen into the hands of the armed anti-Assad rebellion. Abdelaziz fought for moderate rebel factions for several weeks before deeming them too corrupt and ineffective. Then he migrated through various Islamist brigades, joining first Ahrar al-Sham and then Jabhat al-Nusra, which later revealed itself to be the al-Qaeda franchise in Syria. Having earned a reputation as a fearless and religiously devout fighter, Abdelaziz nonetheless grew disenchanted with his Islamist comrades and faced pressure from his family to return to Bahrain. He did at the end of 2012. Once home, Abdelaziz's mother promptly confiscated his passport.

"I walk in the streets [of Bahrain] and I feel imprisoned," Abdelaziz told the authors a year later, still pining for his days as a holy warrior. "I feel tied up. It's like someone is always watching me. This world means nothing to me. I want to be free. I want to go back. People are giving their lives, that's the honorable life."

Abdelaziz's family had moved to Bahrain from eastern Syria in the 1980s. His parents provided him with the means to lead a decent life. "His father raised him well," one relative recalled. "He did not make him need anyone and wanted him to be of a high social status." The relative added that Abdelaziz was "quiet," "refined," and "always behaved like a man."

Abdelaziz stayed in Bahrain for three months before he managed to persuade his mother to give him back his passport. He left for Syria three days later. Once he arrived, Abdelaziz joined the Islamic State of Iraq and al-Sham (ISIS), which was then rising in prominence as one of the most disciplined and well-organized jihadist groups in Syria. Abdelaziz later said that in his last few months in Bahrain he made the decision to join ISIS after speaking with "some of the brothers" in Syria via Skype. His prior experience with other Islamist factions ideologically similar to ISIS was an advantage in joining one that was dominated by foreign fighters. Abdelaziz rose through the ranks of ISIS, first becoming a coordinator among local emirs and other rebel groups, then delivering messages and oral agreements on behalf of his leader. When ISIS seized enormous swaths of territory in both Syria and Iraq in the summer of 2014, Abdelaziz was promoted to a security official overseeing three towns near the Syrian-Iraqi border town of Albu Kamal, long a portal between the two countries for men like him.

In ISIS, Abdelaziz discovered new things about himself. He learned that he was violent, brutal, and determined. He beheaded enemies. He kept a Yazidi girl in his house as a *sabiyya,* or sex slave. She was his prize for his participation in battles against the Iraqi Kurdish peshmerga forces and other Kurdish militias in Sinjar, Iraq, near the Syrian border. According to ISIS's propaganda magazine, *Dabiq,* one-fifth of the sex slaves taken from Sinjar was distributed to ISIS's central leadership to do with as it so chose; the remainder was divided amongst the rank and file, like Abdelaziz, as the spoils of war.

Abdelaziz showed us a picture of his sabiyya. She was in her late teens. She "belonged" to Abdelaziz for about a month before she was handed off to other ISIS commanders.

Being a rapist didn't seem to impinge on what Abdelaziz considered his moral obligations as a pious Muslim. One of his fellow warriors said that during news broadcasts Abdelaziz would cover the television screen to avoid seeing the faces of female presenters. He fervently quoted the Quran and hadith, the oral sayings attributed to the Prophet Muhammad, and spoke pompously about *al-Dawla*, the "state," which is the term ISIS uses to refer to its project. Asked what he would do if his father were a member of Jabhat al-Nusra and the two met in battle, Abdelaziz replied promptly: "I would kill him. Abu Obeida [one of the companions of the Prophet] killed his father in battle. Anyone who extends his hand to harm al-Dawla will have his hand chopped off." Abdelaziz also called his relatives in the Bahraini army or security forces "apostates" because his adoptive country's military was by then involved in a multinational coalition bombing campaign against ISIS led by the United States.

Before he went off to join the jihad in Syria, Abdelaziz had been a theological novice who barely finished a year of Islamic studies at a religious academy in Saudi Arabia. He had dropped out of high school in Bahrain and traveled to the city of Medina to study sharia, Islamic jurisprudence. In school, according to one of his family members, he avoided nondevout peers and mingled primarily with hard-line students. Soon he started to resort to "jihadi speak," constantly referring to the dismal conditions in which Sunni Muslims in Africa, the Middle East, and Southeast Asia persist.

In Syria, his metamorphosis continued on the battlefield. He called himself Abu al-Mu'tasim, after the eighth Abbasid caliph, al-Mu'tasim Billah, who is known for leading an army to avenge the insulting of a woman by Byzantine soldiers. Abdelaziz said he wanted to emulate the Abbasid caliph in supporting helpless Muslims in Syria and Iraq. Even though he was appointed as a security official, he always looked for any chance to fight on the front lines. "I cannot sit down," he told us. "I came here seeking martyrdom, and I have chased it everywhere."

On October 23, 2014, Abdelaziz found it. He was shot dead by a Syrian regime sniper in the al-Hawiqa district of Deir Ezzor.

Fighters customarily write a will when they join a group, to be given to their families only after they die. Abdelaziz had addressed his to his mother: "As you know and watch on television channels, the infidels, and *rafida* [a bigoted term used to describe the Shia] have gone too far in their oppression, killing, torture and violations of Muslims' honor. I, by God, cannot see my Muslim sisters and brothers being killed, while some of them appeal to Muslims and find nobody coming to their help, and I sit without doing anything. I wanted to be like al-Muta'sim Billah. And the most important reason is that I longed for heaven, near the Prophet Muhammed, peace be upon him, and I wanted to ask for forgiveness for you in the afterlife."

When ISIS stormed the city of Mosul, the capital of Iraq's Ninewah province, in mid-June 2014, the world's response was one of confusion as much as shock. Men very much like Abdelaziz had conquered an expanse of land in the Middle East roughly equivalent to the size of Great Britain. Only a thousand of their number had overthrown a city in central Iraq guarded by as many as thirty thousand American-trained Iraqi soldiers and policemen who vanished, forfeiting to ISIS tens of millions of dollars in American-made Humvees and Abrams tanks. What kind of terrorists drive armored vehicles and tanks? Is ISIS an organization, or is it more like an army?

Five months before the fall of Mosul, President Obama had rather regrettably dismissed ISIS in an interview with the *New Yorker*'s David Remnick as the "jayvee squad" of terrorists. Now the jayvee squad had razed the berm barriers separating the modern nation-states of Syria and Iraq that had been in place for a little less than a hundred years. They declared that this physical and symbolic act of recombination was the end of a British-French colonial compact that had helped draw the map of the contemporary region even before the official terminus of World War I. There would no longer be any Western fingerprint on that map, according to ISIS. Instead, there would only be the caliphate. Eventually, intoned ISIS's leader, Abu Bakr al-Baghdadi, if Muslims were strong, the caliphate would again reach Spain and even conquer Rome.

This book is personal. One of the authors is a native Syrian from the border town of Albu Kamal, which has long been a portal for jihadists moving into, and now out of, Iraq. The other author has reported from the Aleppo suburb of al-Bab, once a cradle of Syria's independent and pro-democratic civil society; today, it is a dismal ISIS fief ruled by Sharia law. We set out to answer a simple question asked repeatedly on cable news shows in the haunting summer and fall of 2014: "Where did ISIS come from, and how did it manage to do so much damage in so short a period of time?" The question was understandable, given the images and videos then circulating around the world, most notoriously the horrifying propaganda beheadings of several Western hostages, beginning with the American journalist James Foley. But the question was also a strange one, because the United States has been at war with ISIS for the better part of a decade under its various incarnations, first as al-Qaeda in Iraq (AQI), then the Mujahidin Advisory Council, and then the Islamic State of Iraq (ISI). It was as if the Vietcong had returned under a different banner and laid siege to a third of Southeast Asia in 1985, only to be marveled at and sensationalized as a surprising and unknown guerrilla insurgency by everyone from the Reagan administration to CNN. If ever there was a familiar foe, ISIS was it.

And yet much about this totalitarian and theocratic enemy remains forgotten or occluded or simply underexamined. Debates about its ideology, war strategy, and internal dynamics persist in every country committed to its defeat. Is ISIS greater or less than the sum of its parts? Is it winning or losing seven months into a concerted multinational air campaign, backed by the provision of arms to select allies and proxies? Is the stated US objective articulated by President Obama to "degrade and ultimately destroy" ISIS feasible given the current US policies in Syria and Iraq? Or will this latest iteration of war in the Middle East last for thirty years, as former defense secretary Leon Panetta recently suggested, spreading into North Africa and no doubt into our own backyard, as we may already be seeing in the January 2015 attacks in Paris?

We begin by examining ISIS as it is now but also as it evolved and adapted over the past decade. The early chapters deal mainly in this complex history of ISIS's prior incarnations, drawing on dozens of original interviews conducted with former US military intelligence and counterterrorism officials and Western diplomats who tracked and fought and jailed al-Qaeda in Iraq. ISIS is actually the latest front in a bloody culmination of a long-running dispute within the ranks of international jihadism. Namely, how should this holy war be waged, and against whom? Are Shia, Alawites, and other minority sects and ethnicities viable targets for attack, or should they be spared in light of the more pressing evils of combating the Americans and their "Zionist-crusader" allies? The more fanatical side of this dispute was embodied by Abu Musab al-Zarqawi, the Jordanian founder of al-Qaeda in Iraq, while the more "moderate" side was embodied by his own patron and nominal superior—Osama bin Laden. The recent split between al-Qaeda and ISIS was inevitable ever since al-Zarqawi and bin Laden first laid eyes on each other in Afghanistan in 1999. Allied they helped tear Iraq apart, inspired Shia counteratrocities, and took a bloody toll in American and allied lives. It is this history that ties together the past decade of conflict with the agendas of regimes in Iran and Syria, and without which we cannot truly understand ISIS today. Although it's impossible to determine which side in the jihadist argument will ultimately win out, or even if there will *be* a winner, the fact that al-Qaeda has for the past year been in a state of fratricidal conflict with its former subsidiary will surely determine how the West continues to fight both.

We then look at the origins of the Syrian revolution, showing how the Assad regime, which had long facilitated and suborned al-Qaeda terrorism next door, attempted to portray itself not only as the victim of its erstwhile ally, but also perversely created the fertile conditions for such terrorism to take root inside Syria. Finally, we look at ISIS as it is today, under al-Baghdadi and his willing executioners, relying on interviews with active or now-deceased ISIS militants, spies, and "sleeper agents" and also their victims—Syrian tribesmen, rebels, and activists, and one brave and defiant schoolteacher in Raqqa who said "enough." One of the main recruitment centers and organizing hubs for ISIS is prisons. Whether by accident or design, jailhouses in the Middle East have served for years as virtual terror academies, where known extremists can congregate, plot, organize, and hone their leadership skills "inside the wire," and most ominously recruit a new generation of fighters.

ISIS is a terrorist organization, but it isn't *only* a terrorist organization. It is also a mafia adept at exploiting decades-old transnational gray markets for oil and arms trafficking. It is a conventional military that mobilizes and deploys foot soldiers with a professional acumen that has impressed members of the US military. It is a sophisticated intelligence-gathering apparatus that infiltrates rival organizations and silently recruits within their ranks before taking them over, routing them in combat, or seizing their land. It is a slick propaganda machine effective at disseminating its message and calling in new recruits via social media. ISIS is also a spectral holdover of an even earlier foe than al-Qaeda. Most of its top decision-makers served either in Saddam Hussein's military or security services. In a sense, then, "secular" Baathism has returned to Iraq under the guise of Islamic fundamentalism—less a contradiction than it may appear.

Most important, ISIS presents itself to an embattled Sunni minority in Iraq, and an even more persecuted and victimized Sunni majority in Syria, as the sect's last line of defense against a host of enemies—the "infidel" United States, the "apostate" Gulf Arab states, the "Nusayri" Alawite dictatorship in Syria, the "rafida" one in Iran, and the latter's satrapy in Baghdad. Even here, as with all conspiracy theories, ISIS relies on kernels of truth and awkward geopolitical realities to depict a satanic global enterprise ranged against it. Syria's warplanes are now flying the same skies as America's, purportedly bombing the same targets in eastern Syria—while the US government maintains that Assad has no future in Damascus. In Iraq, Iranian-built Shia militia groups, some of them designated by the US government as terrorist entities (because they have American blood on their hands), now serve as the vanguard of the Iraqi Security Forces' ground campaign to beat back ISIS, with the advertised supervision and encouragement of Iran's Revolutionary Guards Corps, another US-designated terrorist entity. These militias are also committing acts of ethnic cleansing in Sunni villages along the way, earning the censure of Amnesty International and Human Rights Watch—all while US warplanes indirectly provide them with air cover. Whatever Washington's intentions, its perceived alliance of convenience with the murderous regimes of Syria and Iran is keeping Sunnis who loathe or fear ISIS from participating in another grassroots effort (like the earlier Iraqi "Awakening") to expel the terrorists from their midst. Those who have tried have been mercilessly slaughtered; others have simply been co-opted and pledged fealty to the slaughterers.

At once sensationalized and underestimated, brutal and savvy, ISIS has destroyed the boundaries of contemporary nation-states and proclaimed itself the restorer of a lost Islamic empire. An old enemy has become a new one, determined to prolong what has already been an overlong war.

ISIS

1

FOUNDING FATHER
ABU MUSAB AL-ZARQAWI'S JIHAD

"Rush O Muslims to your state. Yes, it is your state. Rush, because Syria is not for the Syrians, and Iraq is not for the Iraqis." Abu Bakr al-Baghdadi—by then anointed Caliph Ibrahim—heralded the end of ISIS and the birth of the Islamic State on June 28, 2014, the first day of Ramadan. He preached from the pulpit of the Great Mosque of al-Nuri in Mosul, a city his forces had taken control of days earlier. Although a native-born Iraqi, al-Baghdadi was abolishing his and all forms of citizenship. As he saw it, the nations of the Fertile Crescent and indeed the world no longer existed. Only the Islamic state did. Moreover, humanity could neatly be divided into two "camps." The first was the "camp of the Muslims and the *mujahidin* [holy warriors] everywhere"; the second was "the camp of the Jews, the Crusaders, their allies." Standing there, draped in black, al-Baghdadi presented himself as the heir to the medieval Abbasid caliphate as well as the embodied spirit of his heroic predecessor, Abu Musab al-Zarqawi, who had spoken in much the same revolutionary terms and who had revered the mosque from which Abu Bakr al-Baghdadi was preaching the fulfillment of a darkling vision eleven years in the making.

THE BOY FROM ZARQA

The scruffy burg of Zarqa lies about twenty-five miles to the northeast of Amman, Jordan. Before its most notorious native son adopted the name of the town for his nom de guerre, it had two main associations, one liturgical and the other humanitarian. Zarqa was the biblical staging ground of Jacob's famous struggle with God and is today the location of al-Ruseifah, the oldest Palestinian refugee camp in Jordan. Ahmad Fadhil Nazzal al-Khalaylah, as al-Zarqawi was born, hailed not from a nationless people but from the Bani Hassan tribe, a confederation of Bedouins who resided on the East Bank of the Jordan River and were known for their loyalty to the Hashemite Kingdom. Al-Zarqawi's father was a *mukhtar*, a village elder, municipally empowered to arbitrate local disputes, although his son was more fond of getting into them. Al-Zarqawi was an unpromising student who wrote Arabic at a semiliterate level, dropped out of school in 1984, the same year his father died, and resorted immediately to a life of crime. "He was not so big, but he was bold," one of al-Zarqawi's cousins later recounted to the *New York Times*. He drank and bootlegged alcohol; some contemporaries also say that he was a pimp. His first stint in prison was for drug possession and sexual assault.

Worried that her son was descending into an underworld from which he'd never escape, al-Zarqawi's mother, Um Sayel, enrolled him in religious courses at the Al-Husayn Ben Ali Mosque in Amman. The experience was transformative. Faith had the intended effect of supplanting the lawlessness, but not in the way Um Sayel might have hoped.

It was in the mosque that al-Zarqawi first discovered Salafism, a doctrine that in its contemporary form advocates a return to theological purity and the traditions of the Prophet Muhammad. Salafists deem Western-style democracy and modernity not only fundamentally irreconcilable with Islam, but the main pollutants

2

of the Arab civilization, which after World War I stagnated under the illegitimate and "apostate" regimes in Egypt, Jordan, Syria, and Iraq. At the most extreme end of their continuum, the Salafists are also adherents of jihad, a word that denotes "struggle" in Arabic and contains a multitude of definitions. When the Soviets invaded Afghanistan in 1979, however, its primary definition meant "armed resistance."

THE HAYATABAD MILIEU

Hayatabad is a city on the outskirts of Peshawar, Pakistan, that rests at the base of the Khyber Pass, the slipway for multiple empires that have entered, and then exited, Afghanistan. In the late 1980s, the city had become a kind of Casablanca for the Soviet-Afghan war, then winding down. It was a city of perpetual waiting and planning, host to soldiers, spies, peddlers, crooks, warlords, smugglers, refugees, black marketeers, and veteran and aspiring holy warriors.

It was also the operational headquarters of Osama bin Laden, one of the scions of a billionaire Saudi industrial family, who was busy laying the groundwork and amassing the personnel for his own start-up organization, al-Qaeda. Bin Laden's mentor at the time was also one of Hayatabad's leading Islamist theoreticians, a Palestinian named Abdullah Azzam, who in 1984 had published a book that became a manifesto for the Afghan mujahidin. It argued that Muslims had both an individual and communal obligation to expel conquering or occupying armies from their sacred lands. Certainly galvanized by Israel's military occupation of his birthplace, Azzam explicitly made the anti-Soviet campaign the priority for all believing Muslims, not just Afghans. Like al-Baghdadi's exhortations decades later, Azzam's was a global casting call for mujahidin from around the world to join one camp against another. Though not quite advocating a transnational caliphate, Azzam did think

3

that Afghanistan was where a viable Islamic state could be constructed on the ashes of Communist hegemony. This war, after all, was still a purist one, not yet diluted by a cocktail of competitive and paradoxical ideologies, which the Palestinian cause had lately been, thanks to the secular nationalism of Yasser Arafat and the jet-set Leninist terrorism of Carlos the Jackal.

So when Azzam relocated to Peshawar, he and bin Laden became den mothers to the arriving "Arab-Afghans," as the foreign mujahidin were colloquially known, who were eager to wage holy war but clueless as to how or where to begin. Together they founded Maktab al-Khadamat, or the Services Bureau, which operated out of a residence bin Laden owned. If Azzam was the Marx, a grand philosopher articulating the concept of a new revolutionary struggle and drawing in the necessary disciples to realize it, then bin Laden was his Engels, the wealthy scion who paid the bills and kept the lights on while the master toiled on texts that would change the world.

About three thousand Arab-Afghans passed through this jihadist orientation center, where they were provided food, money, and housing, as well as acculturated to a strange and ethno-linguistically heterodox North-West Frontier. Untold millions of dollars passed through the Services Bureau as well, much of it raised by bin Laden and Azzam, and some of it channeled by the Saudi government, with which bin Laden—through his family's construction empire—had close ties. Some of the world's most notorious international terrorists gained their most valuable commodity—contacts—under the patronage systems set up by bin Laden and Azzam.

Azzam and his pupil eventually fell out, owing to bin Laden's closeness to another rising celebrity in the jihadist firmament: Ayman al-Zawahiri, an Egyptian surgeon who had done three months of medical work for the Red Crescent Society in Pakistan in the summer of 1980 and had even taken short jaunts into Afghanistan to observe the war firsthand. By the end of the decade, al-Zawahiri had earned global notoriety for being among the hundreds imprisoned and tortured for his alleged complicity in the assassination of Egyptian president Anwar Sadat. He had been the emir, or prince, of Jamaat al-Jihad, or the Jihad Group, which had sought a coup d'etat in Cairo and the establishment of an Islamic theocracy in its place.

After his release, al-Zawahiri returned to Peshawar in 1986 to resume his medical work at a Red Crescent hospital, and to reconstitute al-Jihad. His Salafism by that time had grown more extreme; he had been flirting with the concept of *takfirism*—the excommunication of fellow Muslims on the basis of their supposed heresy, and an injunction that almost always carried with it a death sentence. Thus, when al-Zawahiri befriended bin Laden, he was put on a direct collision course with Abdullah Azzam, who was opposed to Muslims killing other Muslims. For Azzam, jihadism's true target was the irreligious and depraved West, which of course included the state of Israel. Al-Zawahiri and Azzam hated each other and competed for bin Laden's attention and good graces. Most of all, they competed for his money.

In late November 1989 Azzam and two of his sons were killed after a roadside bomb blew up their car on the way to a mosque. (Theories as to the likely culprits behind the bomb ranged from the KGB to Saudi intelligence to the CIA to bin Laden and/or al-Zawahiri.) The very next month, one of Azzam's other sons, Huthaifa Azzam, went to the Peshawar airport to collect a group of mostly Jordanian Arab-Afghans who were arriving late in the day to fight the Red Army, then about two months shy of a categorical withdrawal from Afghanistan. One of the arrivals was al-Zarqawi.

CLAUSEWITZ FOR TERRORISTS

In the spring of 1989 Abu Musab al-Zarqawi made his way from Hayatabad eastward into the city of Khost, Afghanistan, arriving just in time to see the Red Army defeated. Rather than return to Jordan as the man who had missed the holy war, he stayed on in the North-West Frontier region until 1993, establishing more useful contacts among those vying to determine the fate of a post-Soviet Afghanistan. Among those were the brother of Khalid Sheikh Mohammed, the 9/11 mastermind, and Mohammed Shobana, who published a jihadist magazine called *Al-Bunyan Al-Marsus* (the *Impenetrable Edifice*). Despite his remedial Arabic, and solely on the basis of his referral by a well-regarded cleric, al-Zarqawi was hired as one of the magazine's correspondents. He also met his future brother-in-law, Salah al-Hami, a Jordanian-Palestinian journalist affiliated with Abdullah Azzam's *Al-Jihad*, the in-house magazine of the Services Bureau. Al-Hami had lost a leg to a land mine in Khost, and he later claimed that it was during his convalescence in a hospital, after complaining that he would never find a wife with his deformity, that al-Zarqawi offered one of his seven sisters to al-Hami for the purposes of marriage. She traveled to Peshawar for the wedding, an event that furnished the first and only footage of al-Zarqawi until April 2006, when his al-Qaeda franchise in Iraq released a propaganda video showing its black-clad commander firing a machine gun like Rambo.

According to al-Hami, al-Zarqawi's reportage consisted mostly of interviews with veterans of the Soviet-Afghan war, through whom he lived vicariously. At night, he would try to memorize the Quran.

Al-Hami returned to Jordan after a few months with his new bride, but his brother-in-law stayed on, participating in what was then an incipient civil war for the fate of a newly liberated Afghanistan. He cast his lot with the Pashtun warlord Gulbuddin Hekmatyar, who served intermittently as the prime minister in Kabul before his administration was eventually usurped by the Taliban, whereupon Hekmatyar fled to Iran. Al-Zarqawi's days as a chronicler of other people's war stories were at an end. He wanted to make his own.

He attended a series of training camps on the Afghanistan-

Pakistan border, including Sada al-Malahim ("the Echo of Battle"), which was essentially the Fort Dix for al-Qaeda. It graduated the masterminds of the two separate World Trade Center attacks, Ramzi Yousef and Khalid Sheikh Mohammed. As recounted by Loretta Napoleoni in her book *Insurgent Iraq: Al-Zarqawi and the New Generation*, bin Laden's ex-bodyguard, Nasir Ahmad Nasir Abdallah al-Bahari, described camp life at Sada al-Malahim as three distinct phases of training and indoctrination. The first was "the days of experimentation," which lasted for fifteen days, during which a recruit was subjected to "psychological, as well as moral, exhaustion"—this, evidently, to separate the softies from the real warriors. The second was the "military preparation period," which lasted for forty-five days, during which a recruit was taught first how to wield light weapons, then graduated on to shoulder-borne surface-to-air missiles and cartography courses. The third and final phase was "the guerrilla war tactics course," which taught military theory. Clausewitz for terrorists.

HOMECOMING

Al-Zarqawi returned to Jordan in 1992 and was placed immediately under surveillance by the kingdom's General Intelligence Directorate (GID), who were then worried that repatriating Arab-Afghans would redirect their attention to the enemy at home. GID was right to be worried. Their fears were proven out in 1993, when Jordan's peace talks with Israel exacerbated Islamist antipathy against the kingdom and those fighters newly returned from the Afghan front began founding jihadist start-ups of their own, such as Jaysh Muhammad (the Army of Muhammad) and al-Hashaykkah (the Jordanian Afghans).

Al-Zarqawi's return to civilian life was inevitably abortive. He visited Abu Muhammad al-Maqdisi, a Jordanian-Palestinian Salafist whom he had met in Hayatabad, and who had been the one to refer him as a suitable correspondent for Shobana's magazine.

Al-Maqdisi had recently published a blistering anti-Western screed, *Democracy: A Religion*, which drew a stark line between the political economy of the "pagans" and Allah's divine law. Together, in a Levantine shadow play of the bin Laden and Azzam double act, al-Zarqawi and al-Maqdisi proselytized in makeshift salons around Jordan, inveighing against their government's warming relations with Israel and America's meddling, imperialistic role in the Middle East. Al-Maqdisi was a pedantic scholar, full of invective about the perceived shortcomings of contemporary politics; al-Zarqawi was charismatic but an intellectual lightweight. "He never struck me as intelligent," Mohammed al-Dweik, al-Zarqawi's future lawyer, said years later.

Al-Maqdisi founded his own Jordanian jihadist cell known as Bayt al-Imam (the House of the Imam) and enlisted al-Zarqawi. Their first foray into homegrown terrorism smacked more of a Keystone Kops farce than of a grisly tragedy. Weapons discarded by the retreating Iraqi army at the end of the First Gulf War had furnished a thriving Kuwaiti market for matériel. Al-Maqdisi, who had lived in the Persian Gulf for a time and had the relevant connections, purchased antipersonnel mines, antitank rockets, and hand grenades and had them smuggled into Jordan for future terrorist attacks against the kingdom. Al-Maqdisi gave al-Zarqawi the contraband to hide, then asked for it back; al-Zarqawi obliged, save for two bombs, which he would later claim were for "use in a suicide operation in the territories occupied by the Zionists." Aware that the GID was tracking their movements and knew about their illicit wares, both terrorists had tried to flee Jordan before they were caught. In March 1994 both were arrested—al-Zarqawi after the GID raided his house and found his stockpile of weapons. Discovered in bed, he tried to shoot one officer and then commit suicide. He managed neither. He was charged and convicted with illegal weapons possession and belonging to a proscribed terrorist organization.

At their trial, al-Zarqawi and al-Maqdisi decided to transform the dock into a pulpit, much as al-Zawahiri had in Egypt. They denounced the court, the state, and the monarchy for violating the laws of God and Islam. According to Judge Hafez Amin, Bayt al-Imam "submitted a letter of accusation in which they claimed that we were acting against the teachings of the Holy Koran." Amin was further instructed to pass on a message to King Hussein himself, accusing him of sacrilege. Al-Zarqawi was still junior to al-Maqdisi and was dwarfed by the cleric's easy way with turning due process into propaganda. Both were sentenced in 1994 to fifteen years in prison and transferred to a desert-based maximum-security prison called Swaqa.

"PRISON WAS HIS UNIVERSITY"

Time in prison made al-Zarqawi more focused, brutal, and decisive. As a member of the Bani Hassan, he occupied a station above other inmates, even al-Maqdisi, who was nonetheless ennobled by his comradeship with al-Zarqawi. In Jordan, as elsewhere, the gemeinschaft of a jailhouse only emphasized the privileges and perks enjoyed by outlaws beyond their concrete boxes. Al-Zarqawi leveraged his influence with malleable or crooked guards to make his faction, made up of fellow Bayt al-Imam convicts, thrive. He got his underlings out of wearing standard-issue uniforms and morning roll call in the prison yard. "He could order his followers to do things just by moving his eyes," a prison doctor recalled.

By means of coercion or persuasion, al-Zarqawi sought to singularize his interpretation of Islamist ideology, with himself in the role of supreme jurisprudent. He beat up those he didn't like, such as a contributor to the Swaqa magazine who had turned out articles critical of him. Another inmate, Abu Doma, recalled that al-Zarqawi had once caught him reading *Crime and Punishment*, a "book by a heathen." Al-Zarqawi followed up to ensure Abu Doma abandoned his interest in profane Russian literature, writing him a hectoring letter in which he spelled Dostoyevsky's name "Doseefski." ("The note was full of bad Arabic, like a child wrote it," Doma recounted.) Unable to develop arguments, al-Zarqawi instead developed his body, using his bed frame and olive oil cans filled with rocks for weights. He didn't always get his way with the guards, however. When he stood up to them, he was sometimes beaten, further impressing those who looked up to him as a leader of men. At one point, he was thrown into solitary confinement for eight and a half months.

It was in prison that al-Zarqawi also eclipsed al-Maqdisi and assumed the title of emir, a swapping of honorifics that the latter later insisted he bestowed upon the former. The mentor-scholar helped the protégé-commander cultivate ideology as well as brawn; both men composed fatwas, or religious edicts, that then got uploaded to the Internet. A few of these even caught the attention of bin Laden, who had followed the trial of the two Jordanians with great interest from Pakistan. According to "Richard," a former top-ranking counterterrorism official at the Pentagon who asked to be quoted under an alias, al-Zarqawi's experience in prison was akin to Boston organized crime boss Whitey Bulger's: "We sent him to the Harvard of American penitentiaries. He was a wily criminal who had a little IQ and put together some good streams of income. He comes out of the pen with great street cred that helped him form his own gang, which ran Boston for four or five years. Same with al-Zarqawi. Prison was his university." Much the same would be said of Abu Bakr al-Baghdadi twenty years later, as fellow ISIS inmates recounted his similar leadership qualities and maneuverability with the guards at Camp Bucca, the US-run detention facility in southern Iraq.

Ultimately al-Zarqawi served only a fraction of his sentence, owing to a dynastic succession in the government when Jordan's King Hussein died and was succeeded by his son Abdullah II, a Western-educated reformist who instituted a policy of reconciliation with the Muslim Brotherhood, the largest opposition bloc in Jordanian parliament. In March 1999, the new king declared a general amnesty for around three thousand prisoners, excepting the worst offenders such as murderers, rapists, and traitors. Many Islamists who hadn't actually committed terrorism against the crown were freed, al-Zarqawi among them.

MEETING BIN LADEN

Al-Zarqawi left Jordan in the summer of 1999, headed once more for Pakistan to pick up where he left off several years before. Al-Zarqawi was arrested briefly in Peshawar and spent eight days in detention, evidently because his visa had expired. Told that he would only receive his passport back if he used it to return to Jordan immediately, he instead smuggled himself across the border to Afghanistan, winding up in a jihadist "guest house" in a village west of Kabul in an area then under the sway of Gulbuddin Hekmatyar.

Al-Zarqawi's first meeting with Osama bin Laden took place in the Taliban's de facto capital of Kandahar. It went quite badly. Bin Laden suspected him and the cabal of Jordanians he had arrived with of being infiltrated by the GID. Also, the ex-con's many tattoos, which al-Zarqawi had amassed in his less pious days and then tried and failed to erase with hydrochloric acid in prison, also disturbed the puritanical Saudi. More than anything, however, it was al-Zarqawi's arrogance, his "rigid views," that offended bin Laden. Al-Zawahiri was present at the meeting and agreed that the Jordanian was not a prime candidate for membership in al-Qaeda.

ENEMIES, NEAR AND FAR

In 1996 bin Laden issued a fatwa, "Declaration of Jihad Against the Americans Occupying the Land of the Two Holiest Sites," the two sites being Mecca and Medina, in Saudi Arabia, where US and coalition forces were still stationed after the First Gulf War. The declaration was in a sense a fusion of Azzam and al-Zawahiri's exegesis for holy warfare. As with Afghanistan, al-Qaeda claimed to be fighting another infidel occupier of Muslim land, only this time, the "occupier" was there at the invitation and pleasure of a Muslim government, bin Laden's erstwhile collaborator against the Russians.

In the early 1990s al-Qaeda had targeted American soldiers throughout the Middle East and Africa, from Yemen to Saudi Arabia to Kenya and Tanzania, putting the organization firmly in the "far enemy" camp of jihad, albeit with the added dispensation for killing any Muslims who collaborated with the democratic superpower. So in wanting to bring terrorism back to Jordan, for use against *exclusively* Muslim targets, al-Zarqawi was still firmly in the "near enemy" camp. In other words, he was exactly where the elder al-Zawahiri had been a decade earlier, a divergence as much generational as it was ideological. Al-Zarqawi also had a much more promiscuous definition of *kuffar* ("unbelievers"), which he took to include all the Shia and any fellow Sunnis who did not abide by a strict Salafist covenant. Bin Laden had never drawn a bull's-eye on these categories before, no doubt for filial reasons: his own mother was a Syrian Alawite, or a member of the offshoot of the Shia sect.

From such inauspicious beginnings, then, a marriage of convenience was forged between the two jihadists. Saif al-Adel, al-Qaeda's security chief, seems to have been the reason, owing to one of Islamic terrorism's greatest tools: Rolodex pragmatism. Al-Zarqawi by then had extensive contacts in the Levant, which al-Adel convinced bin Laden would be useful to al-Qaeda. One of these contacts was Abu Muhammad al-Adnani, who is today the official spokesman for ISIS.

TAWHID WAL-JIHAD

By 2000 al-Zarqawi was put in charge of a training camp in Herat, Afghanistan's third-largest city, situated on the border with Iran. The camp was built with al-Qaeda start-up money, according to former CIA analyst Nada Bakos, who estimates that bin Laden granted al-Zarqawi $200,000 in the form of a "loan," a pittance compared to what al-Qaeda was financially capable of disbursing. "All you needed was a patch of land, a couple of chin-up bars, and guys running around with AK-47s," Richard, the ex-Pentagon official said. "We're not talking about high-end training or even Marine Corps basic training. The physical activity at Herat was to determine who had the stomach for the fight."

Al-Zarqawi fielded mainly Palestinian and Jordanian recruits for what he called Jund-al-Sham (Soldiers of the Levant), although the banner above the entrance to the camp carried the slogan that would later become the name of his terrorist cell in Iraq: "Tawhid wal-Jihad" ("Monotheism and Jihad"). As the name implied, the Soldiers of the Levant were being groomed for future terrorist operations in Israel/Palestine, Jordan, and other Arab countries, with the ultimate goal being regime change. Some of the camp's graduates did indeed partake in "spectaculars," including the 2002 assassination of Laurence Foley, an officer for the US Agency for International Development in Amman; and another well-publicized plot to set off chemical bombs in the Jordanian capital in 2004, targeting the prime minister's office, the GID headquarters, and the US embassy. The Jordanian authorities claimed that had this attack been successful, it might have killed as many as eighty thousand people; al-Zarqawi accepted responsibility for the abortive attacks but denied that they featured any chemical weapons.

Jund al-Sham grew exponentially, deeply impressing al-Adel, who visited Herat monthly to report back to bin Laden on the grantee's progress. Bin Laden's appraisal of al-Zarqawi might have changed slightly during that period. Repeatedly between 2000 and 2001, the al-Qaeda leader had asked al-Zarqawi to return to Kandahar and make *bayat*—or pledge allegiance—which was the sine qua non for full al-Qaeda enlistment. Repeatedly al-Zarqawi refused. "I never heard him praise anyone apart from the Prophet, this was Abu Mos'ab's character, he never followed anyone, he only ever went out to get what he felt was just to do," a former associate recollected. Whether owing to his arrogance or his difference of opinion with his benefactor, al-Zarqawi retained an arm's-length and opportunistic relationship with al-Qaeda until 2004.

ANSAR AL-ISLAM

One of al-Zarqawi's lieutenants at Herat was a fellow Jordanian, Abu Abdel Rahman al-Shami, who was tasked with expanding his network into northern Iraq via Iran in order to create a Taliban-style fief in the semiautonomous region of Kurdistan, which was then protected from Saddam's army and air force by an internationally enforced no-fly zone. The jihadist group that al-Shami formed was known as Jund al-Islam, and it occupied a five-hundred-square-kilometer area in the mountainous north of the region, lording over some two hundred thousand people, who were suddenly barred from alcohol, music, and satellite television.

After the September 11 attacks and the start of the US invasion of Afghanistan, Jund al-Islam merged with other terrorist cells to become Ansar al-Islam. The targets of this conglomerate were two: the Baathist regime in Baghdad and the Patriotic Union of Kurdistan (PUK) led by Jalal Talabani, who would become president of a post-Saddam Iraq.

On February 3, 2003, just weeks before the Iraq War began, Secretary of State Colin Powell addressed the United Nations and claimed that Ansar al-Islam's perch in northern Iraq, which had been detailed by Kurdish intelligence, was proof of al-Qaeda's ties to Saddam's regime. Al-Zarqawi's network, Powell insisted, was manufacturing ricin and chemical weapons in its five-hundred-square-kilometer district, while al-Zarqawi, whom the top diplomat wrongly referred to as Palestinian, had spent months receiving medical treatment in Baghdad, under state auspices. He had allegedly needed a leg amputated and replaced by a prosthetic after sustaining a major injury in an aerial assault in Afghanistan.

Many of the minor and major details of Powell's speech were later debunked after US forces invaded Iraq and recovered scores of Iraqi intelligence files and interrogated plenty of former Iraqi intelligence officers, although there were those who worked in the Bush administration who never bought Powell's argument. "We first knew of Zarqawi in '98 or '99 and we knew what he was about," Richard told us. "He was going to be a very brutal guy when he was flushed out of Afghanistan, but we didn't know he was going to head to Iraq. We assumed he was going to go back to Jordan. As for his 'hosting' in Iraq, I don't believe the whole Baghdad hospital story the way the administration sold it—that seems to fall in the 'Dick Cheney imagination' category."

Although he had dispatched al-Shami and other Herat trainees into Kurdistan, al-Zarqawi's relationship with Ansar al-Islam was more informal than the United States made out. In fact, it was based on exactly the kind of Rolodex pragmatism that led to al-Zarqawi's own association with bin Laden. "Jihadists gain more from friendships and acquaintanceships than they do from being on a list together that says they're part of the same terrorist cell," Richard said. "Look at ISIS today or look at all the groups in Syria, how fungible they are. Ansar al-Islam gave Zarqawi refuge in [Iraq] Kurdistan because they knew him and they liked him. Remember, he was always good at cutting deals with various criminal and tribal entities."

When the United States and NATO went to war in Afghanistan, al-Zarqawi's camp in Herat was besieged by the Western-backed Northern Alliance, and al-Zarqawi fled to Kandahar, where he did sustain a mild injury from a coalition air strike. But he didn't mangle a leg; he only broke a few ribs, according to Iyad Tobaissi, one of his former trainees. Al-Zarqawi and his convoy of around three hundred militants then departed the country for Iran, where they stayed for a week in the city of Zahedan before migrating to Tehran under the auspices of an old friend: Gulbuddin Hekmatyar, yet another useful contact al-Zarqawi had made on his first trip to the North-West Frontier.

NUR AL-DIN AND IRAQ

According to a member of al-Zarqawi's entourage, "Abu Mos'ab saw in Iraq a new arena for his jihad, a wide space; he was expecting to confront the Americans there once the war in Afghanistan was over, and God Almighty gave him the strength to become the new jihadist leader in Iraq. . . .He had been planning for this for a long time." Saif al-Adel, the al-Qaeda security chief who had lobbied to keep al-Zarqawi closely tethered to the organization, later claimed the Jordanian's decision to move to Iraq was actually rooted in the antique glories of Islamic history: "I think that what [al-Zarqawi] read about Nur al-Din and the launching of his campaign from Mosul in Iraq played a large role in influencing [him] to move to Iraq following the fall of the Islamic Emirate in Afghanistan." He was, it seems, inspired by the story of the twelfth-century ruler Nur al-Din Mahmud Zangi, who ruled over both Aleppo and Mosul and was celebrated as a hero of the Second Crusade. He destroyed Frankish forces in southern Turkey and defeated the Christian prince Raymond of Poitiers in Antioch. Later, Nur al-Din unified Syria by marrying the daughter of the *atabeg* of Damascus.

His vassal, the Kurdish military commander Saladin, a man whom many contemporary jihadists still channel, would become the overlord of Mosul. Before going off to join the Second Crusade, Saladin preached from the Great Mosque of al-Nuri. The location for al-Baghdadi's sermon on June 28, 2014, was thus carefully chosen. He was not only paying homage to ISIS's founding father, al-Zarqawi, but also implicitly heralding the reunification of Aleppo and Mosul under the black banner of the restored Islamic caliphate.

IRANIAN PATRONAGE

For a year or so following his flight from Afghanistan, al-Zarqawi was based in Iran and northern Iraq, although he traveled throughout the region. He visited a Palestinian refugee camp in southern Lebanon, where he recruited members to his burgeoning jihadist network, and he moved around the Sunni-majority communities of central and northern Iraq. Shadi Abdalla, bin Laden's former bodyguard, later told German authorities that al-Zarqawi was arrested in Iran for a short time during this period before being released—an allegation that Jordanian officials claim to have corroborated on a trip to the Islamic Republic in 2003. Al-Zarqawi also went to Syria, where the GID believes he plotted Foley's assassination, with the connivance of Bashar al-Assad's security services.

Amman's own file on the state sponsorship of al-Zarqawi's terrorist activities during the lead-up to the Iraq War stood in marked contrast to what Powell had presented earlier. It wasn't Baghdad America should have been looking at, the Jordanians said; it was Tehran. A high-level GID source told the *Atlantic* magazine in 2006:

"We know Zarqawi better than he knows himself. And I can assure you that he never had any links to Saddam. Iran is quite a different matter. The Iranians have a policy: they want to control Iraq. And part of this policy has been to support Zarqawi, tactically but not strategically. . . .In the beginning they gave him automatic weapons, uniforms, military equipment, when he was with the army of Ansar al-Islam. Now they essentially just turn a blind eye to his activities, and to those of al-Qaeda generally. The Iranians see Iraq as a fight against the Americans, and overall, they'll get rid of Zarqawi and all of his people once the Americans are out."

There's a triple irony behind this observation.

First, al-Zarqawi's coming reign of terror in Iraq was distinguished by its focus on killing or tormenting the country's Shia-majority population; this, he believed, would create a state of civil war that would force Sunnis into reclaiming their lost power and prestige in Baghdad and restore the glory of Nur al-Din.

Second, Iran later tried to "get rid" of al-Zarqawi's far more formidable disciples in Iraq, transparently and boastfully leading the ground war against ISIS using both its own Revolutionary Guards Corps as well as its proxies, the heavily trained and armed Iraqi Shia militias. Iranian warplanes even reportedly bombed ISIS positions in Iraq.

Third, the Islamic Republic's underwriting of al-Zarqawi's activity in 2001–2002 more adequately meets the accusation leveled by the Bush administration against Saddam's regime, of maintaining a tactical alliance or entente cordiale with al-Qaeda. By nice coincidence, this fact was even owned by al-Zarqawi's colleague and ISIS's current spokesman Abu Muhammad al-Adnani in a message directed at Ayman al-Zawahiri in May 2014, months after al-Qaeda formally announced its breakup with its former franchise. It was in deference to al-Zawahiri and other jihadist bigwigs, al-Adnani said, that "ISIS has not attacked the Rawafid in Iran since its establishment. . . .It has kept its anger all these years and endured accusations of collaboration with its worst enemy, Iran, for refraining from targeting it, leaving the Rawafid there to live in safety, acting upon the orders of al Qaeda to safeguard its interests and supply lines in Iran. Let history record that Iran owes al Qaeda invaluably."

Al-Zarqawi and bin Laden may not have trusted or even liked each other, but their partnership was forged in a common objective: snaring the United States and its Western allies in Iraq. As early as October 2002 al-Zawahiri had anticipated the war, which he said was being perpetrated not to spread democracy, but to eliminate all military opposition to the state of Israel in the Arab and Islamic world. A year later, bin Laden wrote a letter to the people of Iraq in a communiqué aired on Al Jazeera, telling them to prepare for the occupation of an ancient Islamic capital and the installation of a puppet regime that would "pave the way for the establishment of Greater Israel." Mesopotamia would be the epicenter for a Crusader-Jewish conspiracy that would engulf the entire Middle East. In opposition bin Laden advocated urban warfare and "martyrdom operations," or suicide bombings, and he put out a global casting call for a mujahidin army on a scale not seen since the days of the Services Bureau. However, this appeal carried an intriguing postscript. The "socialist infidels" of Saddam Hussein's Baathist regime, bin Laden said, were worthy accomplices in any fight against the Americans. To hurt the "far enemy," jihadists were thus encouraged to collaborate with the remnants of a "near enemy" until the ultimate Islamic victory could be won. The consequences of this sanctioning of an Islamist-Baathist alliance would be lethal and long-lasting.

2

SHEIKH OF THE SLAUGHTERERS

AL-ZARQAWI AND AL-QAEDA IN IRAQ

"Corrupt regimes and terrorists keep each other in business," Emma Sky, a British adviser to the US military in Iraq, says. "It's a symbiotic relationship." Indeed, for all its posturing as an unbeatable fighting force, ISIS has relied more than it cares to admit on unlikely ideological allies and proxies. When the United States invaded Iraq, al-Zarqawi found some of his most enthusiastic champions in the remnants of one of the very "near enemies" he had declared himself in opposition to: the Baathist regime of Saddam Hussein. Today, ISIS's stunning advance across northern and central Iraq has benefited from much of the same convenient, proximate deal-making.

SADDAM'S GHOST

Bin Laden's injunction was fully realized in the early months of the occupation of Iraq, when the US military painfully discerned the hybridized nature of the insurgency it was confronting. Saddam

Hussein had not anticipated an invasion of Baghdad. But he had very much prepared his regime for a different doomsday scenario: another domestic rebellion from either Iraq's Shia majority or its minority Kurds. At the prompting of the United States, both of these sects had risen up at the end of the First Gulf War only to be brutally slaughtered (with US acquiescence). Determined not to witness any such revolutionary ferment again, Saddam in the intervening decade constructed an entire underground apparatus for counterrevolution and took precautions to strengthen his conventional military deterrents. He beefed up one of his praetorian divisions, the Fedayeen Saddam, and licensed the creation of a consortium of proxy militias. In their magisterial history of the Second Gulf War, Michael Gordon and General Bernard Trainor note that long before the first American solider arrived in Iraq, "networks of safe houses and arms caches for paramilitary forces, including materials for making improvised explosives, were also established throughout the country. . . . It was, in effect, a counterinsurgency strategy to fend off what Saddam saw as the most serious threats to his rule."

The man who anatomized this strategy, and who understood that the post-invasion insurgency actually comprised holdover elements from the ancien regime—not the "pockets of dead-enders" as US Defense Secretary Donald Rumsfeld had called them—was Colonel Derek Harvey, a military intelligence officer working for General Ricardo "Rick" Sanchez's Combined Joint Task Force 7, the American headquarters in Iraq.

Harvey estimated that between sixty-five and ninety-five thousand members of Saddam's other praetorian division, the Special Republican Guard, the Mukhabarat (a catchall term encompassing Iraq's intelligence directorates), the Fedayeen Saddam, and state-subsidized militiamen were all rendered unemployed with the stroke of a pen after Paul Bremer, the Bush-appointed head of the Coalition Provisional Authority (CPA), chose to disband the Iraqi military. Many of the sacked officers joined a nascent campaign to expel their expropriators. Added to their ranks were more disaffected Iraqis, victims of the controversial policy of "de-Baathification" that Bremer announced ten days after his touchdown in Baghdad.

Making matters worse, Saddam had licensed a gray market in Iraq designed to evade UN sanctions—in effect, a state-tolerated organized crime network, headed by Izzat Ibrahim al-Douri, his vice president. A member of the Sufi Naqshbandi Order, which claimed direct descent from the first Islamic caliph, Abu Bakr, al-Douri had been born in al-Dawr, near Saddam's own hometown of Tikrit, in the northern Salah ad-Din province of Iraq. As such, he proved an adroit Baathist operator within the country's Sunni heartland. And as vice president he was also able to stock arms of the regime's intelligence services and military with his fellow Sufis. This was a form of ethnic patronage that in 2006, after Saddam's execution, manifested itself in the creation of the Army of the Men of the Naqshbandi Order—one of the most powerful Sunni insurgency groups in Iraq, which later helped ISIS take over Mosul in 2014.

Al-Douri was an expert smuggler; he ran a lucrative stolen car ring, importing luxury European models into Iraq via the Jordanian port at Aqaba. It was a vertically integrated racket, Harvey told us, because al-Douri also maintained the auto body shops in which these illicit cars were worked on, furnishing both the factories and conveyances for the construction of vehicle-borne improvised explosive devices (VBIEDs), one of the deadliest weapons used against American troops in Iraq.

Saddam employed other counterrevolutionary measures before the war. We tend to remember his regime as "secular," which it was up to a point. But after the First Gulf War, he sought to fortify his regime against foreign fundamentalist opponents, such as Iran's mullahs, and also against domestic ones that might challenge his rule on Islamist "near enemy" grounds. Thus he Islamized his regime, adding the phrase "Allahu Akbar" ("God Is Great") to the Iraqi flag and introducing a host of draconian punishments, most of which were based on Sharia law: thieves would have their hands amputated, while draft dodgers and deserters from the military would lose their ears. To distinguish the latter from disfigured veterans of the Iran-Iraq War, Saddamists would also brand crosses into the amputees' foreheads with hot irons.

Ramping up state religiosity had an ancillary purpose: to deflect or distract criticism from an economy battered by international sanctions. The regime thus introduced a proscription on female employment, hoping to artificially lower Iraq's lengthening jobless rolls. Most significant, however, was Saddam's inauguration of the Islamic Faith Campaign, which endeavored to marry Baath ideology of regime elites with Islamism. The man he tasked with overseeing this conversion curriculum was none other than his car-smuggling *caporegime*, al-Douri.

Predictably, the Faith Campaign was a Frankenstein patchwork of proselytization and mafia economics. Some of Iraq's new-minted faithful had their hajj, or annual religious pilgrimage to Mecca, subsidized by the state, while others were bribed with real estate, cash, and—naturally—expensive cars. Colonel Joel Rayburn, another US military intelligence officer who served in Iraq and has written a history of the country, observes that one of the unintended consequences of the Faith Campaign was also its most predictable: "Saddam believed he was sending into the Islamic schools committed Baathists who would remain loyal as they established a foothold in the mosques from which the regime could then monitor or manipulate the Islamist movement. In actuality, the reverse happened. Most of the officers who were sent to the mosques were not deeply committed to Baathism by that point, and as they encountered Salafi teachings many became more loyal to Salafism than to Saddam."

Many graduates of the program, Rayburn notes, found that they had much to confess and atone for in their pasts and so turned against the very ideology the Faith Campaign was meant to inculcate, and against the regime itself. Some of these "Salafist-Baathists" even went on to hold positions in a new American-fostered Iraqi government while continuing to moonlight as anti-American terrorists. One such person was Khalaf al-Olayan, who had been a high-ranking official in Saddam's army before becoming one of the top leaders of Tawafuq, a Sunni Islamist bloc in the post-Saddam Iraqi parliament. Mahmoud al-Mashhadani showed the folly of the Faith Campaign even before the American invasion: he became a full-fledged Salafist and was subsequently imprisoned for attacking the very regime responsible for the Faith Campaign. (Al-Mashhadani went on to serve as speaker of the Council of Representatives of Iraq in 2006, a year before both he and al-Olayan were implicated in a deadly suicide bombing—against Iraq's parliament.)

"The Faith Campaign wasn't just about having people in the Baath party go to religious training one night a week and do their homework and such," Harvey told us, more than a decade removed from his first analysis of who and what constituted Iraq's insurgency. "It was about using the intelligence services to reach into the society of Islamic scholars and work with a range of religious leaders such as Harith al-Dari," a prominent Sunni cleric from the Anbar province and the chairman of the Association of Muslim Scholars. "Even Abdullah al-Janabi," Harvey added, referring to the former head of the insurgent Mujahideen Shura Council in Fallujah, "was an Iraqi intelligence agent, although originally he wasn't a Salafist as we portrayed him, but rather a Sufi linked to al-Douri and the Naqshbandi Order. We didn't recognize al-Janabi's true nature. He wasn't a religious extremist at all; he was an Arab nationalist. The thing all these guys had in common was the desire for their tribe, their clan, and themselves. That's a unifying principle. It was the Sunni Arab identity, this search for lost power and prestige, that motivated the Sunni insurgency. Many people miss that when they characterize it. If you talk to the Shiites, they understand it for what it is."

After the US invasion, al-Douri and much of his Baathist network fled to Syria, where they were harbored by Bashar al-Assad's regime. Despite his father Hafez's decades-long enmity with Saddam, al-Assad viewed these fugitives as useful agents for mayhem, for terror-in-reserve, for disrupting Bush's nation-building experiment next door. For his part, al-Douri had wanted to fuse the Iraqi and Syrian Baath parties into one transnational conglomerate, but al-Assad refused and for a time even tried to catalyze his own alternative Iraqi Baath party to rival al-Douri's. (Syria, as we'll examine later, became one of the leading state sponsors of both Baathist and al-Qaeda terrorism in Iraq.)

What Saddam, al-Assad, al-Zarqawi, and bin Laden all understood, and what the United States had to discover at great cost in fortune and blood, was that the gravest threat posed to a democratic government in Baghdad was not necessarily jihadism or even disenfranchised Baathism; it was Sunni revanchism.

Sunni Arabs constitute at most 20 percent of Iraq's population, whereas Shia Arabs constitute as much as 65 percent. A plurality of Sunni Kurds (17 percent), plus smaller demographics of Christians, Assyrians, Yazidis, and Sunni and Shia Turkomen make up the fabric of the rest of the country's society. But Saddam had presided over decades of a sectarian patronage system that broadly favored the minority at the expense of a much-impoverished and restive majority. It was for this reason that George H. W. Bush, in prosecuting the First Gulf War, never pursued a policy of total regime change in Iraq, only (fitfully) one of regime decapitation, which failed. The elder Bush had hoped that a Baathist coup, encouraged by the routing of Iraqi forces in Kuwait, would put an end to Saddam once and for all, giving way to a more reformist or Western-amenable dictatorship.

The violent implementation of democracy meant the demographic inversion of Iraq's power; it destroyed what many Iraqi Sunnis saw as their birthright. In his book, Rayburn recounts what one told him: "At first no one fought the Americans; not the Baath, not the army officers, and not the tribes. But when the Americans formed the Governing Council [in July 2003] with thirteen Shiite and only a few Sunnis, people began to say, 'The Americans mean to give the country to the Shia,' and then they began to fight, and the tribes began to let al Qaeda in." Disenfranchised Saddamists, who had melted back into their native cities and villages along the Euphrates River, were only too happy to accommodate the new arrivals, seeing them as agents for the Americans' expulsion and their own restoration. The jihadists, however, had different ambitions for Iraq.

AL-ZARQAWI VS. AMERICA

Abu Musab al-Zarqawi's grisly debut in Iraq was on August 7, 2003, when operatives from Tawhid wal-Jihad ("Monotheism and Holy War"), the new name for his network, taken from a banner that hung at the entrance to the Herat training camp, bombed the Jordanian embassy in Baghdad. (As ever, he saw his homeland's government as a primary target.) A little more than a week later, al-Zarqawi orchestrated an attack on the UN headquarters in the same city. It was carried out by a twenty-six-year-old Moroccan man, Abu Osama al-Maghribi, who drove a VBIED into a wall right underneath the window of Sérgio Vieira de Mello, the UN's special representative to Iraq, killing him and twenty-one others, and wounding more than two hundred. Al-Zarqawi said that he had targeted de Mello personally for "embellish[ing] the image of America, the crusaders, and the Jews." This "embellishment" evidently included the diplomat's role in overseeing (Christian) East Timor's independence from (Muslim) Indonesia—a fact that did little to dissuade some of al-Zarqawi's Western apologists' characterization of his terrorism as an expression of anti-imperialism.

Al-Zarqawi had help. "Originally, the Baathists cooperated in the bombing of the UN and in other suicide bombings in 2003," Harvey said. "The safe houses of the suicide bombers were adjacent to compounds and residences of the Special Security Organization [SSO] officers." The SSO was the most powerful security apparatus in prewar Iraq and was in charge of the Special Republican Guard and Special Forces. According to Harvey, it provided Zarqawi's men the cars that were fashioned into VBIEDs; they also transported the suicide bombers. "The reason we know so much is that one of the suicide bombers didn't die, and we were able to debrief him and backtrack."

By October 2003 bin Laden's casting call for foreign mujahidin had been heeded, thanks in part to the socialist infidels. The Saddamists had already established the "rat lines"—corridors for foreign fighters—to transport them into Iraq from a variety of terrorist cells and organizations around the Middle East and North Africa. "These jihadists had maintained a relationship for at least three years—in some cases longer—with the SSO and a general by the name of Muhammed Khairi al-Barhawi," Harvey said. "He was responsible for their training. The idea was, if you understood who the terrorists were and kept them close to you, you wouldn't have to worry about them striking you."

Al-Barhawi was later appointed police chief in Mosul by Major General David Petraeus, then head of the 101st Airborne

Division, stationed in the city. Petraeus insisted that al-Barhawi's turn to the dark side was coerced rather than voluntary. Harvey disagrees: "Barhawi had managed his familial relationships into al-Qaeda when he was police chief, then into Mosul's police force, then into local Awakening councils when they developed. From a tribal perspective, it was the smart thing to do: have that accretion in as many places as possible."

KILLING THE SHIA

Between 2003 and 2005, the Zarqawists were still a minority in Iraq's terrorism. According to a study conducted by the Jamestown Foundation, a Washington-based think tank, a mere 14 percent of what the United States had dubbed "Sunni Arab rejectionists" belonged to al-Zarqawi's network. However, this contingent was overrepresented in the media because of the prominence Colin Powell gave to al-Zarqawi, and the fact that al-Zarqawi's terrorism accounted for a full 42 percent of all suicide bombings—the mode of violence with the bloodiest toll—perpetrated in Iraq.

The same month Tawhid wal-Jihad bombed the Jordanian embassy and the United Nations, it also assassinated Ayatollah Mohammed Baqir al-Hakim, the leader of the Supreme Council for Islamic Revolution in Iraq (SCIRI) with a VBIED. In fact, it was al-Zarqawi's father-in-law, Yassin Jarrad, who carried out the suicide VBIED, which struck the Imam Ali Mosque, one of Shia Islam's holiest shrines, outside the city of Najaf, and killed somewhere around a hundred people. Al-Zarqawi made no secret of his pathological hatred of Iraq's demographic majority.

A letter said to have been written by him and addressed to bin Laden was intercepted by the Kurds in January 2004. It made al-Zarqawi's Machiavellian plot quite clear: The Shia, it read, were "the insurmountable obstacle, the lurking snake, the crafty and malicious scorpion, the spying enemy, and the penetrating venom." It went on to state, "The unhurried observer and inquiring onlooker will realize that Shi'ism is the looming danger and the true challenge," its practitioners grave-worshippers, idolaters, and polytheists.

Genocidal rhetoric was followed by genocidal behavior. Though al-Zarqawi had also exploited what was then an incipient but real problem in Iraq's political evolution: namely, the creeping takeover of state institutions by chauvinistic Shia politicians, many of whom were either spies or agents of influence of Iran's Islamic Revolutionary Guards Corps (IRGC). One of al-Zarqawi's named nemeses was the Badr Corps, the armed wing of the SCIRI, a political party whose very name indicated its Khomeinist foundations. By isolating Badr, which was targeting and abusing the Sunnis, al-Zarqawi managed to translate real sociopolitical grievances into an eschatological showdown. "[T]he Badr Brigade . . .has shed its Shi'a garb and put on the garb of the police and army in its place," he wrote. "They have placed cadres in these institutions, and, in the name of preserving the homeland and the citizen, have begun to settle their scores with the Sunnis."

Al-Zarqawi's prescription was to start a civil war by "targeting and hitting [Shia] in [their] religious, political, and military depth [to] provoke them to show the Sunnis their rabies and bare the teeth of the hidden rancor working in their breasts. If we succeed in dragging them into the arena of sectarian war, it will become possible to awaken the inattentive Sunnis as they feel imminent danger and annihilating death at the hands of these Sabeans."

ISIS has couched its current campaign in Syria and Iraq in exactly this sectarian-existential grammar, fondly recalling al-Zarqawi's war strategy in its official propaganda. And it has followed in his footsteps by targeting Shia to prompt their counterreaction (and overreaction), in order to drive Sunnis into ISIS's protective arms. In June 2014, after sacking Camp Speicher, the former US military base in Tikrit, al-Baghdadi's jihadists boasted, for instance, that they had executed seventeen hundred Shia soldiers the Iraqi army had surrendered. That figure may have been exaggerated, but not by much: Human Rights Watch later confirmed the existence of mass execution sites of Shia, with a collective death toll of 770. In Mosul, the very same day ISIS took the city, it stormed Badoush Prison and hauled off some fifteen hundred of its inmates. It drove them all out to a nearby desert and separated the Sunnis and Christians from the Shia. Members of the first two categories were then carted away elsewhere; the Shia were first abused and robbed, then lined up and shot over a ravine after they each called out their number in line.

TELEVISED BEHEADINGS

Al-Zarqawi proved a dire pioneer in another important respect: marriage of horrific ultraviolence and mass media Like ISIS commanders today, he was especially fond of beheadings and the attention they get in the West. He very likely personally decapitated the American contractor Nicholas Berg in 2004 in a video posted online and circulated around the world. The staging of this grotesque event was also significant.

As with James Foley, Steven Sotloff, and Peter Kassig, ISIS's latest American victims, Berg was dressed in a Guantanamo-style orange jumpsuit, forced to his knees, and compelled to identify himself. An imprecation was then recited by his captors, before a knife was applied to his throat, with one editing discrepancy: in Berg's case, the full beheading was featured on-screen, whereas ISIS has preferred (no doubt for added international media exposure) to keep most of the gore offscreen. Also, Berg's body was discovered and his family notified before his snuff film ever got exhibited.

In its August-September 2004 issue, *Voice of Jihad*, a magazine published by the Saudi branch of al-Qaeda, carried an endorsement of the practice by Abd El-Rahman ibn Salem al-Shamari, who referred specifically to the beheading of an Egyptian by the Zarqawists: "O sheikh of killers Abu Musab al-Zarqawi, continue to follow the straight path with Allah's help, guided by Allah, Fight together with the monotheists against the idol-worshipers, together with the warriors of jihad against the collaborators, the hypocrites, and the rebellious . . . show him [any soldier from among the Saudi king's legions] no mercy!" Al-Zarqawi's trademark earned him the name "Sheikh of the Slaughterers."

Though Al-Zarqawi retained an audiovisual squad of reportedly three people who were fluent in computer editing software and comparatively cruder Internet technology, ISIS has dramatically improved on al-Zarqawi's media savvy, employing its own channel and social media feeds for disseminating information. The spectacle of murder most foul, however, had the same intended effect at the hands of both perpetrators.

Not all jihadists approved of al-Zarqawi's murder of Muslims, no matter if they were Shia. His former mentor al-Maqdisi was an outspoken critic. Writing to his former protégé from his latest Jordanian prison cell, where he still languished, the cleric chided al-Zarqawi: "The clean hands of mujahedin should be protected from being tarnished with the blood of the protected people." However, as former CIA analyst Bruce Riedel has observed, these sentiments may not have been genuine: shortly after the letter was published, Jordan let al-Maqdisi out of jail and placed him under house arrest, prompting allegations by jihadists that his rebuke of al-Zarqawi may have been edited or ghostwritten by the GID as a form of psychological warfare against the insurgency.

Although al-Zarqawi professed to be profoundly hurt by his former teacher's criticism (he claimed to have wept when he read the letter), al-Maqdisi's counsel did nothing to lessen Tawhid wal-Jihad's violence against Muslims. Al-Zarqawi told him to take care with issuing such restrictive fatwas in the future. Today, al-Maqdisi has lambasted ISIS as "deviant" and criticized its much-publicized atrocities, as well as its alienation of the local Muslim communities and armed groups in Syria. However, that has not stopped ISIS from trying to curry favor with al-Maqdisi's followers. As scholar Michael W. S. Ryan has noted, the first issue of ISIS's propaganda magazine, *Dabiq*, features an extensive discussion of Millat Ibrahim, or the path of Abraham, which is not coincidentally the title of the 1984 tract al-Maqdisi published, inspiring any number of mujahidin to sojourn to Afghanistan.

AL-ZARQAWI'S APPEAL

Before Blackwater attained international notoriety for the lethal shooting of seventeen Iraqis in western Baghdad's Nisour Square in 2007, its mercenaries made headlines three years earlier as corpses horrifically hung upside down from a railroad bridge in Iraq's Anbar province. Then, as now, Fallujah was a byword for hell on earth to scores of American soldiers—and tens of thousands of Iraqi civilians.

Fallujah and Anbar's provincial capital, Ramadi, were meant to have had a sizable US troop presence after the 2003 invasion. However, the ease with which the military cut through the country and straight into Baghdad altered the military's plans. Instead, the cities that would become the main hot spots for Sunni rejectionism had the lightest American "footprint." The failure of foresight seems staggering in retrospect, given that the Euphrates River Valley consists of what Derek Harvey says was not only the Sunni heartland, but also the national wellspring of Baathism.

Uday and Qusay Hussein, Saddam's sons, fled to Anbar province when their father's high command quit Baghdad in advance of the approaching US army. According to Wael Essam, a Palestinian journalist who was embedded with insurgents in Fallujah, many former Baathists, Mukhabarat officers, and Republican Guardsmen who took up arms to fight coalition forces "all affirmed they were not fighting for Saddam but for Islam and Sunnis." The beheading of Nicholas Berg, US intelligence believed, took place in Jolan, a neighborhood in northwest Fallujah, which Tawhid wal-Jihad had established as one of its earliest garrisons.

An initial attempt to retake Fallujah in the spring of 2004—named, somewhat infelicitously, Operation Vigilant Resolve—ended in calamity. Integral to the Bush administration's reconstruction project for Iraq was the swift transfer of sovereignty and governance to the Iraqis themselves. This included the extraordinary responsibility of national security for a nation still very much in the throes of war. The Iraqis were hardly ready, willing, or able to assume that role, and so US Marines bore the brunt of the fighting instead. An attempt to stand up to a local Iraqi Fallujah Brigade ended in failure: the entire outfit disintegrated, and 70 percent of its recruits wound up joining the insurgency instead.

The main American weapon against Zarqawists in Anbar was Predator drone air strikes, waged by the Joint Special Operations Command (JSOC), domiciled at Balad Air Base north of Baghdad and headed by Major General Stanley McChrystal. JSOC reckoned it had killed six out of fourteen "major operators" by September 2004, including al-Zarqawi's newest "spiritual adviser." Regardless, the organizational structure of Tawhid wal-Jihad remained intact despite intense aerial bombardment, and if anything, the group only grew in strength, number, and popular appeal after the battle, which became known as the First Battle of Fallujah, showed how a combination of domestic and foreign insurgencies could bleed a mighty superpower. McChrystal assessed that the threat posed by al-Zarqawi's network was much greater than what the military had dismissively taken to calling "former regime elements"—an assessment that was greatly bolstered in October 2004 when al-Zarqawi finally did what he had refused to do four years earlier: make bayat to bin Laden.

By then adept at the uses of psychological warfare and propaganda, al-Zarqawi chose to broadcast his pledge of allegiance to the al-Qaeda chief, and did so two weeks after Donald Rumsfeld claimed that he did not believe al-Zarqawi was allied with bin Laden (a reversal of the allegation Colin Powell had advanced a year earlier at the UN).

The Jordanian's bent-knee subordination resulted in the Tawhid wal-Jihad's name change to Tanzim Qaedat al-Jihad fi Bilad al-Rafidayn, or "al-Qaeda in the Land of the Two Rivers," which Washington shortened to al-Qaeda in Iraq (AQI). So where the Jordanian entered Iraq a mere affiliate or ally of al-Qaeda, he was, a year into the war, fully enlisted as bin Laden's field commander. It would be the Saudi billionaire's enterprise, he insisted, that would inherit Mesopotamia.

A month after making bayat, al-Zarqawi attempted to put this proposition to the test with the Second Battle of Fallujah, which began in early November 2004. Dwarfing its predecessor, this operation saw ten American army battalions mobilized, including two marine regiments, and several hundred Iraqi soldiers, many acting as scouts for viable targets. It was also accompanied by F/A-18 Hornet jets, which dropped two-thousand-pound bombs on points around the city.

The marines also discovered what the AQI franchise had gotten up to by way of community outreach in Fallujah. In addition to a calendar for video-recorded beheadings, soldiers uncovered kidnapping victims who had had their legs removed. In total, three "torture houses" were uncovered in the city, along with an IED-manufacturing facility that gave US forces a clue as to the route taken by foreign fighters: a recovered GPS device showed that its owner had entered the country from the west, via Syria.

Ten thousand homes, or about a fifth of total residences in Fallujah, were destroyed in two weeks' worth of intense urban warfare, matched by punishing air strikes. The aftermath was a pocked moonscape, uninhabitable for many—not that many were left. Fallujah had largely been evacuated, with hundreds of thousands of refugees fleeing before the start of major fighting. Roughly a quarter of all insurgents killed by US troops in 2004—2,175 out of 8,400—died at the Second Battle of Fallujah, but at a proportionally high price: 70 marines were also killed, and 651 were wounded, in addition to other US casualties.

In other words, another tactical victory for the United States was rendered strategically negligible because of the enormous propaganda boon it delivered to the insurgency. The Second Battle of Fallujah was more Dunkirk than Waterloo for the jihadists and the Baathists who, if anything, scattered their number to other parts of central and northern Iraq, such as Mosul, where the marines believed that al-Zarqawi had fled after the first day of intense combat operations. Bin Laden, too, took the opportunity to transform a setback into a major forward stride, claiming that he had been acquainted with some of the "martyrs" of the battle and laying the responsibility for Fallujah's undeniable devastation at the feet of President Bush. America was waging a "total war against Islam," bin Laden declared, while the Zarqawists had "written a new page of glory into the history of our community of believers."

What began for bin Laden as a wary collaboration premised on Rolodex opportunism and for al-Zarqawi as the need for start-up capital had clearly metamorphosed into an open and celebrated alliance. The al-Qaeda leader's hesitations about his field commander's arrogance and sectarianism were sacrificed to the morale-building blows the latter was delivering to the world's greatest far enemy.

In December 2004 bin Laden answered al-Zarqawi's bayat with warm acceptance, naming him a "noble brother" and calling on the "unification of the jihadi groups under a single standard which recognizes al-Zarqawi as the Emir of al-Qaeda in Iraq."

The title was somewhat deceptive, however, because al-Zarqawi was in fact granted an operational purview that extended well beyond Iraqi territory, into outlying Arab countries as well as Turkey. As Bruce Riedel recounts, some al-Qaeda ideologues even gelled to al-Zarqawi's fanatical anti-Shiism, which was not endorsed (and was later criticized) by core al-Qaeda leadership. One Saudi ideologue in particular praised the Jordanian for characterizing the Shia as part of a long, uninterrupted line of perfidious collaborators dating back to the Mongol invasion of the Middle East—an invasion that resulted, infamously, in the obliteration of Baghdad in the thirteenth century. Here the thirteenth-century Islamic theologian Ibn Taymiyyah—the godfather of Salafism—was invoked for his commandment, "Beware of the Shiites, fight them, they lie." The Mongols in the contemporary context were the American occupiers, and also the "Jews," who were said to be standing right behind them in Iraq. Al-Zarqawi was thus seen as upholding a seven-hundred-year-old tradition of Islamic resistance. According to this framework, a Muslim has to abide by three criteria of *tawhid*, or monotheism: to worship God, to worship *only* God, and to have the right creed. In the medieval period, Ibn Taymiyyah used the foregoing criteria of tawhid to excommunicate the Shia and Sufis after he established that their practices and beliefs—including the veneration of imams—compromised their worship of God alone.

As Riedel puts it, al-Zarqawi was also being celebrated not just as a great descendant of Ibn Taymiyyah's line, but as the ultimate strategic trap-layer for the infidels of the West. He portrayed the United States and its European allies, the United Nations, and the Shia-dominant Iraqi government as coconspirators in a plot of antique vintage, the aim of which was the violent disinheritance of 1.3 billion Sunnis of the Islamic world. He had, according to his Saudi admirer, "such capabilities that the mind cannot imagine. He prepared for fighting the Americans over a year prior to the American occupation of Iraq. He built the camps and arsenals," and he recruited and enlisted people from all over the region—from Palestine to Yemen.

ISIS today relies on much of the same triumphalist discourse about a coming civilizational showdown in the Middle East. Every issue of *Dabiq* opens with this quote from al-Zarqawi: "The spark has been lit here in Iraq, and its heat will continue to intensify—by Allah's permission—until it burns the crusader armies in Dabiq." Dabiq refers to the countryside of modern-day Aleppo, where ISIS also continues to have an entrenched and expanding military presence. "This place was mentioned in a hadith," *Dabiq* (the magazine) notes, "describing some of the events of the Malahim (what is sometimes referred to as Armageddon in English). One of the greatest battles between the Muslims and the crusaders will take place near Dabiq."

In other words, the next trap being laid for America, as al-Zarqawi originally envisioned it, was in northern Syria.

THE SUNNI TRIANGLE

The disbursal of Islamic militants from Fallujah into other parts of Iraq meant that the "spark" of al-Zarqawi's apocalyptic ideology caught fire throughout the rest of the country, particularly where anti-American sentiment was especially high: where US forces were in densest concentration. One insurgent stronghold was Haifa Street, a thoroughfare that ran parallel with the Tigris River, just north out of the Assassins' Gate, the entrance to the Green Zone. Haifa Street in particular was a totem of Sunni disenfranchisement: residents living in luxury apartments along this Babylonian Champs-Élysées had been the well-paid elites favored by the Saddam regime. But many were unemployed and unemployable in transitional Iraq, thanks to de-Baathification, and so were being drawn into the insurgency in one form or another. It made no difference that Ayad Allawi, a onetime Baathist turned enemy of the party and a secular shia well-respected by Sunnis, was now the interim prime minister of Iraq. Gordon and Trainor recount how on one inoperable US Bradley fighting vehicle that sat along the street in September 2004 "insurgents had hung a black Tawhid wal-Jihad flag on its 25mm gun, and the battalion tasked with controlling the place, from the 1st Cavalry Division, began calling Haifa 'Little Fallujah' and 'Purple Heart Boulevard,' after the medal that would be awarded to 160 of the unit's 800 soldiers by the time they went home in early 2005. In Dora [yet another district of Baghdad infiltrated by insurgents], another 1st Cavalry battalion began to see new graffiti as Second Fallujah inflamed the Sunni population and the January election loomed: 'No, No, Allawi, Yes, Yes, Zarqawi.'"

THE FALL(S) OF MOSUL

Iraq's second-largest city, Mosul, had seemed relatively stable during the early days of the occupation, when it was first secured by Petraeus's 101st Airborne. But the calm was illusory. Al-Zarqawi had made the city his fallback base, and just days into major combat operations for the Second Battle of Fallujah, Mosul fell to the insurgency.

Ninewah's provincial capital had always been susceptible to Sunni rejectionism, given its cocktail composition of Saddamists and Salafists. Unemployment in Mosul hovered at around 75 percent, according to Sadi Ahmed Pire, the Patriotic Union of

Kurdistan's security chief in the city, and thus locals could be hired to carry out terrorist operations for as little as fifty dollars. As in prior battles, the local Iraqi police and army disappeared, their stations either stormed by insurgents facing little resistance or set ablaze. The ease with which Mosul collapsed also seemingly vindicated Derek Harvey's prior assessment to the US military: namely that the city's US-appointed police chief, Muhammed Khairi al-Barhawi, had been quietly playing for both teams.

Though al-Barhawi may have been an Iraqi intelligence asset all along, the Zarqawists certainly didn't make it easy for other Mosulawis to sincerely partner with the Americans. They were especially brutal to any Iraqi soldier or policeman who didn't abandon his post; in one notorious episode, they even tracked a wounded major to the hospital where he was being treated and beheaded him there. In the end, as with Fallujah, it took another overwhelming commitment of US firepower and manpower—joined by an unusually competent contingent of the Iraqi Special Police Commandos—to regain control of Mosul in the face of a combined Baathist–al-Qaeda onslaught of machine guns and rocket-propelled grenades.

A decade later, history repeated itself, as Mosul once again fell to a hybridized insurgency made up of al-Zarqawi's disciples and the Baathists of al-Douri's Naqshbandi Army. Only this time, there was no US military presence to retake the city. ISIS sacked Mosul in less than a week. The jihadists rule it to this day.

3

THE MANAGEMENT

OF SAVAGERY

BIRTH OF THE ISLAMIC STATE OF IRAQ

Al-Zarqawi's sinister strategy hewed closely to a text titled *Idarat al-Tawahhush*, or *The Management of Savagery*, published online in 2004 as a combined field manual and manifesto for the establishment of the caliphate. Its author, Abu Bakr Naji, conceived of a battle plan for weakening enemy states through what he called "power of vexation and exhaustion." Drawing the United States into open as opposed to "proxy" warfare in the Middle East was the whole point, because Naji believed that once American soldiers were killed by mujahidin on the battlefield, the "media halo" surrounding their presumed invincibility would vanish. Muslims would then be "dazzled" at the harm they could inflict on a weak and morally corrupted superpower as well as incensed at the occupation of their holy lands, driving them to jihad. He urged that they should then focus on attacking the economic and cultural institutions (such as the hydrocarbon industries) of the "apostate" regimes aligned with the United States. "The public will see how the troops flee," Naji wrote, "heeding nothing. At this point, savagery and chaos begin and these regions will start to suffer from the absence of security. This is in addition to the exhaustion and draining (that results from) attacking the remaining targets and opposing the authorities."

Naji was using the time-honored jihadist example of Egypt, but he was also implicitly referring to Iraq, where he urged the fast consolidation of jihadist victory in order to "take over the surrounding countries." One ISIS-affiliated cleric told us that Naji's book is widely circulated among provincial ISIS commanders and some rank-and-file fighters as a way to justify beheadings as not only religiously permissible but recommended by God and his prophet. For ISIS, *The Management of Savagery*'s greatest contribution lies in its differentiation between the meaning of jihad and other religious matters. Naji at one point lectures the reader, arguing that the way jihad is taught "on paper" makes it harder for young mujahidin to understand the true meaning of the concept. "One who previously engaged in jihad knows that it is naught but violence, crudeness, terrorism, frightening (others), and massacring. I am talking about jihad and fighting, not about Islam and one should not confuse them. . . .[H]e cannot continue to fight and move from one stage to another unless the beginning stage contains a stage of massacring the enemy and making him homeless. . . ."

THE SUNNI BOYCOTT

To succeed in Iraq, al-Zarqawi needed to both massacre and dispossess the enemy (the Shia and Americans) and keep Sunnis divested of any stake in what he saw as their conspiratorial project: the creation of a democratic Iraqi government. Both the Baathists and the Zarqawists undertook a campaign to enforce a Sunni boycott of the forthcoming January 2005 Iraqi election. It worked.

Less than 1 percent of Sunnis cast ballots in a key province in central Iraq—Anbar. The result conformed exactly to the dire scenario outlined by al-Zarqawi in his letter a year earlier: the Shia parties won the election by an overwhelming percentage, and Ibrahim al-Jaafari, a Dawa Party candidate who had received millions in campaign funding from Iran, became prime minister in a government that would draft Iraq's new constitution and thus determine the country's postwar fate. The boycott marked the climax of Sunni rejectionism but also, paradoxically, the beginning of the end for the insurgency's popular appeal, because it transformed what had hitherto been a numerically minimal element—AQI—into the dominant one.

The Sunni loss at the ballot box unsurprisingly coincided with a sharp uptick in attacks on "Shia" targets, which included state institutions and the Iraqi Security Forces (ISF). On February 28, 2005, a suicide bomb killed more than 120 people in the Shia-majority city of Hilla, just south of Baghdad, targeting young men tendering job applications with the ISF. In the crucial border town of Tal Afar, which jihadists used as a gateway to import foreign fighters from Syria, AQI ethnically cleansed mixed communities, "attacking playgrounds and schoolyards and soccer fields," as Colonel Herbert "H. R." McMaster later recalled. In one horrifying instance, they used two mentally disabled girls—ages three and thirteen—as suicide bombers to blow up a police recruitment line.

THE DESERT PROTECTORS

Military progress in Iraq began as improvisation—the innovative thinking of local military actors who apprehended early on that the war for "hearts and minds" wouldn't be won by adhering to a strategy cooked up by strategists who stayed in the Green Zone or, in some cases, inside the walls of the Pentagon. Integral to the insurgency's success was the failure by the Americans to engage with arguably the most important demographic in Sunni Iraq—the tribes. They had suffered enormously from de-Baathification. Saddam had understood the importance of these ancient confederations of families and clans and had thus made them a large part of his state patronage system: the tribes ran smuggling rings, gray-market merchant businesses, all under the auspices of al-Douri.

It wasn't for a lack of trying that the tribes failed to persuade the coalition of their bellwether status for defeating the insurgency. A sheikh from the influential Albu Nimr tribe had offered to work with the Iraqi Governing Council and the CPA in establishing a much-needed border guard as early as 2003, an offer that was reflected in a memo prepared for the Joint Chiefs of Staff in October of that same year. "Leaders of these tribes—many of whom still occupy key positions of local authority—appear to be increasingly willing to cooperate with the Coalition in order to restore or maintain their influence in post-Saddam Iraq," the memo read. "If they perceive failure, they may take other actions, to include creating alternate governing and security institutions, working with anti-Coalition forces, or engaging in criminal activity to ensure the prosperity and security of their tribes." Nothing came of the memo.

Al-Zarqawi again proved more adept at navigating Iraqi culture than the CPA or US military—at least at first. "Zarqawi, or the Iraqis he had working for him, understood who was who in the tribes and he worked them," Derek Harvey told us. "That's how he controlled territory in Anbar and the Euphrates River Valley."

His fatal error, however, was in overplaying his hand by turning AQI's protection racket into an asphyxiating mode of jihadist governance. The tribes chafed at the implementation of a seventh-century civil code in areas ruled by fundamentalists, many of whom were foreign-born and behaved exactly as the colonial usurpers they were meant to expel. Tribal businesses were disrupted or taken over by those seeking their own monopoly on smuggling, and AQI protected its confiscated interest with a mafia's thuggish zeal. It justified killing on the basis of market competition.

So when it assassinated a sheikh from the Albu Nimr tribe in 2005, Major Adam Such, who commanded the Army Special Forces Operational Detachment Alpha 555 Company under the 1st Marine Division, seized the opportunity to make AQI a pariah among its most important constituency. He recruited tribesmen to join an ad hoc militia to monitor the roads near the Anbar city of Hit—another strategically vital town that ISIS later seized in 2014. It was an inspired idea, although it lacked the necessary structural support to become wholly transformative. At the time, there was no permanent US military presence in the area to convince the locals that the routing of AQI wouldn't be a flash in the pan, but the prelude to a long-term counterinsurgent policing mission. Still, the fact that Iraqis suddenly *wanted* Americans to stay in their midst indicated that the jihadists had worn out their welcome.

Another city where this proved to be so was Qa'im, which al-Zarqawi had made the capital of his Western Euphrates "emirate" for obvious geostrategic reasons. The Sunni and Bedouin town abuts the Syrian border town of Albu Kamal and is also situated along a main road connecting Iraq to Jordan. It also contains the largest phosphate mines in the Middle East, with an enormous subterranean cave system, which became a guerrilla network for moving men and materiél through undetected.

US Marines moved in to take Qa'im in September 2005, followed by subsequent sorties in subordinate AQI bases in the Western Euphrates. They constructed concrete-fortified outposts to mark an indefinite presence and thereby forestall a jihadist resurgence. Building on Adam Such's experience in Hit, they also reached out to Qa'im's tribes, some of which had already grown so horrified by AQI's practices that they took up arms against the

Zarqawists. In the Albu Mahal's Hamza Battalion, the marines discovered a volunteer army that proved as committed to hammering the insurgents as they were.

Discounting corruption, the main reason why the ISF often proved inept or simply unwilling to duke it out with AQI was that many recruits were Shia, who understandably had little interest in fighting in Sunni-majority territory where they were viewed with suspicion or outright contempt. Sunni tribesmen had no such compunction, however, and were fired by self-interest to rid their areas of what may have started out as an applauded anti-American "resistance" but had devolved into a gang of obscurantist head-loppers. The graduates of the Qa'im program were turned into a battalion called the Desert Protectors, a name more than a little redolent of Lawrentian romanticism but accurate insofar as the battalion safeguarded the December 2005 parliamentary election from terrorist sabotage.

By 2006 security incidents in Qa'im had plummeted. Even in success, though, US forces still failed to discover that the tribes weren't motivated by anything so grandiose as patriotism; they only wanted to ensure peace and quiet in their own communities, not in the entire country. A third of the Desert Protectors' members quit after being told that it constituted a *national* defense force and not just a local Qa'im gendarmerie and so was duly slated for redeployment elsewhere in Iraq.

That said, Iraq's national parliamentary election yielded unforeseen and welcome developments. One of these was the transformation of Dr. Muhammad Mahmoud Latif, a long-sought-after insurgent leader, into a partner of the United States. Appalled by how the Sunni boycott of the January election for a constituent assembly had deprived Sunnis of their say in Iraq's self-determination, Latif realized that al-Zarqawi's plan for delegitimizing the new government was backfiring. He also had political ambitions of his own. In the lead-up to the parliamentary vote, he gathered a collection of Ramadi tribal sheikhs who were eager to declare war on AQI and, more daringly, work with the Americans to do so, on one condition. Like the Desert Protectors, the Ramadi tribesmen wanted a guarantee that the security portfolio for Anbar's provincial capital would devolve to themselves after AQI was no more.

Assured of the Americans' good faith in that respect, the Anbar People's Council was born. Its first initiative was to encourage Sunnis to join the Iraqi police, which was about to hold a large recruitment drive at a local glass factory. The council's certification of the effort yielded hundreds of fresh applicants, who in turn became an unavoidable target for al-Zarqawi's jihadists. On the fourth day of the glass factory drive, a suicide bomber exploded a device that killed as many as sixty Iraqis and two Americans. AQI then announced all-out war on the Anbari sheikhs who had joined the council, hunting them down individually for weeks after the bombing. Latif fled Iraq to avoid being caught in the terrorists' dragnet. Still too vulnerable to al-Zarqawi's strong-arm tactics, the council folded weeks later.

It took another two years for the US military to make strategic sense of what had transpired in Hit, Qa'im, and Ramadi. Pockets of wholly spontaneous and unforeseen tribal backlashes against the same foreign-led terrorist organization made sense in light of tribal history. For centuries, these clans had survived by cutting pragmatic deals with perceived dominant powers in their midst. They had done it with Saddam, and they had done it with al-Zarqawi, and they were ready to do it with the Americans. And while they still regarded the United States warily, they saw in its army a possible ally against a greater common enemy.

"I had a Marine Corps captain," a former top US military official told us. "He was a Sioux. He didn't know shit about Anbar or Iraq. He got out there, and he understood it immediately. The Iraqis could see he knew what was going on, and they loved him for it."

For Derek Harvey, understanding the way Iraq's tribes functioned was the key to all mythologies in understanding Iraq itself. "There were a lot of regime organizations that we didn't figure out very well. The key person might not have been the head guy, but the second or third guy—and this rule of not knowing exactly who's running the show applied to the Saddamists as much as it applies to ISIS today. The tribes had professional and in some cases religious networks that determined informal hierarchies in everything that happened in that country. Our difficulty was in learning who did what."

4

AGENTS OF CHAOS
IRAN AND AL-QAEDA

Iraqi's Sunnis had just as much of a learning curve to adapt to as did the US military. Having squandered most of their political power through a disastrous boycott of the January 2005 election, they were not about to repeat the blunder again at the one in December 2005. The about-face was statistically staggering. In December, in Ramadi, Sunni voter turnout was around 80 percent, whereas in January it had been a measly 2 percent. The letdown, then, was commensurately disappointing. Shia political blocs again came out on top, albeit with a small margin of victory, which did little to dissuade many Sunnis of the conspiracy theory that al-Zarqawi had cleverly capitalized on and that suddenly appeared wholly realized: an Iranian-American alliance was purposefully keeping them from their rightful place as the true masters and custodians of Baghdad.

Sunni participation in the December election also had another disconcerting side effect: because many of the more nationalistic or "moderate" insurgents quit the battlefield in favor of trying their luck at the ballot box, AQI's role in Iraq's terrorism grew more concentrated. Additionally, less moderate non-AQI insurgents, such as the 1920 Revolution Brigades, opted to cast their lot with the Zarqawists, who appeared to be the champions of Sunni rejectionism. And though Jaysh al-Islami (the Islamic Army), was vying with the Zarqawists for control of territory in Mosul, it was not yet ready to abandon Sunni rejectionism for reconciliation. AQI's overreach had alienated many, but al-Zarqawi was still able to exploit demographic anxieties, which long predated the war.

Kanan Makiya, a scholar of Baathist Iraq, had forecast a dire scenario for a post-Baathist state in his 1993 book *Cruelty and Silence*: "After Saddam is gone, when people's lives and those of their loved ones look as if they are on the chopping block, Sunni fears of what the Shi'a might do to them in the name of Islam are going to become the major force of Iraqi politics. The more Iraq's Shi'a assert themselves as Shi'a, the greater will be the tendency of Iraq's Sunni minority to fight to the bitter end before allowing anything that so much as smells of an Islamic republic to be established in Iraq. They see in such a state—whether rightly or wrongly is irrelevant—their own annihilation."

Al-Zarqawi's choice to Iraq's Sunnis was therefore "My barbarism or theirs." In order to make his option even more persuasive, he needed to dispel one of the greatest liabilities to AQI's popular appeal—its perception as a foreigner's jihadist army. He thus needed to "Iraqize" his franchise. In January 2006 al-Zarqawi announced the creation of the Majlis Shura al-Mujahidin fi al-Iraq (the Mujahidin Advisory Council of Iraq). Initially, this consortium consisted of six different Salafist groups, five of which were Iraqi in composition, leaving AQI as the sole outlier, albeit with central control over the council's operations. Contributing to what was, in effect, a new marketing or "branding" strategy for takfirism was the chauvinistic and authoritarian behavior of the newly elected Iraqi government.

SHIA MILITIAS, IRANIAN PROXIES

Given the world's current preoccupation with ISIS and the current US campaign against it, it's easy to forget that a decade ago, the American military saw as formidable a terrorist threat in the portly, demagogic Shia cleric Muqtada al-Sadr. The son of the revered Muhammad Sadiq al-Sadr, who was killed by Saddam's Mukhabarat in 1999, the younger al-Sadr by rights ought to have been confined to the lower rung of Shia religious leaders. He ruled an impoverished and overcrowded ghetto in northeast Baghdad formerly known as Saddam City and renamed Sadr City after the invasion. He founded his own paramilitary organization, the Jaysh al-Mahdi (Mahdi Army), not long after the regime's fall, seeing it as Iraq's counterpart to Hezbollah ("the Party of God"), the Iranian proxy paramilitary in Lebanon that had long straddled the fault line between US-sanctioned terrorist entity and internationally legitimized political party, occupying posts in the Lebanese cabinet and wielding furtive influence within the country's ostensibly independent intelligence services and armed forces. The Party of God proved the perfect template for carving out a similar terrorist "deep state" in Iraq.

Like all warlords, al-Sadr wanted to rule his fief uncontested. Left largely alone by US forces, he created his own sphere of influence with the help of the Iranians. The Sunni conspiracy theory of a Washington-Tehran plot to destroy Iraq can have been met only with anger and bemusement by GIs who experienced firsthand how Iran sought to make life as bloody and difficult for them as possible. The Battle of Najaf in August 2004 was essentially a proxy war between the United States and Iran's elite foreign intelligence and military apparatus, the Revolutionary Guards Corps-Quds Force (IRGC-QF), coordinated on the Iraqi side by an Iranian operative named Sheikh Ansari, who US intelligence concluded was embedded with the Mahdi Army in Najaf and was helping it conduct its combat operations. Ansari was an operative for the Quds Force's Department 1000, which handled Iran's intelligence portfolio in Iraq.

Iran's hegemony in Iraq began well before the regime change. The devastating eight-year war with Iraq had turned the Islamic Republic into a place of refuge for hundreds of thousands of Iraqi Shia who fled Saddam. With Saddam gone, many of these exiles were able to return home to a country where the Shia were enfranchised by nascent democracy and to launch both political and paramilitary apparatuses upon an infrastructure that had been quietly and covertly built up for years under Baathist rule.

The Supreme Council for Islamic Revolution in Iraq (SCIRI) was in fact a wholesale creation of Iranian intelligence and Mohammed Baqir al-Hakim. SCIRI's armed wing, al-Zarqawi's hated Badr Corps, operated as Tehran's fifth column in Iraq. "The mullahs ran a very subversive campaign against Saddam long before we got into that country, and we were dealing with those same lines of communications before we got there," said Colonel Jim Hickey, the former commander for the 4th Infantry Division brigade that captured Saddam in December 2003—an operation in which Hickey played a key role.

When the Americans arrived, Tehran's campaign of sabotage and terrorism fell principally to IRGC-QF's commander Brigadier General Qassem Suleimani, who answered directly to Iran's Supreme Leader Ayatollah Ali Khamenei. A former CIA officer not long ago described Suleimani, who has understandably been promoted to major general in the years since, as "the single most powerful operative in the Middle East today and no one's ever heard of him."

David Petraeus, when he became the top US general in Iraq, got to know Suleimani quite well, referring to the master spy as "evil" and mulling whether or not to tell President Bush that "Iran is, in fact, waging war on the United States in Iraq, with all of the US public and governmental responses that could come from that revelation." For Petraeus, Iran had "gone beyond merely striving for influence in Iraq and could be creating proxies to actively fight us, thinking that they [could] keep us distracted while they [tried] to build WMD and set up [the Mahdi Army] to act like Lebanese Hezbollah in Iraq."

In 2007, five American servicemen were killed in an ambush in Karbala carried out by agents of Asa'ib Ahl al-Haq (the League of the Righteous), a splinter militia of the Mahdi Army set up with al-Sadr and Iran's assistance. Not only had the Quds Force officer stationed at the Iranian consulate in Karbala quit his post shortly before the ambush took place, but one of the leaders of Asa'ib Ahl al-Haq, Qais al-Khazali, confessed to Iran's masterminding of the entire operation.

Suleimani's deputy in bleeding America in Iraq was Abu Mahdi al-Muhandis, an Iraqi national who had lived in Iran and had been tied to the 1983 bombing of the US embassy in Kuwait. Al-Muhandis had gone from being a Badr Corps member to a full-fledged Quds Force operative *before* he was elected to Iraq's parliament. He also set up another so-called Special Group— the American euphemism for Sadrist breakaway militias—called Kata'ib Hezbollah, which similarly targeted US forces.

Suleimani had spent his career in the 1990s stopping the flow of narcotics into Iran from Afghanistan; he'd spend the subsequent decade in the Iraqi import business. Al-Muhandis was selected to oversee trafficking one of the deadliest weapons ever used in the Iraq War: a roadside bomb known as the explosively formed pene-trator, or EFP for short. When detonated, the heat from the EFP melts the copper housing of the explosive, turning it into a molten projectile that can cut through steel and battle armor, including tank walls. The US military reckoned that these devices constituted 18 percent of all coalition combat deaths in the last quarter of 2006. They were manufactured in Iran and smuggled across the border by Iranian agents working with the Badr Corps, then used by all manner of Shia militias, earning them the sobriquet "Persian bombs." In July 2007 two-thirds of US casualties were suffered at the hands of these Shia militias, prompting Petraeus to assess the Mahdi Army as "more of a hindrance to long-term security in Iraq than is AQI," as he wrote to US Defense Secretary Robert Gates. For this reason, many in the military advocated bombing the EFP factories in Iran, regardless of the diplomatic fallout. And whatever Petraeus considered telling the president, America *was* at war with Iran in Iraq.

General McChrystal's JSOC arrested Mohsen Chizari, the head of the Quds Force's Operations and Training staff, along with the Quds Force's station chiefs for Baghdad and Dubai, in late 2006. (Chizari had just come from a meeting at SCIRI headquarters and been spotted by a US surveillance drone.) Another JSOC raid in Erbil, the capital of the Kurdistan Regional Government, intended to net Brigadier General Mohammad Ali Jafari, a senior Quds Force commander, but instead captured five lower-ranking Iranian officers. Eventually, "countering Iran's influence" in Iraq got to be such a full-time job that JSOC bifurcated its task forces according to quarry. Task Force 16 would hunt down AQI, while Task Force 17 would go after Suleimani's operatives and their proxies in the Special Groups.

In some cases, the United States discovered, its two enemies were secretly collaborating with each other. Suleimani intermittently helped AQI for the simple reason that any agent of chaos and destruction that hastened the American departure from Iraq was deemed a net positive for Tehran. In 2011 the US Treasury Department had sanctioned six Iranian-based al-Qaeda operatives, who had helped transport money, messages, and men to and from

Pakistan and Afghanistan via Iran. "Iran is the leading state sponsor of terrorism in the world today," Under Secretary for Terrorism and Financial Intelligence David S. Cohen said at the time. "By exposing Iran's secret deal with al-Qa'ida allowing it to funnel funds and operatives through its territory, we are illuminating yet another aspect of Iran's unmatched support for terrorism."

Former US Ambassador to Iraq Ryan Crocker told the *New Yorker* in 2013 that a decade earlier US intelligence confirmed the presence of al-Qaeda in Iran—itself no great revelation, given that al-Zarqawi had made the Islamic Republic his fallback base after fleeing Kandahar the previous year. (According to the London-based Saudi newspaper *Asharq al-Awsat*, Suleimani is even reported to have boasted in 2004 that al-Zarqawi and Ansar al-Islam were free to move in and out of Iran at will through multiple border crossings—and that al-Zarqawi had even trained at an IRGC camp in Mehran.) However, Crocker claimed that al-Qaeda in Iran was seeking to strike at Western targets in Saudi Arabia in 2003. He enjoyed a somewhat amenable back channel with Iranian officials given the latter's quiet assistance to the United States in routing the Taliban: a case of enemy-of-my-enemy logic that proved opportunistic and fleeting. When Crocker traveled to Geneva the same year that the United States invaded Iraq and prevailed upon them to halt al-Qaeda's terrorism against America in the Gulf, they refused. On May 12, 2003, three compounds in Riyadh were blown up in a combination attack involving gunfire and VBIED bombings. Dozens were killed, including nine Americans. "They were there, under Iranian protection, planning operations," the ex-diplomat recounted to the *New Yorker*.

Meanwhile, the sectarian deep state of al-Sadr's fantasy and the Sunnis' nightmare was indeed emerging with the collusion of the new Iraq government. After December 2005 SCIRI was placed in charge of Iraq's Ministry of Interior, which commanded sixteen thousand troops. The outgoing Interior Minister was Falah Naqib, a Sunni who, along with his uncle Adnan Thabit, had cobbled together the first post-Saddam gendarmeries put to use by the Americans in the form of the Special Police Commandos and the Public Order Brigades. Naqib saw nothing but trouble in Iran's fifth column running the national police force of Iraq. "We either stop them or give Iraq to Iran," Naqib reportedly told George Casey Jr. "That's it."

Naqib's replacement was Bayan Jabr, an SCIRI functionary whom the Americans viewed as less extremist in orientation than others members of the party. But, by way of trying to limit the damage he could still do, they arranged for Thabit to remain on as head of the Ministry of Interior's armed forces. This posed no problem for Jabr, whose workaround solution was not to deal with or through Thabit at all and to simply replace the paramilitary forces under his command with loyal Badr Corps and Mahdi Army militiamen. The counterpart brigade in charge of West Baghdad menacingly patrolled the streets, blasting Shia songs on December 15, 2005, just as Sunnis took to the polls to participate in what was for many their first democratic election. A Ministry of Interior uniform conferred authority and impunity on active members of sectarian death squads.

A Badr-influenced Special Police Commando unit, better known as the Wolf Brigade, was one of the worst offenders. The Islamic Organization for Human Rights, an Iraqi nongovernmental organization (NGO), found that that Ministry of Interior was guilty of twenty cases of detainee abuse, six of which resulted in death and most of which were carried out by the Wolf Brigade in Mosul. According to a State Department cable from the US embassy in Baghdad, the NGO "described practices such as use of stun guns, hanging suspects from their wrists with arms behind back, holding detainees in basements with human waste, and beatings."

Other Iraqi government institutions also fell under the sway of Shia sectarians such as the Health Ministry, the deputy head of which was Hakim al-Zamili, a Mahdi Army agent. Ambulances were used not to transport the sick and injured but to ship weapons. Hospitals, meanwhile, were refashioned into execution sites for Sunnis, driving many in Baghdad to travel outside the capital to seek medical treatment.

Iraq's prime minister, Ibrahim al-Jaafari, created his own intelligence agency, the Ministry of State for National Security Affairs, headed by Shirwan al-Waeli, a man who funneled intelligence on US troop movements to the Mahdi Army and gave the Sadrists practical oversight over much of Iraq's travel industry—the commercial airline sector especially. Right under the noses of US civilian and military authorities, then, the Mahdi Army was doing in Baghdad what Hezbollah had done in Beirut: seizing control of the major international airport and its attendant facilities. It ran the customs office, the sky marshal program, even its contracted cleaning company, existing employees of which the Sadrists murdered to create job vacancies for themselves. It imported weapons hidden in cargo holds of planes from Iran. It also had ready access to the international comings and goings of Sunnis—knowledge that, unsurprisingly, led to many kidnappings and murders.

No single episode better characterized for Sunnis the new republic of fear being constructed atop the ruins of the former one than Jadriya Bunker. A detention facility situated just south of the Green Zone, the bunker's Special Interrogations Unit was run by Bashir Nasr al-Wandi, nicknamed "Engineer Ahmed." A former senior intelligence operative for the Badr Corps, Engineer Ahmed was, like Hadi al-Amari, seconded to Suleimani's Quds Force. When US soldiers finally opened the door to this dungeon prison, they found 168 blindfolded prisoners, all who had been held there for months, in an overcrowded room filled with feces and urine.

Nearly every prisoner was a Sunni, and many bore signs of

torture—some were so badly beaten that they had to be taken to the Green Zone for medical treatment. Because it fell under the Ministry of Interior's purview, Bayan Jabr was forced to answer for what had transpired. He claimed never to have visited the prison and dismissed the human rights abuses in a press conference. Only the "most criminal terrorists" were detained, Jabr said, and by way of showing how gently they had been dealt with, added "no one was beheaded, no one was killed." Testifying to the grim cooperation between Shia-run ministries in al-Jaafari's Iraq, Jabr's predecessor, Falah Naqib, who lived only a few blocks from the Jadriya Bunker, claimed to have seen ambulances coming and going from the building, and speculated that prisoners were being transported in them.

"The Iraq War upset the balance of power in the region in Iran's favor," Emma Sky, the former adviser to the US military, told us. "It is common in the Arab world to hear talk of secret deals between Iran and the United States, and laments that the US 'gave Iraq to Iran.'" This geopolitical perception, Sky said, accounts for one of the primary reasons that Sunnis have been attracted to ISIS.

RICHER THAN BIN LADEN

In 2006 the US government found that AQI, along with other Sunni insurgent factions, could collect between $70 and $200 million annually from criminal enterprises. According to Laith Alkhouri, a specialist on al-Qaeda at Flashpoint Partners, an intelligence firm, al-Zarqawi's gangland past clearly influenced his career as a terrorist warlord. "AQI resorted to any number of methods to make money, from stealing US military weapons and trading them with other insurgent groups, to kidnapping and ransoming hostages. They'd raid the houses of top-ranking Iraqi army officers, then interrogate them inside their own homes. They'd tell them: 'Give us the names, addresses, and phone numbers of other high-ranking army officers.'

Some of these kidnapping victims were very rich, and their families would pay. When that didn't work, al-Qaeda would simply kill the officers in their houses."

From 2005 to 2010 subsidies from Gulf Arab donors and dubious Middle East "charities" accounted for at most an insignificant 5 percent of AQI's overall budget. Oil smuggling from the Bayji Oil Refinery, in Salah ad-Din province, was keeping al-Zarqawi's apparatus in clover.

A Defense Intelligence Agency (DIA) assessment conducted in 2006 found that "[e]ven a limited survey of revenue streams available to the insurgency strongly suggests revenues far exceed expenses." AQI's resources had by then eclipsed those of its Pakistan-based leadership, forcing Osama bin Laden into the embarrassing position of cadging for cash from his reluctant subordinate.

Nor would al-Zarqawi's nominal junior status in the al-Qaeda hierarchy make him more eager to acquiesce to the instructions of his superiors. In July 2005 al-Zawahiri sent him a letter, couched in tones of fraternal advice, though the message was unmistakable: stop murdering Iraq's Shia. The Egyptian believed that AQI ought to be pursuing a three-phase strategy. First and foremost, expel the American occupier; second, establish an Islamic emirate in the Sunni parts of Iraq; third, use this terrain to plot terrorist attacks against other Arab regimes. Al-Zawahiri counseled al-Zarqawi to avoid the "mistakes of the Taliban," which he believed collapsed too quickly because it had played only to its support base in Kandahar and Afghanistan's southern region at the expense of the rest of the country.

Al-Zawahiri was in effect flirting with a kind of jihadist nationalism, at least as a tactical tool to keep a parasitical organization from alienating its host country. Al-Zawahiri was the patient planner, whereas al-Zarqawi was the foolhardy warrior who thought he could battle any and all comers at once. There was one enemy that al-Zawahiri didn't think it wise to take on, at least not yet: Iran.

Fearing that the Islamic Republic's response to any AQI provocations in Iraq would be formidable (it already was that in response to the US occupation) al-Zawahiri told al-Zarqawi that "we and the Iranians need to refrain from harming each other at this time in which the Americans are targeting us." This letter, composed in July 2005, reflected what ISIS spokesman Abu Muhammad al-Adnani would remind the Egyptian of in May 2014; that "Iran owes al Qaeda invaluably."

The letter was never intended for public dissemination; as far as the rest of the world was supposed to know, al-Qaeda high command looked on their Mesopotamian emir's performance with something less than unmixed enthusiasm. The CIA leaked the critical missive in part to aggravate what was then still a deep fissure running between the Sheikh of the Slaughterers and his masters in Central Asia. A lot of good it did.

On February 22, 2006, four AQI terrorists, dressed in the uniforms of the Iraqi Ministry of Interior, detonated several explosives inside the al-Askari Mosque in Samarra, one of the holiest shrines in Shia Islam and a mausoleum for two of the sect's twelve revered imams.

The mosque had been built in 944 AD and remodeled in the nineteenth century, although its celebrated gilt dome, which was ruined in the explosions, was only added at the turn of the twentieth century. The day of the bombing, Iraq's vice president, Adel Abdul Mahdi, a Shia, likened it to 9/11. Grand Ayatollah Ali al-Sistani called for peaceful protests, while hinting that if the Iraqi Security Forces couldn't protect other sacred sites, then Shiite militias might have to. One of Iraq's NGOs found that after the bombing several hundred terrified Shia families fled Baghdad, while US forces announced an emergency mission, Operation Scales of Justice, to mitigate the anticipated wave of retaliatory violence against Sunnis.

The al-Askari Mosque bombing accomplished in the

international imagination what al-Zarqawi had intended and what most Iraqis had already been living through for three years—a civil war.

Al-Sistani's plea for restraint was not heeded by the Sadrists and Iranian-run Special Groups, whose weapons of choice for use on Sunni captives included power drills and electrical cords. Bodies were dumped in the Tigris River. The Mahdi Army also set up checkpoints in Ghazaliya, one of several strategically key towns that ran along a major highway from Baghdad to Anbar. Uniformed Iraqi policemen were enlisted to stop cars passing by and check the identity papers of the passengers; if they were Sunni, they'd be disappeared in an elaborate show of officialdom that was in fact a Sadrist form of ethnic cleansing.

Sunni insurgents paid the Shia back in the same coin. AQI and other Islamist insurgent groups, including ones that would eventually turn on AQI, used every horrific means at their disposal to push the Shia out of Ameriya Fallujah, a Sunni-majority town in western Baghdad that had been choked off and partially starved by the Sadrists. The Iraqi army and police, all answerable to newly installed prime minister Nouri al-Maliki, another Dawa party member, were seen as accomplices to the rampant killings and abductions, which al-Maliki appeared to be tolerating. This was the issue put forth in a classified memo, subsequently leaked, from Stephen Hadley of the White House National Security Council to President Bush in 2006, after Hadley's visit to Baghdad.

"Reports of nondelivery of services to Sunni areas," the memo read, "intervention by the prime minister's office to stop military action against Shiite targets and to encourage them against Sunni ones, removal of Iraq's most effective commanders on a sectarian basis, and efforts to ensure Shiite majorities in all ministries—when combined with the escalation of [Mahdi Army] killings—all suggest a campaign to consolidate Shiite power in Baghdad."

THE DEATH OF AL-ZARQAWI

Al-Zarqawi's whereabouts had been a mystery to coalition forces since the Second Battle of Fallujah, although, according to Bruce Riedel, he'd actually been captured a few times by Iraqis who had no idea of the identity of their prisoner. He may even have once escaped from US custody on the sly. To find al-Zarqawi through his underlings, JSOC and the British Special Air Service (SAS) began rounding up lower-level AQI members in the spring of 2006. In one raid, during which the group's leader in the town of Abu Ghraib was captured, US commandos found the unedited propaganda video of al-Zarqawi clumsily handling a machine gun. This detainee and another mid-ranking AQI operative captured separately outlined the jihadist network in detail, providing the Americans with the name of al-Zarqawi's latest spiritual adviser, Abd al-Rahman. From there, it was a matter of reverse-engineering al-Rahman's mode of communication with al-Zarqawi, via a series of couriers. US forces discovered that their target had been hiding in plain sight all along: al-Zarqawi's safe house was in Hibhib, a town northeast of Baghdad and just twelve miles away from JSOC's own headquarters at Balad Air Base.

On June 7, 2006, a US drone quietly surveilled al-Rahman making contact with al-Zarqawi. By early evening, an F-16 had dropped a five-hundred-pound laser-guided bomb on the location, followed by a second, satellite-guided munition. Iraqi soldiers found al-Zarqawi first, still alive but mortally wounded. He died as McChrystal's men reached the scene. Jordanian intelligence, which had claimed to know al-Zarqawi better than he ever knew himself, took partial credit for his discovery.

In death, the Sheikh of the Slaughterers earned the kind of panegyrics from al-Qaeda's core leadership that had eluded him in life. He was a "knight, the lion of jihad," bin Laden announced in a bit of revisionist canonization. All foregoing words of caution to the contrary, he suddenly fully endorsed al-Zarqawi's mass murder of Iraqi Shia as payback for their collaboration with the "Crusaders."

THE NEW WAR STRATEGY

The death of al-Zarqawi hardly meant the demise of AQI. The Mujahidin Advisory Council he installed as a way to domesticate an expat-heavy franchise appointed another non-native emir: Abu Ayyub al-Masri, an Egyptian national who used another nom de guerre, Abu Hamza al-Muhajir.

He knew al-Zawahiri and al-Zarqawi personally. Al-Masri had belonged to al-Jihad in the 1980s. He traveled to Afghanistan the same year as al-Zarqawi, whom he met at an al-Qaeda training camp. When al-Zarqawi headed to Iraq in 2003, al-Masri went with him.

Al-Masri's appointment was at once a continuation and repudiation of al-Zarqawi's legacy. For one thing, he took the Iraqization program further when, in October 2006, he declared that his franchise was part of a mosaic of homegrown Islamic resistance movements, which he named the Islamic State of Iraq (ISI). Its demesne was Ninewah, Anbar, and Salah ad Din provinces, but also areas where Sunnis didn't have numerical strength, such as Babil, Wasit, Diyala, Baghdad, and Kirkuk, an oil-rich and once cosmopolitan city that had been "Arabized" by Saddam in the 1980s and that the Kurds to this day consider their "Jerusalem." ISI's appointed leader, Abu Omar al-Baghdadi, al-Masri added, was a native Iraqi, whom the Mujahideen Shura Council had voted on to be its leader, yet who never appeared in videos or audio files, presumably for security reasons. Some doubted he even existed at all, until his corpse confirmed that he did.

But al-Masri had a different outlook on the purpose of terrorism than did his predecessor. After his succession became public, US forces captured AQI's emir for southwestern Baghdad, who, in the course of his interrogation, spelled out what divided the two jihadist commanders. Al-Zarqawi, he said, saw himself in messianic terms, as the defender of all Sunnis against the Shia; al-Masri saw himself as a talent scout and exporter of terror, for whom Iraq was but one staging ground in the fight against "Western ideology worldwide." In this respect, al-Masri was closer to al-Zawahiri as a grand strategist. "He came from outside, he was the guy sent by al-Zawahiri and bin Laden to be their man in Iraq," Joel Rayburn told us. "But he joined up with al-Baghdadi, who was an Iraqi Salafist, so there was this inside-outside partnership. Al-Baghdadi lent the street cred to the operation; al-Masri was the supervisory mujahid standing behind him." AQI was thus becoming more adept at navigating Iraqi power politics: the person said to be in charge isn't the one necessarily in charge.

The al-Masri–al-Baghdadi duo served practical purposes, too. The Egyptian was the point of reference for an uninterrupted supply of foreign fighters, whereas the Iraqi didn't want to openly marry himself to al-Qaeda for fear of losing Sunni support among insurgents who believed they were fighting a more nationalistically oriented jihad. Both men wanted to establish an Islamic emirate on the ashes of the Americans and their Shia helpmeets, but the difference was one of emphasis. Most of the Sunni groups that joined ISI protested, as military historian Ahmed Hashim notes, on the grounds that "they were interested in liberating Iraq and not in creating an Islamic state."

Moreover, ISI focused on hitting what Laith Alkhouri calls "soft targets" like Iraqi military bases and Shia religious leaders. "This was intended as a PR campaign to remaining Salafist factions outside the al-Qaeda fold," said Alkhouri. "The message was: 'We are the only group that is looked upon as legitimate by all jihadi groups around the world. You guys are losing men every day. Why don't you just join us?' Jaysh al-Islami refused to join them, which is true to this day. So al-Masri and al-Baghdadi simply intensified their PR. Ultimately, they resorted to killing jihadists who didn't join ISI in order to take over their operational territory. It was rather like a mafia turf war."

In keeping with its name, the Islamic State of Iraq also transformed the Mujahideen Shura Council's remit by creating and populating various other "ministries" such as one for agriculture, oil, and health. It was nation-building, or at least giving that impression. Most controversially, al-Masri, while reaffirming his commitment to bin Laden, also made bayat to al-Baghdadi, placing AQI hierarchically under the patronage of a newly formed umbrella. In jihadist terms, this was like taking a mistress and presenting her as your second wife to your first.

Al-Masri was indeed trying to have it both ways: to remain the emir of AQI while also flirting with outright secession from it to command his own independent operation in Iraq. It wasn't until ISIS formally broke with al-Zawahiri in early 2014 that the deep and irreparable fissure created by al-Baghdadi's pretensions of statehood and al-Masri's subordination of his faction to ISI was at last revealed—by a very angry Ayman al-Zawahiri. In May 2014 he issued a statement in which he quoted an unknown third party who had characterized al-Baghdadi and al-Masri as "repulsive" fools. If al-Qaeda had ever reserved such animadversions for al-Zarqawi, it never publicized them.

THE NEW VBIEDS

The rise of ISI also coincided with the rise in frequency, and sophistication, of VBIED attacks. According to Jessica Lewis McFate, an Iraq analyst at the Institute for the Study of War, one reason why

ISIS today projects a much larger military strength than it actually has owes to its expert use of these devices. Not only is the carnage from VBIED bombings extensive, but the weapon is as much about psychologically discombobulating the enemy in advance of a major military push. "We see them at checkpoints mostly," Lewis said. "We're looking more at VBIEDs or suicide VBIEDs as a tool to catalyst an attack or drive tension for an one. So, for instance, ISIS will conduct a VBIED bombing somewhere in Baghdad or along the Euphrates River Valley, and then will test to see how the Iraqi Security Forces and Shia militias respond to those attacks."

From 2006 onward al-Masri had specialized in pursuing these kinds of attacks in and around Baghdad; factories for the outfitting of cars and trucks with ordnance were discovered in the Baghdad "belts"—the towns and villages that surrounded the capital and where, up until the "surge," the United States had maintained a relatively light footprint.

ISI divided Baghdad and the belts into six zones, five centered around the city. Each zone was ruled by its own local emir. Digital intelligence on ISI, obtained in a JSOC raid, found that one such emir, Abu Ghazwan, who lorded over the thirty-thousand-man town of Tarmiya, managed a number of AQI cells in northern Iraq, including ones that were recruiting women and children for suicide bombing missions. Abu Ghazwan was also intimately acquainted with the schedules of US and Iraqi patrol units, how to avoid them, and how to lay traps for them. The *Wall Street Journal* reported that in mid-February 2007, a "massive truck bomb sheared off the front of the soldiers' base in Tarmiya, sending concrete and glass flying through the air like daggers. The soldiers at the small outpost spent the next four hours fighting for their lives against a force of 70 to 80 insurgents." (More recently, ISIS has targeted Tarmiya with VBIED attacks: in June 2014 it blew up the houses of high-ranking Iraqi Security Forces personnel and a former tribal Awakening leader.)

Abu Ghazwan's overview of how his mini emirate functioned suggested that ISI wasn't just using Tarmiya as a base of terror operations—it was actively building a statelet. "We are running the district, the people's affairs, and the administrative services, and we have committees to run the district headed by my brother Abu Bakr," he said with not a little self-satisfaction. Indeed, AQI's occupation of Tarmiya was redolent of the kind of Islamic fief that had characterized Ansar al-Islam's five-hundred-square-kilometer zone in Iraqi Kurdistan, or ISIS's rule in the eastern Syrian province of Raqqa. Abu Ghazwan even had his municipal conveyances for his Tarmiya emirate. He drove around in a white Nissan truck confiscated from the Iraqi police force and repurposed as an ISI car. He also piloted a ferryboat taken from a water treatment plant along the Tigris River.

Abu Ghazwan's personal history also highlighted another alarming trend of ISI warfare—recidivism. He had once been a detainee of the coalition, as had another man by the name of Mazin Abu Abd al-Rahman, who was newly released from Camp Bucca, one of the largest US-run prisons in Iraq based in Basra and named for a New York City fire marshal who had perished in the Twin Towers on 9/11.

As with al-Zarqawi's Swaqa, Camp Bucca gained a deserved reputation for serving as much as a terrorist academy as a detention facility. Islamists reaffirmed their bona fides by preaching to the converted, but also by proselytizing to new inmates from the general population of criminals who may have gone into the clink as secularists or mildly religious, only to emerge as violent fundamentalists. In Bucca, al-Rahman not only learned the finer points of sharia, he also made friends with AQI bomb-makers and thus graduated from US custody as a new-minted expert in the construction of VBIEDs. Another AQI member later recalled how al-Rahman's time in the facility also acquainted him with the necessary contacts to start his own jihadist cell in the northern Baghdad belt once he was released. As Michael Gordon and Bernard Trainor recount: "It took [al-Rahman] and two other men two days to build each car bomb in the Tarmiya farmhouse they used as a workshop . . .using stolen cars driven up from a parking lot where they were stored in Adhamiya and a combination of plastic and homemade explosives. The evening before an attack, the completed car bomb would be driven from Tarmiya back into Baghdad, where it would be stored overnight in a parking lot or garage before the bomber drove it to its final destination and blew it up."

The founder of AQI had been found and killed thirteen miles away from JSOC's headquarters at Balad Air Base. A major cottage industry for car bombs was thriving some forty miles north of Camp Victory.

5

THE AWAKENING

"The history of the Anbar Awakening is very bitter," a former high-ranking official in the Iraqi government told us toward the end of 2014. "The people who fought al-Qaeda were later abandoned by their government. Many of them were also executed by al-Qaeda, and some of them were even arrested by Iraqi forces. Until there is a perceivable change [in] the way business is done by Baghdad, I strongly doubt that people are willing to risk their lives and start something similar against ISIS." His point, which is reflective of many Iraqi Sunnis we have interviewed, is better illuminated by the origins of the Awakening. Like most propitious discoveries, this one happened by accident.

SAHWA

The Desert Protectors program had been a short-lived but useful exercise in American alliance-building with the tribesmen of Ramadi. By 2006, however, the provincial capital of Anbar had fallen again to AQI's dominance.

The jihadists were so entrenched in the city that they resorted to US Army Corps of Engineers–type innovations for laying undetectable IEDs to deter or kill US and Iraqi columns. They used power saws to cut away large chunks of asphalt in the road and fill the resulting craters with ordnance before reapplying a seemingly untouched blacktop. To the naked eye, it looked like normal road—until the bomb went off, damaging or destroying a Bradley fighting vehicle or Abrams tank and killing or maiming the occupants inside. The holes these inlaid IEDs left in the ground also caused severe infrastructure damage, bursting the city's sewage pipes and flooding the streets with filth.

As elsewhere in Iraq, the provincial government in Ramadi had been keeping two sets of books, one for its official duties on behalf of Baghdad, the other for AQI, which bribed and cajoled Iraqi Security Forces and municipal officials, using its greatest asset outside of murder: oil-smuggling revenue. Barrels of purloined crude were imported into Ramadi on a regular basis from the Bayji Oil Refinery up north, then exported for resale on Iraq's black market. This had been the tribes' arrangement with the Saddamists for years. But the new bosses proved more difficult to work with.

Locals bridled at medieval rule, for starters, especially since one of AQI's self-arrogated entitlements was sharia's answer to droit du seigneur: just like ISIS today, the jihadists in 2006 raped Iraqi women at their pleasure. Tribal elders, too, were susceptible to kidnapping or murder. Two sheikhs from the Albu Aetha and Albu Dhiyab tribes had been killed already, and others were being targeted as competition to what had become the AQI's thriving war economy.

The people of Ramadi turned slowly against terrorism. Nighttime vigilantism gained enough of a following among families of the group's victims, who were joined by vengeful Iraqi policemen and even rival insurgents fed up with takfiris, that soon a bona fide civil resistance movement was born under the banner of Thuwar al-Anbar, or the Revolutionaries of Anbar. It was the beginning of what became known as Sahwa—"Awakening." These native revolutionaries proved so successful in Ramadi that AQI even attempted to negotiate with them.

What made Ramadi different was that, when the city was retaken by American and Iraqi forces, a post-battle strategy of police recruitment was wisely implemented not in the vulnerable city center, which, as with the glass factory episode two years prior, was an easy target for insurgent attack, but in the adjoining rural tribal districts. Keeping Sahwa confined to the countryside encouraged what was already a growing insurrection to build enough to become an officially sanctioned one, fostered by growing mutual trust between the Americans and the tribes. One of the key tribal allies was the charismatic Abdul Sattar al-Rishawi, whose compound had actually been raided twice before by US forces after allegations that he was cooperating commercially with the insurgents. Suddenly, out of the very self-interest and pragmatism that had catalyzed the temporary alliance, al-Rishawi was ready to cut a new deal with the enemy of his enemy. "People with ties to the insurgents have us over for tea," a US lieutenant had told the journalist George Packer about a similar experience in Tal Afar in 2005, when H. R. McMaster had overseen that border town's temporary turnaround on much the same principle. Al-Rishawi would prove one of the most significant allies the United States ever made in Iraq.

AQI's attempt to undermine his efforts failed because tribal disaffection had already grown into a significant groundswell. Along with his brother, Al-Rishawi formed the Anbar Emergency Council, which claimed to represent seventeen Anbari tribes ready to partner with coalition forces against AQI. The council quickly expanded and was rebranded the Anbar Awakening. Al-Rishawi oversaw the recruitment of four hundred men to the Iraqi police force in October 2006, and then another five hundred in November.

He was also farsighted enough to realize that recruitment did not necessarily translate into immediate security: these cadets all had to be sent off to Jordan for training, creating a vacuum that AQI was sure to exploit. Al-Rishawi convinced Nouri al-Maliki to authorize the formation of makeshift paramilitary battalions to serve in their stead. And so the Emergency Response Units were born, led not by corrupt or incompetent neophytes but by tribesmen who had served in the former Iraqi army and knew how to fight. Just before New Year 2007, the Units numbered a little more than two thousand men.

To make these ad hoc solutions permanent, the United States also shrewdly set up new police substations throughout the Ramadi region, creating a further psychological bolster for the tribes—that US-imposed and Iraqi-maintained law and order was there to stay—which served as a deterrent for the insurgents. VBIED attacks in the outskirts of the city dropped as a result. Al-Rishawi's general success led him into fits of hyperbole and overconfidence, although both were surely welcome to American ears at the time. "I swear to God, if we have good weapons, if we have good vehicles, if we have good support, I can fight Al Qaeda all the way to Afghanistan," the sheikh told the *New York Times*, and evidently also President Bush, who met him on a visit to Baghdad in 2007. In the end, Al-Rishawi wasn't able to finish seeing al-Qaeda run out of Iraq. He was assassinated by the jihadists just days after his encounter with the president.

The Anbar Awakening was bottom-up rather than top-down, and thus seized upon at the brigade level by other quick-thinking and improvisational commanders who were ready to negotiate with those who only the day before were sharing tea with the insurgents. The December 2005 election had already proved that some Sunni terrorists were reconcilable to Iraq's political system and didn't need to be captured or killed.

Lieutenant General Graeme Lamb, General Casey's British deputy, had long held that it was only a matter of a time until AQI's presence proved too noxious for Sunnis and some of the jihadists' less extremist battlefield partners turned to the coalition for help. The question was determining who could be approached in return and who was too far gone. AQI operatives were off-limits, clearly, but what about the organization's more ideologically flexible "affiliates" in the Islamic State of Iraq? Lamb met with an emir from Ansar al-Sunna, a Salafist faction that had recently begun to doubt ISI's methods. The emir told him that while foreign occupiers could and must be fought, Ansar al-Sunna knew that the more exigent evil facing Iraq was al-Masri and al-Baghdadi's head-loppers and rapists. "We have watched you in Anbar for three and a half years," he told Lamb. "We have concluded that you do not threaten our faith or our way of life. Al-Qaeda does."

THE SURGE

Solidifying an incipient popular revolt against AQI meant adding to the conventional military capability in Iraq. Much has been written and debated about the "surge" of US forces in Iraq, which began in 2007 under a cloud of domestic political controversy in Washington. Overseen by Petraeus, the policy adopted by the president called for the injection of five additional combat brigades—up to thirty thousand more troops—and a completely overhauled war strategy. The new strategy demanded confronting not only AQI but also the vast network of state-backed Shia militias and Iranian proxies that posed just as much of a security threat to US forces and the Sunni civilians suddenly being asked to help rout jihadism. Not coincidentally, the architect of that strategy was the man in charge of implementing it.

Petraeus and Marine Lieutenant General James Mattis had

coauthored a new field manual on counterinsurgency (COIN), a 282-page guidebook for beating back a Maoist-style guerrilla resistance by turning the communities it lived among and cooperated with against it—or, to use the oft-cited Maoist metaphor, turning the sea against the fish. A mixture of soldiering and policing, COIN's magic ratio, as codified by the Petraeus-Mattis manual, was 20-to-1,000—twenty soldiers for every one thousand civilians. (That math incorporated Iraqi army soldiers and policemen.)

The Sunni tribes didn't have to be persuaded that hunting AQI was in their interest—they were already doing so more bravely and ably than most of the Iraqi army. Petraeus had seen that firsthand. He had been in charge of the training program of the Iraqi Security Forces, a program that had been beset by dysfunction and corruption. Many of the cadets proved incompetent or unwilling to fight. Others stole equipment and ran off to resell it—in some cases, to the very enemy America had hired them to beat. In 2007 the US Government Accountability Office released a report stating that close to 190,000 AK-47s and sidearms had disappeared from registered stocks. That meant weapons purchased by the American taxpayer were very likely floating around Iraq and killing American servicemen.

The first two surge brigades were dispatched to Baghdad, the hornet's nest for AQI, which wasted no time trying to sabotage the new COIN strategy. AQI was strongest in the belts surrounding the capital, where newly established US outposts were attacked by coordinated VBIED assaults. In a single day in February, five such operations killed around five hundred people. Conditions were particularly nightmarish in areas with mixed Sunni-Shia populations, where Special Groups and insurgents kidnapped, tortured, killed, and ethnically cleansed each other. The US military's solution was a partition: it built enormous and extensive concrete walls to keep one sect away from its rival.

"The key to Baghdad is this terrain, especially the north and south," Jim Hickey told us. "Sunni tribes and families—they were the support bases AQI used in 2005 and 2007. We ultimately won the battle for Baghdad because we cleared out the supporting belts they spent years building."

DIYALA, THEN AND NOW

US failure in destroying AQI's purchase on Iraq's capital was actually rooted in some of its deceptive successes. When al-Zarqawi was killed in Hibhib in June 2006, JSOC recovered a cache of AQI intelligence that suggested that the jihadists believed they were losing their chief stronghold, the so-called Triangle of Death in southern Baghdad, to the Americans. Al-Zarqawi had contemplated yet another change of venue for his headquarters just before he was killed. But the coalition's territorial victories were Pyrrhic because they were tactical, not strategic. Did defeat for AQI in one place mean defeat nationwide? On that, competing camps within the US defense establishment disagreed. A military intelligence analysis commissioned by George Casey Jr., Petraeus's predecessor, concluded that all the trademarks of Zarqawist violence—suicide bombings, sniper attacks, IED detonations—were noticeably fewer, and the jihadists seemed to be too. Furthermore, the overwhelming cluster of attacks was confined to only four provinces out of Iraq's eighteen; but half the national population resided in twelve of the remaining ones, which collectively experienced just 6 percent of all attacks. That meant that AQI was losing badly throughout Iraq, according to Casey.

The rebuttal to Casey's sanguine appraisal was offered by Derek Harvey. Harvey thought the methodology of the general's study was wrong and was mistaking short-term advances for long-term ones. He cited a DIA-commissioned plebiscite that had found that Iraqis had minimal confidence in their own government's defense establishment but were still full of admiration for the "armed resistance." That didn't bode well, since popular support was its own force multiplier, and one that could keep Iraq's national security in a state of turmoil. Harvey also noted that the way the military was counting terrorist attacks was highly misleading, because it only scored ones that were successful, i.e., that resulted in casualties. But what about the *failed* attacks, the near misses? If a detonated IED turned out to be a dud or if it didn't injure or kill people, did it still not constitute an attack and indicate AQI's enduring ability to terrorize and operational capability to do so?

Harvey's more depressing analysis proved correct. Since AQI kept relocating its command centers from city to city, what had been Casey's strictly counterterrorism-focused strategy was an agonized game of Whac-a-Mole.

By 2007 AQI had set up new headquarters in Baqubah, the provincial capital of Diyala province. As they had done the prior year in Ramadi, the jihadists took over not only downtown Baqubah but the outlying rural areas in the south as well, which ran parallel to the Diyala River and afforded them a verdant canopy to mask their movements and activities. The group's fallback base was in nearby Buhriz, a former Baathist redoubt where it had resorted to publicly executing or kidnapping locals, if not booting them from their homes. As for AQI's "governance," it seized the bread mills outside of the city and rationed food to command the fealty of those it didn't dispossess or murder. Buhriz subsequently became the site of one the most intense battles of the entire Iraq War.

It started in March 2007, when a US Stryker battalion and a paratrooper squadron moved in to take the city, encountering a storm of RPG and sniper fire. The enemy targeted US forces "in small numbers," using "subterfuge," Sergeant 1st Class Benjamin Hanner told the *Washington Post*. "They're controlled, their planning is good, their human intel network and early-warning networks are effective." They were also skillful at using decoys. They laid twenty-seven IEDs in a one-mile expanse of road but ensured that only one out of every three or four bombs was operational. "I have never seen, before or since, organization like that," Shawn McGuire, a staff sergeant recalled to Gordon and Trainor. "They were organized. They were well trained. They shot. They could hit things. Instead of just poking around corners and shooting and running, they would bound and maneuver on you. It was almost like watching US soldiers train."

The jihadists also made heavy use of another weapon of choice: house-borne improvised explosive devices (HBIEDs), which were built into the walls of Buhriz residences and set to explode as soldiers entered. In 2013 ISIS deployed HBIEDs with devastating effect—this time against Iraqi soldiers and policemen in Ninewah to coerce them into defecting or deserting. Given how easily ISIS sacked Mosul the following year, these attacks clearly weakened an already underwhelming Iraqi authority.

Long after the battle of Buhriz was over, Diyala saw a return to sectarian warfare, with Shia militias competing against new Sunni *sahwats* who were committed to opposing the repressive al-Maliki government. The province also represents a crucial battleground for ISIS. Abu Bakr al-Baghdadi belongs to the Bobadri tribe in Diyala, where a new ISIS *wilayat* (province) was announced in December 2013. Al-Adnani, the ISIS spokesman, also said that the jihadist war on Iraq's Shia would be most concentrated there.

LIONS FOR LAMB

The battle for Buhriz also showed the wisdom of Graeme Lamb's attempt to co-opt the less fanatical Sunni insurgents and use them against AQI. Of all the groups for which this eventually proved feasible, none turned on their former jihadist colleagues with more fervor than the Islamic Army.

In an interview with the *Washington Post* conducted in 2004, not long after the Second Battle of Fallujah, the group's leader, Ishmael Jubouri, a Sunni tribesman, insisted that his army was all Iraqi, made up of Sunnis, Shia, and Kurds, and committed only to the expulsion of the occupiers. Maybe, but the Islamic Army was also the largest Salafist-Baathist insurgency in Iraq, and by April 2007 it had grown so tired of AQI that it appealed directly to bin Laden to rein in his runaway franchise. When that didn't work, it appealed to the Americans.

Abu Azzam, an Islamic Army commander, offered to help the US military regain control of the overrun Baghdad belts—especially Abu Ghraib, where Sunnis faced the pincer of AQI and the Shia militias. Azzam arranged a meeting between US forces and the three thousand volunteers who signaled their willingness to join an Awakening-style gendarmerie. Among them was a 1920 Revolution Brigades member named Abu Marouf, who had been number seven on the coalition's most-wanted list for Abu Ghraib. Reluctant though they were to collaborate with a top-level terrorist who, not weeks earlier, was hunting and killing their own, the Americans agreed to put Abu Marouf's overtures to the test. After being handed a list of the top-ten AQI operatives in the belt city of Radwaniyah, Abu Marouf returned days later with a cell phone video showing the capture and execution of one of them.

Abu Marouf was backed by the powerful Zobai tribe in the Baghdad region, with which he waged daring raids against AQI, further proving his bona fides. In Ameriya, a neighborhood west of Baghdad, an Iraqi volunteer group known as Forsan al-Rafidayn (Knights of the Two Rivers) called in coordinates of jihadist targets for American warplanes to bomb.

Eventually, Sahwa went from being a collection of localized civic actions to an institutionalized part of Petraeus's COIN strategy, with regional Awakening Councils answering directly to the

US military and to the Iraqi provincial governments. Initially billed as the Concerned Local Citizens program, it soon became known by the more evocative Sons of Iraq. No doubt leery of seeing a replay of the first Iraqi Security Forces train-and-equip debacle, Petraeus tracked the Awakening volunteers by taking their biometric data and cataloging it on a central database.

"The surge is poorly understood," Ali Khedery, the longest continuously serving American diplomat in Iraq, told us. "It was less about a surge of troops and more about a surge of diplomacy with Iraq's national leadership to force it to work together and hammer out political deals. The goal was to buy time for the politicians to reach an accommodation with one another. That's why you saw a reduction in violence by ninety percent from pre-surge highs to the time of provincial election in 2009."

Not coincidentally, that election was largely won in the Sunni provinces by the very tribal figures who had cannibalized AQI. Al-Rishawi's brother earned a seat on the Anbar Provincial Council. In Diyala and Ninewah provinces, Sunni coalitions likewise came out on top.

AQI ON THE ROPES

In a June 2010 Pentagon news briefing, General Odierno claimed that in the same three-month period, US forces had "either picked up or killed 34 out of the top 42 al Qaeda in Iraq leaders. They're clearly now attempting to reorganize themselves. They're struggling a little bit. . . . They've lost connection with [al-Qaeda senior leadership] in Pakistan and Afghanistan."

AQI was being battered by a combination of JSOC raids, US surge brigades, Sons of Iraq militias, and their own lousy communications. For years, the National Security Agency had been Hoovering up telephone chatter between and among jihadists in the field, passing the intercepts along to the CIA and JSOC, which then tracked, arrested, or eliminated them.

"It was Darwinism," said Derek Harvey. "All the guys who were stupid enough to use cell phones in Baghdad kept getting hit, hit, hit, and hit. That was their way of culling the herd, though it had the negative side effect of leaving the smarter and more powerful operatives in place, the ones who were good at internal counterintelligence and buffering access to key leaders. The opaqueness of ISIS today is a reflection of this tradecraft."

Distinct from the surge and the Awakening but equally auspicious was the fact that AQI's fortunes began to wane in 2007 in the Iraqi imagination, coinciding with the emergence of something resembling a post-Saddam national identity, which transcended sectarianism and fratricidal bloodletting. In 2007, Iraqi singer Shada Hassoun won *Star Academy*, the Middle East equivalent of *American Idol*, for a heartbreaking rendition of the ballad "Baghdad," which she belted out wrapped in her nation's flag. Later that year, Iraq took the Asian Cup soccer tournament, beating Saudi Arabia. AQI's celebrity, meanwhile, dimmed in its key demographic—young Sunnis. In *Iraq After America*, Joel Rayburn recounts a telling anecdote relayed to him by a police commander in Habbaniyah, a city in Anbar, around that time:

"Stepping from his home on Christmas Eve, 2007, he had been astonished to find the young men of his neighborhood setting off fireworks, with their girlfriends, and drinking alcohol—all distinctly 'Christian' activities that Al Qaeda had banned. The bemused policeman had teased the youths, 'You're celebrating like Christians, but last year you were all Al Qaeda!' The young men had laughed, the police officer later recalled, answering, 'Al Qaeda? That was last year!'"

That the takfiris could be reduced to the level of a passing fad would prove a valuable lesson for the US military's central command

(CENTCOM) to learn in Iraq, and an even harder one for it to remember when that fad returned with a vengeance five years later.

As AQI's reputation sagged externally, its internal decision-making was also apparently in crisis. Mullah Nadhim al-Jibouri was originally from the town of Dhuluiya, just north of Baghdad, and had sat on al-Zarqawi's Mujahideen Shura Council. He then joined the Awakening before moving for a time to Jordan, where a lot of the tribes' Islamic outreach was being conducted remotely. Al-Jibouri appeared on Jordanian national television frequently, denouncing AQI for its atrocities back home. Then, in the spring of 2011, he returned to Baghdad for reconciliation talks with the al-Maliki government. Al-Jibouri gave an interview to an Iraqi television station. The next day, he was murdered in a drive-by shooting in the western part of the capital.

Several months before his death, he had conducted a Skype call with members of the US military. According to one of the officers dialed into the conversation, al-Jibouri confirmed that the creation of the ISI was in effect a putsch by AQI, which had sought to dress up its own foreign jihadism in a nationalist costume. But other Sunni insurgents saw through it. ISI created a backlash among nationalists who had not been fighting and dying just to see a Zarqawist emirate installed in the Green Zone. Many of these insurgents, furthermore, had only ever accepted AQI on an ad hoc military basis. "ISI represented al-Qaeda's attempt to hijack the political channel of the Iraqi insurgency," al-Jibouri said.

All totalitarianisms thrive on myths that transcend or erase national boundaries, even ones that begin as expressions of nationalism and then have to retroactively justify their inevitable anschluss of foreign land. AQI was no different. For the first years of the war, it had created a powerful dual perception of itself—first, as the vanguard of an *Iraqi* insurgency committed to seeing the Western occupiers pummeled and expelled, and second, as the guardian of a stolen Sunni patrimony. In its apocalyptic extremism, it erased both perceptions. Petraeus's army had administered the powerful drug of counterinsurgency warfare, which helped Iraq's own antibodies in turn to destroy a foreign and deadly pathogen.

But that was with nearly 170,000 American soldiers in Iraq. Today, the challenge is far more difficult because the tribes don't trust Baghdad, and with rare exception, they are not about to partner with Shia militias against ISIS. "People don't believe in the term *Awakening* anymore because when the Iraqi government finished using the tribes, it turned against the Sons of Iraq," Dr. Jaber al-Jabberi, a senior political adviser o the former Deputy Prime Minister Rafi al-Issawi, told us. "It didn't give them rights, it didn't pay their salaries, and it put a lot of them in jail. I don't think the tribes will do another Awakening. What they need is a provincial National Guard, which can be part of the Iraqi Security Forces but from the tribal people, who can work as not army or police but as a militia."

ISIS has taken every precaution against seeing anything of the sort occur again. *Sahwat* is a frequent term of abuse in its propaganda; it boasts of destroying the homes of tribesmen who oppose it and of allowing former Awakening militiamen to "repent" and rejoin ISIS. "Nobody has talked to me about a new Awakening, of forming a national guard," Sheikh Ahmed Abu Risha, al-Rishawi's brother, told the *Guardian* in October 2014. That same month a mass grave filled with 150 bodies was uncovered in a ditch in Ramadi. All the corpses belonged to the Albu Nimr tribe.

6

WITHDRAWAL SYMPTOMS

ISI AND AL-MALIKI WAIT OUT THE
UNITED STATES

The success of Sahwa and the counterinsurgency meant that more jihadists were not only being killed in battle, but rounded up as enemy combatants and jailed in American-run detention facilities in Iraq. The current leader of ISIS and a host of his lieutenants were once prisoners of the United States; they were released either because the United States deemed them negligible security threats or because the al-Maliki government had other motives than the military's security concerns. The failure of foresight, many former US officials have told us, had to do with how these prisoners were identified and categorized once in custody. "Guys we ID'd and reported to be this thing in an organization—we did that because it made it easy to understand them," a former Bush administration official told us. "So we'd say, 'Well, he's the emir.' Fuck you, he's the emir. It's the fifth guy standing behind him who counts."

TERROR U.

AQI and ISI weren't only using US-run prisons as "jihadi universities," according to Major General Doug Stone; they were actively trying to *infiltrate* those prisons to cultivate new recruits. In 2007 Stone assumed control over the entire detention and interrogation program in Iraq, with an aim to rehabilitate rehabilitation. Not only had the internationally publicized and condemned torture of detainees at Abu Ghraib prison left a permanent stain on the occupation and America's credibility in the war, but theater detainment facilities had also been used as little more than social-networking furloughs for jihadists. Camp Bucca, based in the southern province of Basra, was especially notorious.

According to one US military estimate, Bucca housed 1,350 hardened takfiri terrorists amidst a general population of 15,000, yet there was little to no oversight as to who was allowed to integrate with whom. Owing to the spike in military operations coinciding with the surge, the detainee number nearly doubled to 26,000 when Stone took command in 2007.

"Intimidation was weekly, killing was bimonthly," Stone recalled in an interview. "It was a pretty nasty place that was out of control when I got there. They used cigarettes and matches to burn down their tents and mattresses, and when we tried to rebuild the tents, they'd just burn them down again. We thought they'd burn the whole goddamn prison down."

Stone introduced a de-radicalization program, featuring lectures by moderate Muslim imams who used the Quran and hadith to try and persuade extremists that theirs was a distorted interpretation of Islam. He started to compartmentalize inmates into what were known as Modular Detainee Housing Units (MDHUs). "Before that, we had guys in thousand-man camp blocs. We used the

MDHUs to segregate those who had been intimidated or beaten from those who did the intimidating and beating up."

During his eighteen-month tenure, Stone either led, oversaw, or consulted on more than eight hundred thousand detainee interrogations, observing several "trends" among the AQI population. In a PowerPoint presentation he prepared for CENTCOM, summarizing his findings, Stone corroborated much of what Mullah Najim Jibouri had told military officials about this period, namely that foreign fighters were looked on unfavorably as "Iraqis [who were] trying to re-assume leadership roles." Baathists were "attempting to use the ISI banner to regain control of some areas." Jihadists cared more about their hometowns or local areas than they did about global or regional terrorism. AQI's use of women and children as suicide bombers had "disgusted" many. Money, not ideology, was the primary motivation for joining AQI. Finally, AQI's emir Abu Ayyub al-Masri was "not an influential figure to most . . .however[,] younger, more impressionable detainees" were swayed by the figure of ISI emir Abu Omar al-Baghdadi.

Early on in his command, Stone noticed a strange phenomenon that pertained exclusively to the takfiri detainees—they would enter Camp Bucca asking to join the AQI bloc, often with foreknowledge of how the prison worked and how detainees were housed. "Sometimes guys would allow themselves to be caught. Then, in the intake process, they'd ask to be put in a specific compound which housed a lot of the al-Qaeda guys. The takfiris were extremely well organized in Bucca; they arranged where their people slept and where they were moved to based on their Friday night prayers. In fact, one of the large cell areas was nicknamed Camp Caliphate. The more I heard it, the more I began to think, *Even if they can't get it done, they sure as shit believe they can.*"

Prison culture in Iraq was such that anyone picked up by US forces without any form of identification would give his name and then have his biometric data processed. Iris scans, fingerprints, and DNA samples were collected from all detainees. But often the names given during the intake were fake. "Some of them would have a different name for every interrogation. It was only through biometrics that we were later able to track recidivism rates," Stone said.

Early on, Stone said, he came across a detainee whose listed surname was Baghdadi. There was nothing inherently eyebrow-raising about that—insurgents often take their city or country of origin (or the city or country they'd like people to think they're from) as a nom de guerre. But this Baghdadi stood apart from others. Stone said, "His name came up on a list of people that I had. They listed him as a guy who had significant al-Qaeda links. The psychologists rated him as someone who was a really strong wannabe—not in the sociopathic category, but a serious guy who [had] a serious plan. He called himself an imam and viewed himself not as a descendant of Muhammad—we had a few of those at Bucca—but someone with a very strong religious orientation. He was holding Sharia court and conducting Friday services from the platform of being an imam."

This Baghdadi was pensive and hardly a jailhouse trouble-maker. "We had hundreds like him in what we termed the 'leadership category,'" Stone said. "We ended up referring to him as an 'irreconcilable,' someone for whom sermons by moderate imams wasn't going to make the slightest difference. So here's the quiet, unassuming guy who had a very strong religious viewpoint, and what does he do? He starts to meet the 'generals.' By that I mean, we had a lot of criminals and guys who were in the Iraqi army who called themselves generals, but they were low-ranking officers in Saddam's army." All the high-level former Iraqi military officials and hard-core Baathists, including Saddam himself, were detained at Camp Cropper, another US-run facility based in Baghdad International Airport. Cropper was also the processing center for Bucca detainees. "Some of the generals shared Baghdadi's religious perspective and joined the takfiris—big beards and all of that."

Stone said he believes that this man was in fact a decoy sent by ISI to pose as the elusive Abu Omar al-Baghdadi to penetrate Bucca and use his time there to mint new holy warriors. "If you were looking to build an army, prison is the perfect place to do it. We gave them health care, dental, fed them, and, most importantly, we kept them from getting killed in combat. Who needs a safe house in Anbar when there's an American jail in Basra?"

A former ISIS member interviewed by the *Guardian* confirmed Stone's appraisal. "We could never have all got together like this in Baghdad, or anywhere else," Abu Ahmed told the newspaper. "It would have been impossibly dangerous. Here, we were not only safe, but we were only a few hundred [meters] away from the entire al-Qaida leadership."

Abu Ahmed recounted how jihadist detainees scribbled one another's phone numbers and hometowns on the elastic waistbands of their underwear and had a ready-made network upon their release. "When we got out, we called. Everyone who was important to me was written on white elastic. I had their phone numbers, their villages. By 2009 many of us were back doing what we did before we were caught. But this time we were doing it better."

That a decoy al-Baghdadi was recruiting from the ranks of the lower or middle cadres of the former Iraqi army made perfect sense to Richard, the former Pentagon official. "We tend to look at the Iraqi army as a joke, but it was a professional army, a very large army," he said. "What we would consider junior officers—such as captains, majors, warrant officers—we'd be dismissive of those guys in Iraq. In Arab armies, usually those are the guys that are the true professionals. The guys that rise higher than major, the real generals in Saddam's military, have tribal connections, family money. They buy their way in. The mid-grade officers are the ones who matter. Those dudes rocked. How else are they going to make money? Their families are starving, they gotta make money. 'I'll put together a convoy ambush, piece together a couple of rounds into an IED, and these guys will pay me.' Eventually they became pretty successful and they joined up with various insurgent groups, including al-Qaeda."

Around 70 percent of Bucca inmates in 2008 were there for about a year or so. "What this meant in reality"—Craig Whiteside, a professor at the Naval War College in Newport, Rhode Island, wrote in an essay for the website War on the Rocks—"is that your average Bucca detainee was incarcerated for a year or two before being released, despite being involved in fairly serious violence against the coalition or Iraqi government. There were even examples of insurgents who were sent to and then released from Bucca multiple times—despite specializing in making roadside bombs."

AL-MALIKI VS. WASHINGTON

Camp Bucca was closed in 2009 in line with the Status of Forces Agreement (SOFA) signed between Washington and Baghdad, which mandated that US-held prisoners either be let go or transferred into Iraqi custody, and that US troops be withdrawn from Iraqi cities by June 30, 2009, handing over all security responsibilities to their Iraqi counterparts. In December 2008 President Bush and Prime Minister al-Maliki signed SOFA in Baghdad at a ceremony more remembered for its violent disruption—an audience member threw his shoes at Bush—than its diplomatic breakthrough.

In reality, by late 2008 US soldiers were already largely confined to the outskirts of Iraq's cities and were acting more as a stopgap on sectarianism than anything else. They protected Sunni and mixed communities from Shia death squads, which operated with state impunity, and they protected the Shia communities from the equally vicious violence of the remaining Sunni insurgency.

SOFA was certainly billed as a major victory by al-Maliki over the United States rather than a mutually agreed compact marking the end to a war. Its implementation date, June 30, 2009, was turned into a national holiday commemorating the "repulsion of foreign occupiers." But it was what the prime minister did with his newfound internment authority that had the direst repercussions for Iraq. "The vast majority of prisoners were just let go, even the crazy Sunni ones," said Joel Rayburn, who has made a close study of SOFA and its consequences for Iraq's security. "Maliki thought that, as of 2008 and 2009, we were just holding innocent people who had been caught up in a sweep. The big problem was, we would capture someone based on intelligence—either signals intelligence or human intelligence—and then not be able to share our methodology with the Iraqis to explain why the captured dude was a bad dude. If it was intelligence where you had to take out all the sources, the Iraqis would say, 'Based on whose say-so?' They'd dismiss it. The entire Iraqi legal system runs on the authority of witness testimony. If you get two witnesses to say something, then it's unshakable."

Plenty of incorrigible AQI jihadists were also let out of jail after the end of US oversight of Iraq's wartime penal system, as the late Anthony Shadid, then a foreign correspondent for the *Washington Post*, reported in March 2009. That month, 106 prisoners were released and headed straight for the Umm al-Qura mosque in Baghdad—among them, Mohammed Ali Mourad, al-Zarqawi's former driver. Despite his likely involvement in two deadly VBIED attacks against a police station, Mourad had been let out of Camp Bucca after he was suspected of having founded a new jihadist cell consisting of fellow detainees. Shadid cited a senior intelligence official at the Iraqi Ministry of Interior who reckoned that 60 percent of freed detainees, be they Sunni or Shia, were getting up to their old habits again and rejoining active insurgencies or Special Groups. "Al-Qaeda is preparing itself for the departure of the Americans," the official said. "And they want to stage a revolution."

Where Baghdad didn't rubber-stamp their freedom, the jihadists took matters into their own hands, mounting jailbreaks of their incarcerated associates, often by paying off or intimidating Ministry of Interior personnel to help them.

"It was easy to capture al-Qaeda people," Rayburn told us. "We'd get them by the dozen, but they had an entire system for getting their guys back out, either by ensuring that their case was dropped in court or that through bribery they could be released early or, in the last resort, that a physical break of the prison could take place. They even had, at one point in 2008 or 2009, a 'detainee emir'—a guy who was responsible for springing jihadis from the clink—just like they had a 'border emir' who'd coordinate the foreign fighter rat lines into Iraq from Syria. 'Hey, Ahmad's trial is coming up, here's a list of the key witnesses. Go around, get them to recant or leave, or just kill them.' Mosul was the worst spot in the country for that. We never got a full handle on the justice and prison systems up there."

THE AWAKENING PUT TO SLEEP

Al-Maliki's definition of the threats to a post-American Iraq derived from his own political and sectarian biases. Detainees whose only crime was fighting US forces were not deemed true criminals necessitating further incarceration. Members of the Awakening, however, who had previously fought Iraqi Security Forces or Shia militias, were not subject to the same magnanimous gloss on rehabilitation.

Long-dormant criminal cases against the Sons of Iraq remained opened even after the suspects had been deputized as state-sanctioned militiamen. No longer useful to al-Maliki, and with ever-diminishing US protection, they were instead harassed and bullied by the government they had served. Many were also arrested on spurious "terrorism" grounds. "Sunnis always talk about the release of prisoners who were convicted illegally or extrajudicially," a former Iraqi government official told us. "The dropping of all these terror cases is a main demand of them now."

Conditions were especially grim in Diyala province, which had been pacified at great expense in the preceding years and yet fell into chaos again after the surge. In August 2008 the prime minister had dispatched personnel from the Iraqi Special Operations Forces—one of the few effective counterterrorism units in the Iraqi security apparatus—into the office of the provincial governor of Diyala to arrest both a local councilman and the president of the University of Diyala, a Sunni. The operation resulted in the killing of the governor's press secretary.

By the summer of 2009 the 3rd Stryker Brigade of the US 2nd Infantry Division had returned to Diyala, where it spent a year observing the crackdown on Sunni political power. It wasn't enough that AQI was hunting Sunnis who had repudiated it; anyone affiliated with the Awakening was targeted for arrest by the state on dubious or nonexistent evidence. Such prejudicial justice didn't apply to Shia prisoners, however, many of whom were released back into society with no questions asked—or so claimed the Diyala governor, who left Iraq in 2012 after a systematic campaign of intimidation by al-Maliki–appointed officials following the murder of his press secretary. More ominously, the Stryker brigade found, the central government was no longer paying the salaries of Awakening members. After a month or two without pay, they'd be liable to quit or even return to the arms of the insurgency they had previously repudiated.

The problem was no better in Anbar. Shadid interviewed Colonel Saad Abbas Mahmoud, the police chief of al-Karmah, northeast of Fallujah. Mahmoud claimed to have been nearly assassinated twenty-five times, by means crude and creative. "He was delivered a Koran rigged with explosives buried in the pages between its green covers, then, less than two weeks later," Shadid reported, "his dish of dulaymiya, a mix of chicken, lamb, a slab of fat, and rice, was poisoned, sending him to the hospital for ten days. When he got out, two bombs detonated near his house in Fallujah." Mahmoud was in charge of three thousand Sons of Iraq in al-Karmah who were paid a measly $130 per month—or were supposed to be. They hadn't received their salaries in three months.

The original plan for the Awakening was to integrate these volunteers into a more official form of government service, hiring them to work in state ministries, for instance. The Iraqi agency tasked with transitioning them was called the Implementation and Follow-up Committee for National Reconciliation (IFCNR), and while it's true that by 2010, nearly thirty thousand volunteers had moved from being volunteer watchmen into certified candidates for state employment, they still had to compete for government jobs, many of which were extremely low-level. Al-Maliki showed little interest in carrying forward a program originally shoehorned into place by the United States.

Mullah Nadim Jibouri claimed before he was assassinated that as of mid-2010, a full 40 percent of AQI was composed of deserters or defectors from the Sons of Iraq. This figure may be exaggerated, but it was certainly plausible given two key events that year that helped deepen the fissures reemerging between the tribes and the central government.

The first was Iraq's national election, which al-Maliki didn't win as easily as he had expected to, and technically didn't win at all. The US assessment of his dictatorial tendencies were such that, even before the polls opened, Odierno feared a defeat for the incumbent might result in his putsch or cancellation of democracy in order to retain power. Many Sunnis say that's exactly what happened anyway.

Even before the election, Iraq's Accountability and Justice Commission—the sequel bureaucracy to the CPA's de-Baathification Commission—banned more than five hundred candidates running for parliament because of their links to the Baath Party. Naturally, the majority of these were Sunnis and part of the Iraqiya alliance led by former interim Prime Minister Ayad Allawi's faction. (Allawi, despite being a Shia, was seen as the mainstream Sunni electorate's best hope for regaining the premiership.) Odierno, with good reason, saw that behind this broad-brush campaign of delegitimization lurked the hand of Iran's Quds Force.

Despite preelection skulduggery, the vote went smoothly on March 7, 2010, with 60 percent turnout and little reported violence throughout the country. The one person it didn't go quite so smoothly for was al-Maliki.

Allawi's Iraqiya bloc won two more seats than did the State of Law Coalition, holding a 91-to-89 margin of victory. Iraqiya even performed remarkably well in the Shiite south, winning some two hundred thousand votes. The new parliament had been increased by fifty seats, from 275 to 325 in total, but the addition of legislators belied the near-categorical housecleaning that the election represented. There were 262 seats that went to first-time candidates, meaning that almost the equivalent of the previous parliament had been sacked. By all accounts, al-Maliki's polling had been way off. He would need to form a government by partnering with any of the other major blocs. Defeat unleashed his paranoia in a grand fashion.

Despite the election being deemed fair by UN monitors, al-Maliki accused the body of conspiring with Iraq's electoral commission to oust him. It was all a neo-Baathist plot, abetted by the United States, and he demanded a recount.

Al-Maliki used every means at his disposable—including legal rereadings of the constitution—to push the election toward power for his government.

Yet the electoral commission certified Iraqiya's win. The following day, Iraq's president, Jalal Talabani, flew to Tehran for negotiations between the State of Law Coalition and the Iraqi National Alliance. Iraqiya was to be stopped at all costs, even if it meant that rival Shia parties had to work together under the supervision and blessing of their foreign state sponsor, Iran. The new government would finally be decided through these negotiations and through more judicial maneuvering. Al-Maliki eventually formed a national unity government that also included Kurds and Iraqiya—but with the incumbent returning as prime minister.

Odierno, for one, saw how flagrant manipulation and Iranian meddling in a sovereign state's election would be viewed by Iraq's Sunnis. So did Ali Khedery, the former US diplomat who arrived in the Green Zone on the back of the invasion in 2003, and served as Ryan Crocker's aide during the surge and Awakening period. Khedery maintains today that the US handling of the 2009 election only exacerbated Sunni grievances in Iraq, convincing many that they *were* being purposefully kept from power. The history of the postelection period did no favors in dispelling this assumption. Ambassador Hill had likened an Iraqiya win to the return of the Afrikaners in South Africa. Vice President Joseph Biden, whom President Obama put in charge of the administration's Iraq policy, is recorded as saying, "Maliki hates the goddamn Sunnis" but nevertheless acceded to the return of this sectarian incumbent. "I know one guy, one of the most peaceful, moderate Iraqis you can imagine," Khedery told us. "He had been a bottom-level Baathist, one of Saddam's engineers. He says, 'Look, I was never sectarian before. I never liked Iran, we fought a war with them. I love my country, I'm a nationalist. But I've become sectarian now because there's nowhere else for a moderate or a secularist to be. We're losers. I've become as sectarian as the people I used to hate.'"

DIPLOMATIC DISENGAGEMENT

As much as the consequences of the surge have been debated in US policy circles, so too has the wisdom (or lack thereof) of a categorical troop withdrawal from Iraq in 2011. Did this enable the easy reconstitution of ISI? Could it have been avoided with more fleet-footed or energetic diplomacy by the Obama administration, which had intended to renew and extend SOFA but had come to the negotiating table late in the day and with the air of being even less interested in maintaining a postwar US garrison than was the supposedly hard-bargaining al-Maliki?

There was actually little debate within the ranks of both the US and Iraqi militaries about the necessity to extend SOFA. Obama's chairman of the Joint Chiefs of Staff, Admiral Mike Mullen, had advocated leaving a minimum of sixteen thousand troops, a figure deemed way too high by the White House's national security team. "I'll bet you my vice presidency Maliki will extend SOFA," Joe Biden had said. But al-Maliki didn't, owing to the fact that the minuscule troop number Obama ultimately decided on—3,500 personnel permanently stationed in Iraq, with 1,500 more rotated in at regular intervals for training Iraqi forces and conducting counterterrorism operations—wasn't worth the cost of wrangling with his own deeply divided parliament, which had to ratify any bilateral agreement.

What the debate over military disengagement obscures, however, is that the United States withdrew *politically* from Iraq even sooner and arguably with more lasting consequence for the country's future instability.

Colonel Rick Welch ran the national tribal leader program for the US military during the Awakening and helped transfer the responsibility for continued Sunni and Shia tribal outreach over to the State Department. What he found was a US foreign service ill-equipped to ensure the Sons of Iraq stayed on the right side of the conflict. As Welch recounted:

"The joke of the day at the embassy was: 'If you want to know what the embassy is doing, go to the [commissary] on Thursday, and look at how much alcohol was on the shelf and compare that to how much was there by Saturday.'

"It was as if Iraq wasn't still a conflict or war zone. The time when it needed the keenest and sharpest minds that understood the country was in that preelection and immediate postelection period because Maliki pulled a fast one with his supreme court. And the Sons of Iraq, the tribal leaders, would complain about what he was doing. They called it the 'purge.' Yet the State Department's talking point was, 'We're really sorry to hear that, but Iraq is a sovereign country. We cannot interfere.'

"I remember this moderate tribal leader, with this look of incredulity on his face. 'You cannot interfere?' he asked. 'Yes, we can't interfere.' 'Didn't I just see President Obama authorize the bombing of Libya? Wasn't that a sovereign country? And didn't I hear President Obama interfere in Egypt and say that Mubarak had to go? And didn't I hear the president intervene in Syria and say that Assad has to go? Don't you have sanctions against Iran, another sovereign country? Didn't you invade our country and aren't you still here? It's not that you can't intervene—we've watched you intervene all around us to remove long-standing dictators. What we hear you say is that you won't intervene to stop a rising dictator right here and restore the democracy you brought to us.'"

Against Obama's rosy prognosis in 2011 that Iraq was a democratic success, Saleh al-Mutlaq, al-Maliki's deputy prime minister, had gone on CNN and said that Iraq was spiraling into "dictatorship." "It is a one-party show and one-man show. Yes, al-Maliki is the worst dictator we have ever seen in our history," al-Mutlaq noted without the slightest trace of irony given the dictator who had been overthrown in 2003. The United States, he charged, was blind and stupid to think it had the kind of leverage over Baghdad it believed it did. "The whole set of the government, from the president to the prime minister, was the decision of Iran," he said.

To counter this criticism from his own cabinet, al-Maliki ordered tanks to surround al-Mutlaq's home, as well as the homes of Rafi al-Issawi, now the finance minister, and his vice president, Tariq al-Hashimi. On December 18, al-Hashimi fled to Iraqi Kurdistan after al-Maliki's security forces held his plane on the tarmac at Baghdad International Airport while he awaited departure. Al-Hashimi was allowed to fly off, but three of his bodyguards were detained for "suspected terrorist activity" (one later died in custody). The next day, an arrest warrant was issued for al-Hashimi himself. He remained in exile in Iraqi Kurdistan before moving to Turkey. In 2012, he was sentenced to death in absentia by hanging by a judiciary widely seen as acting under al-Maliki's personal instructions.

These and other crackdowns on Sunni politicians precipitated Arab Spring–style protests in Sunni areas throughout Iraq—and a counterresponse from al-Maliki, which only aggravated them.

On April 23, 2013, three days after Iraq's provincial elections were held, the Iraqi Security Forces razed one protest site in Hawija, near Kirkuk. They claimed to be searching for the killer of an Iraqi soldier at the site, and although stories differ as to what happened next, the aftermath is not in dispute: twenty Sunnis were killed and more than one hundred were injured. The Hawija violence led to Sunni violence throughout Iraq, targeting police stations and army checkpoints. The speaker of Iraq's parliament, Osama al-Nujaifi, called for al-Maliki's resignation in response to the carnage. Clashes spread to Mosul and Baghdad, where Sunni mosques were blown up and Iraqi security officials were yanked from their cars and murdered, and then to Shia cities, where AQI-style terrorist attacks took place. Sunnis took to calling for an armed national revolution, agitating for al Douri's Naqshbandi Army and Sahwa militias.

BREAKING THE WALLS

It hardly helped Iraq's overall stability during this fraught period that AQI had used 2012–2013 to execute its Breaking the Walls campaign, which was characterized by eight daring attacks on Iraqi prisons, all designed to spring former operatives and replenish the ranks of the organization.

Jessica Lewis McFate of the Institute for the Study of War separated the growth of the ISIS campaign into four distinct phases. The first saw four prison attacks, including one against the Tasfirat prison in Tikrit in September 2012, an operation that freed one hundred inmates, nearly half of whom were believed to be al-Qaeda operatives slated for state execution. The second phase targeted locations along the Green Line—the demarcation point between Iraq proper and the Kurdistan Regional Government's semiautonomous zone—no doubt designed to capitalize on roiling political and economic tensions between Erbil and Baghdad. The third phase saw the return of VBIED sorties in Baghdad and the belts region, targeting Iraqi Security Forces and Shia civilian areas. Here the jihadists sought to exploit another widening gulf in Iraqi society: that between the al-Maliki government and Sunni protestors who, inspired by the Arab Spring but mainly driven by domestic turmoil, had taken to the streets of Fallujah and elsewhere. The fourth and final phase began in mid-May 2013 and was meant to terrorize the Shia, clearly to precipitate another sectarian civil war and the return of Shia militias. Almost half of the VBIED waves during Breaking the Walls, Lewis McFate found, occurred in this phase, coinciding with the Sunni protests, which culminated in the most successful jailbreak of the entire campaign: the July 2013 freeing of five hundred inmates from Abu Ghraib prison. According to the Obama administration, whereas suicide bombings in Iraq averaged between five and ten per month in the years 2011 and 2012, from the period encompassing the last three months of Breaking the Walls, that number jumped to thirty per month.

By the end of the summer, more than seven hundred Iraqis were being killed each month, and the conditions for Sunni rejectionism turning into jihadist extremism in force had returned. At the end of December, in response to an ISIS killing spree, al-Maliki deployed security forces to Ramadi to put an end to the antigovernment protests. They withdrew in the face of tribal resistance. ISIS then sacked Fallujah on New Year's Day 2014 and announced that it had become an "Islamic emirate" committed to defending Sunnis from al-Maliki.

"Maliki pushed the Sunnis so far that they had to rise up," Rick Welch said. "They tried to get reforms, but they couldn't. Tribal honor was on the line and revenge thinking was on the line. Maliki made this crisis."

7

ASSAD'S PROXY

SYRIA AND AL-QAEDA

ISIS's resurgence in Iraq coincided with its takeover of a large swath of territory in next-door Syria, a fact which the regime of Bashar al-Assad had tried to exploit to claim victimhood at the hands of international terrorism. The Assad regime's absurd claim was proved false by the uncovering of undeniable forensic proof that Syria helped keep AQI afloat, before the US withdrawal from Iraq. Al-Rishawi, the Anbar Awakening leader, told the *New York Times* before he was murdered by AQI, "This is all Syria's doing. Syria is doing bad things."

It was. Al-Assad has managed to unite a chorus of varied global accusers—ranging from the US military, the Sons of Iraq, his own former diplomats and security officials, innumerable Syrian rebels, and even the al-Maliki government—in affirming and condemning his state sponsorship of Zarqawism. The proliferation of ISIS in both Iraq and Syria can't be understood without examining Damascus's long-running collaboration with its forerunner organization.

HAFEZ'S ISLAMISM

We have seen how secular Iraqi Baathism had a habit, in the last century, of making an accommodation with Islamism in order to preempt its revolutionary potential. The Syrian counterpart was no different.

The Muslim Brotherhood uprising in Syria, which began in 1976 and was brutally suppressed in 1982 by forces loyal to Hafez al-Assad, had tended to obscure the regime's strategic alliance with a host of Sunni Islamist parties and paramilitaries, alliances premised on mutually beneficial geopolitical needs: chiefly, confronting the United States and Israel. As scholar Eyal Zisser has noted, by the mid-1990s, Hafez al-Assad was no longer the dread nemesis of those seeking a marriage between mosque and state because "Damascus started to see the Islamists as perhaps the only possible means by which to enhance its regional standing, gain influence in neighboring countries, and bring domestic tranquillity to Syria itself."

When the elder al-Assad died in 2000, and his London-trained ophthalmologist son ascended to the presidency, this arrangement increased. Up until recently, for example, despite a national Syrian law banning the Brotherhood as party or organization, Damascus had no qualms about hosting Khaled Mashal, the chairman of the politburo of Hamas. Today, the regime relies overwhelming on the paramilitary assets of Hezbollah and Iran's Islamic Revolutionary Guards Corps—both US-designated terrorist entities—to continue its grueling war of attrition against a legion of domestic and foreign-backed insurgencies. These of course consist of Islamist and jihadist rebels, some of whom are former prisoners of the regime, if not former accomplices of it in Iraq.

Even before the United States toppled Saddam, al-Assad had embarked on a policy of facilitating foreign fighters' movement into Iraq to destabilize the occupation. An office situated across from the US embassy in Damascus even helped would-be insurgents book bus travel to the Syria-Iraq border. In 2007 CENTCOM announced that it had captured a "Saddam Fedayeen leader involved in setting up training camps in Syria for Iraqi and foreign fighters," although the person's name was not released.

That same year, US forces killed Muthanna, a man designated as al Qaeda's emir for the Syrian-Iraqi border region, in the city of Sinjar. According to Major General Kevin Bergner, the spokesman for coalition forces, Muthanna acted as "a key facilitator of the movement of foreign terrorists" from the one country into the other. As with other high-value targets, Muthanna possessed a cache of useful intelligence, which became known as the Sinjar Records. A study published in 2008 by the Combating Terrorism Center at West Point (CTC) analyzed these records and found that more than half of 376 foreign fighters in Iraq listed their occupation as "suicide bomber," indicating again the expendable nature of non-Iraqi jihadists to AQI, and also underscoring one reason why sending such cannon fodder to their deaths abroad wasn't seen as potentially self-defeating for Damascus. The Sinjar Records also confirmed that the foreign fighters were entering Iraq from the Syrian province of Deir Ezzor, typically using the Syrian border town of Albu Kamal, which lies adjacent to the Iraqi city of Qa'im—where al-Zarqawi established his headquarters after fleeing Fallujah in 2004 and where a proto-Awakening got started the following year. The flow, the CTC concluded, came in three distinct "waves."

The first began shortly before the invasion, when Saddam exhorted Arabs from around the region to join in the forthcoming insurgency. This fielded a number of Bedouin tribesmen hailing from Deir Ezzor and Hasaka, as well as other jihadists egged on by Sheikh Ahmad Kuftaro, Syria's mufti, who wasted no time in lending state legitimacy to the incendiary sermons wafting out of mosques and madrassas in his country. "In border villages and cities," the CTC study stated, "houses were donated for volunteers to live in while local notables—both religious and tribal figures—organized transportation and accommodations for them in Iraq. According to local sources, hundreds of fighters passed through Albu Kamal and [Hasaka] just before the US invasion, leading to rapid increases in the cost of housing, food, and weapons—all of which greatly benefited the locals. The Syrian authorities monitored the flow, but made no move to stop it."

The second wave arrived with the First Battle of Fallujah, when the al-Assad regime's new show of trying to stop the rat lines was eclipsed by rampant corruption: Syrian Mukhabarat officers were bribed into letting Syrians cross the border anyway.

The third wave followed the 2005 Cedar Revolution, which brought an end to Syria's military occupation of Lebanon and was prompted by popular revulsion at the assassination of former Lebanese prime minister Rafik Hariri, for which a UN tribunal indicted members of Hezbollah, al-Assad's terrorist ally.

"CALL US"

Al-Assad, of course, has always denied orchestrating or coordinating the jihadist activities in Iraq in any way, and he has even played up his supposed cooperation with Washington in the war on terror. Yet many of his regime's former officials now say his state sponsorship of AQI was hardly a secret and was quite clearly premised on two separate but related motives. The dictator had hoped it would be a severe warning to the Bush administration after Iraq, and as Jason Burke's *The 9/11 Wars* shows, he also wanted to divert Islamists' attention away from his regime by keeping them preoccupied next door.

"For Assad the problem was much bigger than America invading Arab countries for regime change," Bassam Barabandi, a former diplomat at the Syrian embassy in Washington, DC, told us. After the 2011 uprising, Barabandi covertly helped hundreds of dissidents and activists obtain passports for their relatives who were trying to flee a war-ravaged country. "Assad understood that part of Bush's strategy in Iraq was to end minority rule of Sunnis ruling over majority Shiite. He feared that he would be next. From then on, he started to work with mujahidin; he did everything possible to convince the Americans, 'Don't come after me, otherwise I'll send more terrorists next door to kill your soldiers.'"

For about five years, the US reply to this ultimatum was mainly diplomatic, and al-Assad sometimes acceded to Washington's demands, lending the impression that he was dismantling the jihadist networks on his soil. It was all a feint, Barabandi said, part of the strategy to use Syria's facilitation of terrorism as a bargaining chip. The former diplomat described for us how Sabawi Ibrahim al-Hassan al-Tikriti, Saddam's half-brother who had been hiding in Syria and was wanted by both the Americans and Iraqis, finally came to be handed over. "The Americans went to Assad in 2005 and asked for his help in catching Sabawi," Barabandi said. "He was on the border of Syria and Iraq, and he was leading the Baathist terrorists. Bashar was of course hosting him. Practically, the Americans and Iraqis were asking for his help: 'We will try to improve our relations with you in return.' Assad agreed. Imad Moustapha [the Syrian ambassador to the United States at the time] was in the meeting in Damascus with the US under secretary of state, where this was discussed and decided. Imad told us the story. In fact, he told everyone this story. After two days, Assef Shawkat [al-Assad's own brother-in-law and Syria's top intelligence officer] contacted Imad to tell him to tell his American friends that Sabawi would be in such-and-such area of Iraq. They informed the Americans exactly where he was, and they captured him."

Tony Badran, an expert on Syria at the Washington-based

Foundation for the Defense of Democracies, has characterized al-Assad's underwriting of al-Qaeda as a form of attention-seeking. "It's about the regime's conception of its role and position in the region," Badran said. "It believes that its longevity lies in being perceived as an indispensable regional power, and so its foreign policy with respect to the West is: 'You have to talk to us. Just pick up the phone and talk to us; it doesn't matter what's discussed, we just want to hear from you.' For Assad, the ability to boast that the United States is an interlocutor is a matter of power projection. It lets him pretend that he's the linchpin for Arab-Israeli peace or a real force for counterterrorism. He creates the problems he then oh-so-magnanimously offers to solve."

ABU AL-QAQA AND SHAKER AL-ABSI

Badran mentioned, as an example, the curious case of an Islamist Kurdish cleric named Sheikh Mahmoud Gul Aghasi, who more commonly went by the name Abu al-Qaqa. Having called for US soldiers to be "slaughtered like cattle" in Iraq, al-Qaqa was allowed to preach openly in Aleppo—following his brief arrest by the regime after 9/11—despite his loud championship of Syria's transformation into a Sharia-compliant Islamic state. As recounted by journalist Nicholas Blanford, who interviewed the cleric in 2003, al-Qaqa organized "festivals denouncing the [United States] and Jews. Many of these festivals were attended by Syrian officials, and some of al-Qaqa's followers grew suspicious of their leader. Those suspicions hardened when it was learned that al-Qaqa had delivered a list of Wahhabis in Syria to the state security agency. Was al-Qaqa playing a double game, preaching jihad while handing over jihadists to the authorities?"

Blanford argued that al-Qaqa was tolerated by the regime so long as he stayed in the terrorist export business; forswearing attacks at home was the price for running jihadists. This was why on the wall of al-Qaqa's mosque in Aleppo there was a sign displaying "a bomb with a red line drawn through it."

The Mukhabarat's relationship with this demagogue was hardly Syria's best-kept secret. "Abu al-Qaqa was a strange phenomenon," said Muhammad Habash, a former Syrian MP who, in 2008, headed the de-radicalization program at Sednaya prison in Damascus. "He was preaching about jihad in a mosque situation in one of Aleppo's most crowded neighborhoods. In the Sakhour mosque, he not only preached about jihad, but he held military training for young people heading to Iraq. With a sermon like that, an imam would usually spend the rest of his life in prison, along with his family and relatives and those who attended the sermon."

Habash told us that he first met al-Qaqa in 2006.

"I was giving a lecture at the Islamic Research Centre and someone stood up to talk. He spoke with such charisma, so I asked to meet him afterward in my office. I told him, 'I would like to know you, you have such a strong presence when you speak.' He was accompanied by two young men who were listening attentively to what he was saying, and he was engaging them in the talk. He seemed to have strong leadership skills. I told him of my plans in Aleppo since it was announced as the new capital of Islamic culture in that year. I had a project for Islamic reform, and I wanted the help of someone like him in Aleppo. We both agreed that there was some room for such activism under this regime. When he left, someone came out and told me he was Abu al-Qaqa, and asked why I talked to him. I did not believe that. He was wearing a suit and tie, and had a tidy beard. His presence gave no indication of his infamous violent side."

Following that initial encounter, Habash met with al-Qaqa regularly. "He spoke to me proudly about his role in preventing the Americans from entering Syria. He was a tool for the regime, and in the end he was shot."

Yet another famous case was that of Shaker al-Absi, the Palestinian leader of an al-Qaeda–linked militant group, called Fatah al-Islam, who also worked with al-Zarqawi in planning the murder of USAID worker Laurence Foley in 2002. "Shaker al-Absi was the mastermind for the Foley assassination, which was put together in Damascus," said David Schenker, formerly the Pentagon's top policy aide on the Levant and now the director of the Program on Arab Politics at the Washington Institute for Near East Policy. "I am 100-percent convinced that it was planned in Syria with Assad's involvement, tolerance, permission, and support. In fact, I don't think there's any debate about that anymore. The smoking gun isn't Zarqawi, it's al-Absi who was in Syria, and then went to Jordan to oversee the assassination."

The Jordanians sentenced both al-Zarqawi and al-Absi to death in absentia and requested the latter's extradition from Damascus. Al-Assad refused and claimed to have put al-Absi in prison. "According to reports in the Arabic press, he was subsequently released and ended up running a terrorist training camp for al-Qaeda operatives going into Iraq from Syrian territory," Schenker said. Regardless of what happened to him in Syria, he was clearly free to leave the country in 2007, because he led Fatah al-Islam's armed uprising against the Lebanese Armed Forces (LAF) in the Nahr al-Bared Palestinian refugee camp. Although the LAF put down the rebellion, al-Absi was never apprehended. Fatah al-Islam later posted to its website that he returned to Syria, where he may have been killed by the security services. According to Schenker, he had in fact been "exported" to Lebanon in 2007 and maintained ties to the Syrian Mukhabarat throughout the Nahr al-Bared siege. "How do we know that? There was a Lebanese [pro-Assad] cleric named Fathi Yakan from the Tripoli area who went several times into the camp to serve as an intermediary to contact Absi. A week or so later, he showed up in pictures with Assad in Damascus."

THE ASSASSINATION OF ABU GHADIYAH

Most of the insurgents Syria funneled into Iraq had been hosted under the auspices of al-Assad's own brother-in-law, Assef Shawkat, who was killed in a stunning assassination plot in Damascus in 2012 that wiped out the regime's "crisis management cell," the ad hoc security committee tasked with destroying the Syrian revolution. Originally believed to have been the work of Syrian rebels who infiltrated the cell, new evidence had emerged suggesting that this assassination may have been an inside job, waged by Iranian-backed hard-liners against Shawkat, who advocated negotiating with the anti–al-Assad opposition.

Shawkat's history gives no indication of his being a softie. One of his jihadist charges was a man known as Badran Turki Hishan al-Mazidih, or Abu Ghadiyah, a Mosulawi Iraqi whom the US Treasury Department designated as a terrorist in February 2008. Abu Ghadiyah, the Treasury Department alleged, had been appointed AQI's commander of logistics in 2004 by al-Zarqawi and had subsequently taken orders from Abu Ayyub al-Masri upon the Jordanian's death. "As of the spring of 2007, Abu Ghadiyah facilitated the movement of AQI operatives into Iraq via the Syrian border," the designation stated, while also listing and sanctioning the rest of Abu Ghadiyah's Syria-based network. According to a State Department cable, subsequently published by WikiLeaks, "Bashar al-Asad was well aware that his brother-in-law . . .had detailed knowledge of the activities of AQI facilitator Abu Ghadiya."

Abu Ghadiyah was evidently in the family business. His

"right-hand man" was also his cousin Ghazy Fezzaa Hishan, also known as Abu Faysal, who resided in Zabadani, a city northeast of Damascus known for being an important concourse for smuggling and transporting weapons from Syria into Lebanon. As of September 2006 both Abu Ghadiyah and Abu Faysal, according to the Treasury, "planned to use rockets to attack multiple Coalition forces outposts and Iraqi police stations, in an attempt to facilitate an AQI takeover in Western Iraq."

Another member of the network was Abu Ghadiyah's brother Akram Turki Hishan al-Mazidih, or Abu Jarrah, also based in Zabadani and in charge of weapons smuggling and, as the US government noted, "order[ing] the execution of all persons found to be working with the Iraqi Government or US Forces."

Finally, there was another cousin, Saddah Jalut Al-Marsumi, who went by Saddah. He was an al-Qaeda financier who helped his enterprising clan transport suicide bombers from Syria to Iraq.

Abu Ghadiyah's predecessor, the Syrian national Sulayman Khalid Darwish (who was also, rather confusingly, known as Abu Ghadiyah), had been killed by JSOC in Qa'im in 2005. That city's strategic value is that it lies right across from the Syrian border town of Albu Kamal, and functions a bit like El Paso does for Juarez: a transnational portal through which men and money can flow in either direction.

By 2008 numerous diplomatic attempts by the United States to stop Abu Ghadiyah's rat lines had failed. Petraeus had even sought permission from the Bush administration to parlay with al-Assad directly in Damascus, in the hope that another Sabawi-style deal might be arranged. The White House said no. Other attempts to cajole al-Assad via the UN Security Council failed.

In October 2008 the cajoling stopped. Stanley McChrystal's JSOC, overseen by the CIA, was authorized to conduct a covert cross-border raid into Albu Kamal to kill Abu Ghadiyah, which it did on October 26, in a special operation that resembled the assassination of Osama bin Laden in Abbottabad in 2011.

Despite the irrefutable habeas corpus nature of the evidence, al-Assad continued to deny any involvement in sending terrorists into Iraq. Weeks after the raid, British Foreign Secretary David Miliband traveled to Damascus and once again tried the talking cure. He asked al-Assad to end his noxious activities and was met only with further professions of ignorance and innocence. Maura Connelly, the charge d'affaires at the US embassy in Damascus, recounted the meeting in a State Department cable:

"Bashar reportedly complained about the October 26 US military operation at Albu Kamal. Miliband replied the US had hit known [foreign fighter] facilitator Abu Ghadiyah. What Syria needed to do was to cooperate with the US and West. Miliband asked why Syria had not taken action against Abu Ghadiya when the US had provided a lot of information regarding his presence in Syria. 'Even if Abu Ghadiya was there (in Albu Kamal),' the US strike was not the way to deal with the issue, replied [al-Assad]."

Perhaps it was with the foregoing episode in mind that a year later Connelly minuted her overall impression of dealing with a regime whose "officials at every level lie. They persist in a lie even in the face of evidence to the contrary. They are not embarrassed to be caught in a lie."

Although it garnered little media attention at the time, the most damning indictment of the al-Assad–jihadist alliance came in the form of a US Federal Court civil judgment issued in 2008, which found Damascus liable for the kidnapping and murder of Olin Eugene "Jack" Armstrong and Jack Hensley, two American contractors who were beheaded in characteristic grisly fashion by agents of AQI.

The families of Armstrong and Hensley had originally filed their complaint not only against the regime but also against its military intelligence apparatus and al-Assad and Shawkat personally. However, the court, citing the Foreign Sovereign Immunities Act (FSIA)—which places limitations on lawsuits filed in the United States against foreign states—and the fact that al-Assad and Shawkat were never served subpoenas, listed only Syria as the sole defendant. The judgment, written by Judge Rosemary Collyer, brought it all up—Shaker al-Absi, Abu al-Qaqa, the first Abu Ghadiyah, and the Foley assassination—and concluded that "Syria provided substantial assistance to Zarqawi and al-Qaeda in Iraq and that this led to the deaths by beheading of Jack Armstrong and Jack Hensley," and that "Syria's provision of material support and resources was inevitably approved and overseen by President Assad and General Shawkat, acting within the scope of their official duties." The regime appealed this decision in May 2011; it lost.

ROLLED UP?

Conventional wisdom in US counterterrorism circles maintained that al-Assad's alliance with AQI more or less ended in 2008, after Abu Ghadiyah was killed, because the regime "rolled up" its jihadist networks in eastern Syria and arrested returning foreign fighters. New evidence, however, complicates this assessment.

In December 2014 Martin Chulov of the *Guardian* newspaper published an in-depth profile of ISIS, confirming what had long been an allegation put forward by the al-Maliki government—that al-Assad was complicit in a devastating series of attacks against Iraqi state institutions on August 19, 2009. Sequential VBIED operations targeted the Iraqi Finance and Foreign Ministries and a police convoy in Baghdad. More than one hundred people were killed, including government employees and journalists, and around six hundred more were injured.

Al-Maliki had immediately accused the Baathists of being behind both plots. In November 2009 his government aired what it claimed were confessions obtained from three Baathist operatives involved in the August explosions.

At first, Baghdad was reluctant to assign any blame to the al-Assad regime directly, insisting only that the plots had been formulated in Syria. But it recalled its ambassador from Damascus after the regime failed to turn over two fugitive Baathists. Al-Assad responded by yanking his own envoy from Baghdad. One of the men he refused to turn over was Muhammad Younis al-Ahmed, whom he said he had already expelled from his territory. For a short time, al-Assad had tried to make al-Ahmed a Syrian-controlled leader of an Iraqi Baathist insurgency to rival the more established and self-financed Naqshbandi Army led by al-Douri, who was also being hosted on Syrian soil.

As 2009 wore on, Baghdad's allegations against its neighbor grew more serious. Iraqi Foreign Minister Hoshyar Zebari told members of the media in Bahrain, "Intelligence confirms that Saddamist Baathists are working from Syrian soil and enjoy the support of [the Syrian] intelligence services." Major General Hussein Ali Kamal, the director of intelligence at the Iraqi Ministry of Interior, was absolutely convinced that this was so. Well respected by American diplomats and military officials for his professionalism, Kamal, who died of cancer in June 2014, told Chulov that he obtained hard proof of Syria's hosting and supervision of "two secret meetings" between al-Qaeda agents and Iraqi Baathists in 2009. Both meetings were held in Zabadani. Chulov wrote of Kamal's reconstruction of these meetings: "[H]e laid out his evidence, using maps that plotted the routes they used to enter western Iraq and confessions that linked their journey to specific mid-ranking officers in Syria's military intelligence units."

Kamal apparently had an asset who wore a wire at one of the Zabadani meetings, which he said the Baathists led. "He is the most sensitive source we have ever had," he told Chulov. "As far as we know, this is the first time there has been a strategic level meeting between all of these groups. It marks a new point in history."

US forces were still stationed in Iraq at that point, but the objective shared by Syrian intelligence, the Baathists, and al-Qaeda was to instead destabilize al-Maliki's government. Kamal relayed to Chulov that a source inside Syria had told him that the plotters noticed an uptick in Iraqi security around the original targets and so had decided on different ones. The Iraqi general struggled in vain for months trying to figure out where the new targets might be, until the August bombings horribly informed him.

ALI MAMLOUK'S GUIDE TO COUNTERTERRORISM

No one has better explained both the motive and nature of Syria's collaboration with Sunni jihadism better than Ali Mamlouk, al-Assad's director of general intelligence. In February 2010 Mamlouk surprised US diplomats in Damascus by turning up at a meeting between the State Department's Coordinator for Counterterrorism Daniel Benjamin and Syria's Vice Foreign Minister Faisal al-Miqdad. Mamlouk arrived, as he explained, at the prompting of al-Assad, who claimed to be seeking improved Syrian-US relations under the new American president. Obama had come to office promising a new policy of engagement with Damascus, and Mamlouk, obviously capitalizing on the opportunity the regime's destabilization strategy had created, explained that cracking down on terrorism would be contingent on seeing that engagement policy carried through to something approaching a full normalization of bilateral relations. As relayed in a State Department cable about the meeting, Mamlouk and al-Assad sought three dispensations from Washington, all of which confirmed Tony Badran's gloss on the regime's purpose for misbehavior: "(1) Syria must be able to take the lead in any regional actions; (2) politics are an integral part of combating terrorism, and a 'political umbrella' of improved US-Syrian bilateral relations should facilitate cooperation against terrorism; and (3) in order to convince the Syrian people that cooperation with the US was benefiting them, progress must be made on issues related to economic sanctions against Syria including spare parts for airplanes and a plane for President [Assad]."

But then Mamlouk made an interesting admission. He explained his own peculiar method of dealing with jihadists as "practical and not theoretical. . . .In principle, we don't attack or kill them immediately. Instead, we embed ourselves in them and only at the opportune moment do we move." But what constituted an "opportune moment" for Syria didn't necessarily constitute one for the United States, as the preceding decade had amply demonstrated.

Was this acknowledgment of state infiltration of jihadist cells merely edifying, or did it contain an implied threat? The answer to that question lay in Mamlouk's follow-up point to Daniel Benjamin, wherein he reminded the US diplomat that foreign fighters were still slipping into Iraq through Syria—this was about sixteen months after the Abu Ghadiyah assassination and about seven months since the last series of VBIED bombings had rocked Baghdad. However, Mamlouk continued, the regime was cracking down, and "[b]y all means we will continue to do all this, but if we start cooperation with you it will lead to better results and we can better protect our interests."

The Syrian regime has been likened by other US diplomats to a mafia crime family. Mamlouk made the new White House an offer it couldn't refuse.

8

REBIRTH

ISI UNDER ABU BAKR AL-BAGHDADI

ISIS's history, according to *Dabiq*'s reconstruction, was an eleven-year utopian quest made sweeter by suffering, and one which ended in 2014 with the establishment of the caliphate. Abu Omar al-Baghdadi built the "first state in 'modern' times set up exclusively by the mujahidin—the active participants in the jihad—in the heart of the Muslim world just a stone's throw away from" Mecca, Medina, and Jerusalem. And even through Sahwa and the surge, and the elimination of its own leadership, that state had endured, retreating "mostly into the desert regions of al-Anbar, where its soldiers regrouped, planned, and trained."

THE DEATH OF AL-MASRI AND AL-BAGHDADI

In June 2008 Stanley McChrystal had been replaced as commander of JSOC by Vice Admiral William McRaven, a Navy SEAL who later coordinated Operation Neptune Spear, the raid in Abbottabad, Pakistan, that killed bin Laden in 2011. Although by 2010 most JSOC operations were in the AfPak theater—in line with the

114

Obama administration's commitment to drawing down in Iraq and winning the "good war" against core al-Qaeda and the Taliban in Afghanistan—McRaven's team did strike a number of important victories against the Mesopotamian franchise.

The first was the killing of Abu Khalaf, Abu Ghadiyah's kinsman who briefly assumed responsibility for the Syria-based facilitation network after the latter's killing in October. A US official later said, "Khalaf was perhaps the most dangerous AQI facilitator in Iraq," and that his death left a "void in AQI hierarchy."

The second came after Iraqi forces arrested Manaf Abd al-Rahim al-Rawi, al-Qaeda's emir in Baghdad, known to his subordinates as "the dictator." Al-Rawi had collaborated with Baathists and Syrian intelligence to perpetrate the devastating series of bombings in Baghdad in 2009, all aimed at the al-Maliki government rather than the US military. And the Iraqis initially kept his arrest a secret. It was only after the Americans captured his twin brother that they forced al-Maliki to allow them to interrogate the dictator, who duly gave up information about his network. Al-Rawi named two couriers, whom JSOC tracked in April 2010 to a location in the Tharthar region along Salah ad-Din's border with Anbar.

The courier's safe house turned out to contain none other than Abu Ayyub al-Masri, hiding in a secret basement accessible only through a door underneath the kitchen sink. His companion was a man whom some had doubted ever existed: Abu Omar al-Baghdadi.

"Their killing was [a] reflection of ISI's weakness," Laith Alkhouri, the counterterrorism expert, said. "Masri had been preaching on operational cautiousness to Muslims, how to secure their communications and such to avoid being hit by the Americans. The power he held as the head of AQI was more in the realm of public relations. He'd released a document to supporters [that] was a step-by-step guideline showing them how they might burnish the image of global jihad. He wanted his recruits to learn how to hack websites and marry scientific advancement with Islamist ideology."

But this focus on the more Don Draper-ish aspects of takfirism happened to coincide with the nadir of ISI's popularity and prowess, owing to some of the worst tactical decision-making by its commanders since the war started. Eighty percent of the leadership had been killed along with them. Nor was the "Iraqi face" supposedly created by al-Baghdadi's appointment as emir really working anymore. Al-Baghdadi himself had pretensions of something higher than his nominal role as *caporegime* of the Sunni insurgency, at least judging by the name he bestowed upon himself—"Emir of the Believers"—an honorific usually reserved for only the highest positions of Islamic rulership. (Mullah Omar, the fugitive Taliban leader, is called that.) "The adoption of that title," said Laith Alkhouri, "created a huge question for jihadists unsure of where ISI was headed." That question would be answered by Baghdadi's successor, Ibrahim Awwad al-Badari.

THE NEW AL-BAGHDADI

Al-Badari, who assumed the nom de guerre Abu Bakr al-Baghdadi, was in effect appointed by ISI's Shura Council as a singular replacement for two slain commanders. He came seemingly out of nowhere. What is known about him in both Iraq and within US intelligence circles came to light after ISIS reigned triumphant across two countries and in the subsequent media rush to figure out the identity of this tenebrous new figure. As a result, much of the second al-Baghdadi's biography still hovers not far above the level of rumor or speculation, some of it driven, in fact, by competing jihadist propagandists intent on scandalizing or delegitimizing the caliph being presented as more authoritative than Ayman al-Zawahiri. But this cleavage into pro and contra camps took time. "No one thought he wanted competition with al-Qaeda," Alkhouri said. "In secret communication, he not only pledged allegiance to al-Zawahiri, he asked if this pledge should be made public or secret. Al-Zawahiri replied that it should be kept secret to avoid complexities and take some of the pressure off ISI."

Born in 1971 near the city of Samarra, al-Baghdadi became a scholar of Islamic studies, obtaining both a master's degree as well as a doctorate in the subject from the University of Islamic Sciences in Baghdad's Adhamiya suburb. He's said to have lived in modest quarters attached to a local mosque in Tobchi, a western district of Baghdad that was fairly mixed between Sunni and Shiite residents. Like most mass murderers recollected by those who knew them in their nonage, his friends and acquaintances say he was the quiet, retiring type who in no way resembled the dangerous fanatic of recent imagination ("Neighbors Remember Serial Killer as Serial Killer" being a headline confined only to the satirical pages of the *Onion,* apparently.) Al-Baghdadi wore glasses, excelled at soccer, and carried himself in a manner befitting a scholar.

Dr. Hisham al-Hashimi, an expert on ISIS who consults with the Iraqi government, met al-Baghdadi in the late 1990s. "He did not have the charisma of a leader," al-Hashimi told us. "When I met him, he was extremely shy and did not speak much. He was interested in religious studies, and the focus of his interest was the Quran. He was from a poor rural family, and he was not envious of urban people, as others often are. His ambition was limited to obtaining a government job within the Islamic endowment ministry."

According to one of his neighbors, Abu Ali, who spoke to the *Daily Telegraph,* al-Baghdadi came to Tobchi when he was eighteen years old: "The mosque here had its own imam. When he was away, religious students would take his place. [Al-Baghdadi] would sometimes lead the prayers but not give any sermons." He grew more reactionary as time wore on, Abu Ali remembered, recounting al-Baghdadi's reaction to a wedding in Tobchi at which men and women were "dancing in the same room. He was walking past on the street and saw this. He shouted 'How can men and women be dancing together like this? It's irreligious.' He stopped the dance."

Wael Essam, the Palestinian journalist with extensive experience reporting from Iraq, talked to many Sunnis who were al-Baghdadi's colleagues during his academic days at the University for Islamic Sciences. Al-Baghdadi, they claimed, was either a member of the Muslim Brotherhood or an affiliate of it when he matriculated. His Salafist inclinations came later, well into his curriculum. "Al-Baghdadi was close to Mohammed Hardan, one of the Brotherhood's leaders," Essam said. "Hardan had left to fight with the mujahidin in Afghanistan and returned in the 1990s and adopted a clear Salafist ideology. Al-Baghdadi joined Hardan's group organizationally and ideologically. He also briefly joined Jaysh al-Mujahideen [the Army of the Mujhahidin, a Sunni militant group]."

By around 2000 al-Baghdadi had a doctorate, a wife, and a son. By 2003 the United States occupied Iraq, although the future ISIS leader was not yet an insurgent. Abu Ali told the *Telegraph* that al-Baghdadi bore no discernible grievance against US forces at that point: "He wasn't like the hot-blooded ones. He must have been a quiet planner."

So quiet that by late 2003 he had founded his own Islamist faction, Jaysh Ahl al-Sunnah wa al-Jamaah (the Army of the People of the Sunni Community); a year after that, he was enrolled in another sort of university—Camp Bucca.

Contrary to numerous claims in the Western press that suggest that al-Baghdadi was released from Bucca in 2009, when it was shuttered, he actually served only a single yearlong stint in the internment facility, in 2004. "He was visiting a friend of his in Fallujah named Nessayif Numan Nessayif," al-Hashimi recalled to us. "With him was another man, Abdul Wahed al-Semayyir. The

US Army intelligence arrested all of them. Baghdadi was not the target—it was Nessayif. He was arrested on January 31, 2004, and was released on December 6, 2004. He was never arrested again after that. Everything to the contrary is incorrect."

Abu Ahmed, the former high-ranking ISIS member who knew al-Baghdadi at Bucca, told the *Guardian* that prison administrators at first took al-Baghdadi to be something of a problem-solver. His PhD in Islamic studies conferred a jurisprudential wisdom on him to which squabbling jihadist inmates seemed to defer. As such, the Americans let him travel among the different camp blocs at Bucca, ostensibly to resolve conflicts; instead, al-Baghdadi used the indulgence to recruit more foot soldiers. In time, according to Abu Ahmed, he started causing problems in the prison, using "a policy of conquer and divide to get what he wanted, which was status. And it worked."

When al-Baghdadi was released at the end of 2004, owing to US appraisals that he posed a low-level risk to the coalition or Iraqi institutions, he grew even more extremist in orientation, according to Essam. In 2007 he joined the Mujahideen Shura Council, which al-Zarqawi had installed to nationalize the insurgency. However, al-Baghdadi's purism and his mercurial alliance-making meant that he wasn't really interested in working with an ideologically diverse consortium of insurgent groups, even if al-Qaeda was primus inter pares. An AQI commander from Fallujah told Essam that al-Baghdadi turned on just about every faction he ever joined. "He left the Muslim Brotherhood and he then declared them apostates and agents of [former US Ambassador to Iraq Zalmay] Khalilzad. He also left Jaysh al-Mujahideen and he engaged in hostilities against them, especially in al-Karmah [a town northeast of Fallujah]. Al-Baghdadi was always very consistent about his position on fellow Sunni militant groups that were not part of his own organization. He would say: 'Fighting them is more of a priority than fighting the Americans.'"

His insistence on the need for fratricidal warfare—or *fitna* between and among Sunnis—would remain a hallmark of al-Baghdadi's leadership well into the expansion of ISIS into Syria and Iraq. Essem also maintains that, contrary to the popular belief that al-Baghdadi came from nowhere, he was actually well-known to both Iraqis and Americans. "His uncle was Ismail al-Badri, member of Iraq's Muslim Ulema Association, which is considered an apostate organization by his nephew. Al-Baghdadi's sister-in-law is also married to a leader of the Iraqi Islamic Party, the vehicle of the Brotherhood in Iraq. Before the Americans withdrew, he was arrested multiple times because of his kinship to Abu Bakr."

Furthermore, according to al-Hashimi, al-Baghdadi's ascension to ISI emir was decided overwhelmingly, by nine out of eleven members of the Shura Council. There were three reasons for his selection. First, he belonged to the Quraysh tribal confederation, considered one of the most venerable in the Middle East, thanks to its proximity to the Prophet Muhammad. (Abu Omar al-Baghdadi was also said to have hailed from this tribe, the wellspring of all Islamic caliphs.) Second, al-Baghdadi had himself been a member of ISI's Shura Council and was therefore close to Abu Omar. Finally, he was chosen because of his age: he was a generation younger than the other viable candidates for emir and was viewed as someone with more staying power to lead ISI out of the doldrums once US forces had quit Iraq. Today, ISIS reveres him as a "messenger." "Whoever comes to you while your condition is united behind a single man, and intends to break your solidarity or disrupt your unity, then kill him," *Dabiq* proclaimed, exhorting all Muslims to pledge allegiance to al-Baghdadi.

GHOSTS OF SADDAM II

Al-Baghdadi's rise heralded yet another mutation of ISI, or rather a retrogression of it to an earlier period in the Sunni insurgency's history. There were visibly many more former Baathists in the higher ranks, owing no doubt to the continued Iraqization of the organization. As General Odierno noted in his June 2010 Pentagon news briefing, AQI's leadership had been all but destroyed in a very short space of time—thirty-four out of the top forty-two operatives were removed from the battlefield in one way or another—and the franchise had lost its ability to coordinate with al-Qaeda's headquarters in Pakistan. The vacuum this created at the top meant that, before al-Zawahiri and bin Laden could appoint a new emir from afar, the Iraqi wing of ISIS was able to decide on one of its own in Abu Bakr.

According to US officials, that was the internal story told by two disgruntled al-Qaeda members several years later. The reason they were disgruntled was that their perception of the rise of al-Baghdadi, whatever his level of education, represented the takeover of the Salafist-Jihadist movement within ISI of people without strong Salafist-Jihadist credentials—the Baathists.

There is no argument among analysts or those who knew al-Baghdadi that he is a true-believing takfirist. But, as we've seen already, even rock-ribbed terrorists benefit from their own who's who, mainly in the form of filial or tribal connections that enable them to leverage a birthright afforded to them by the very societies or regimes they seek to destroy. Might al-Baghdadi have benefited from his ties to the Baathists? Given what is known of his biography and education, the likelihood is strong.

According to Derek Harvey, "he's clearly not Zarqawi. But the breadth and size of the organization and the things it has going on from financial enterprises to administration to the running of eight separate regional commands, to its tactical partnering with Naqshbandi Army, to its tribal outreach—I see a Baathist style to all of this. And I know that one of Baghdadi's mentors at the University of Islamic Sciences was close to Izzat al-Douri. Al-Douri continually operated from Raqqa and [the] northeastern Syria area early on in ISIS's emergence in Syria."

Al-Hashimi pointed out that al-Baghdadi had sought in his youth to pursue a career at Saddam's Ministry of Islamic Endowments. "I had a talk with a senior former Iraqi official who was a senior official in Saddam's regime and under al-Maliki," an active US military official told us.

> "I asked him specifically about al-Baghdadi. 'Did you know who he was?' Not specifically, but he knew the background that he came from and the extended network he came from. In Saddam's time, where this guy was from and where his family was from was very much a Saddamist-Baathist stronghold. The people who came from Samarra were very tight with the regime. Al-Baghdadi went to the Islamic University of Baghdad at exactly the time of Saddam's Faith Campaign—in other words, at a time when the Baath Party was controlling admissions. There's no way you'd get into the Islamic University at that time without getting vetted and approved by the party, and there's no way you'd get vetted and approved by the party without having an extended family network of uncles and cousins and so on who are in the regime and endorsing you. So yeah, al-Baghdadi may not have been a Baathist himself, but I guarantee you he had a lot of Baathist family members who put him into the Islamic University."

As we've examined, the anti-American insurgency in Iraq drew its strength from Sunni revanchism. One way to view Baathism historically is as one among many exponents of Sunni political power. It competed in its heyday with pan-Arab nationalism, as expounded by Egyptian President Gamal Abdel Nasser, the Islamism of Sayyed Qutb's Brotherhood, and the Salafist-Jihadism of bin Laden. Indeed, the Islamic Faith Campaign was meant to preempt

Salafism's usurpation of Baathism. Today, the secular socialist ideology is in a tenuous state of coexistence and competition with the caliphate-building takfirism of ISIS. Amatzia Baram and Pesach Malovany, two scholars of contemporary Iraq, take this thesis even further and make an intriguing case for viewing al-Baghdadi as the rightful heir to Saddam Hussein. For one thing, they argue, even though he is originally from Samarra, his chosen nom de guerre, al-Baghdadi, immediately situates the Iraqi capital as ISIS's center of gravity, which it was under the Abbasid caliphate, itself an important Islamic touchstone for the dead Iraqi dictator. "Saddam never declared himself to be a caliph," Baram and Malovany write, "but his conceptual connection with the Abbasid caliphate centered in Baghdad was profound. One of the nicknames attached to his name was 'Al-Mansur,' which means 'Victorious by the grace of God,' but that was also the name of the most important Abbasid caliph. . . . Saddam also gave names derived from the Abbasid history to numerous military units he established. . . . So, as far as the central role of Iraq and Baghdad is concerned, Abu-Bakr al-Baghdadi is Saddam's disciple."

"The brutality, the tradecraft, how ISIS is behaving on and off the battlefield—it's really no different from the Saddamists, in my view," said Derek Harvey, who would surely know.

There is also a grim parallel between Saddam and al-Baghdadi's hatred of the Shia. The Baathist slaughtered 150,000 of them during Saddam's thirty-year reign, most notoriously during the suppression of the Shia and Kurdish uprising against his regime in March 1991, at the end of the First Gulf War. When his tanks rolled into Najaf in 1991, they had the slogan "La Shi`a ba`d al-yawm" ("No Shia after today") painted on their sides.

If there is a difference in the ideology of murderous sectarianism, then, it is one of scale. For all his savagery, Saddam did not make it a matter of state policy to seek the wholesale destruction of

the Shia, nor could he—they were still tolerated in the upper echelons of the Iraqi military and in the Baath Party, even after the 1991
massacres. Al-Baghdadi, however, has so far demonstrated nothing
short of annihilationist intention, following in the dark pathological tradition of al-Zarqawi. To ISIS, the Shia are religiously void,
deceitful, and only marked for death.

ALL THE EMIR'S MEN

Harvey's insight is all the more compelling for the fact that ISIS's
high command consists of former or recovering Saddamists, those
who occupied elite posts in the Iraqi military or Mukhabarat. Al-
Hashimi credits two men in particular with helping al-Baghdadi
advance in ISI.

The first is Abu Abdul-Rahman al-Bilawi (real name: Adnan
Ismael Najm), who was killed during ISIS's siege of Mosul in
June 2014. He joined AQI during al-Zarqawi's era and had been
al-Baghdadi's chief of the general military council for ISIS, with a
purview encompassing all of Iraq's eighteen provinces. Originally
from al-Khalidiya in Anbar, Bilawi was formerly a captain Saddam's
army. He, too, had been detained at Camp Bucca, although a year or
so after al-Baghdadi's confinement.

The second influencer, according to al-Hashimi, is Abu Ali
al-Anbari, a native of Mosul and ISIS's man in charge of operations in Syria. Before becoming a jihadist, al-Anbari was also an
officer in Saddam's army. Somewhere in between, according to the
Wall Street Journal, he had been affiliated with Ansar al-Islam before the group kicked him out following accusations of financial
corruption. Iraqi and Syrian militants think al-Anbari was selected
as al-Baghdadi's deputy in the Levant because of his political pragmatism; his "knowledge of Shariah Islamic rules isn't considered as
extensive as that of other senior leaders," the *Journal* reported.

Abu Ayman al-Iraqi, another member of ISIS's Military Council, was formerly a lieutenant colonel in Saddam's air force intelligence, according to a cache of internal documents recovered by Iraqi forces. Another former US detainee, his previous nom de guerre, under Baathist rule, was Abu Muhannad al-Suweidawi. So entrenched in his native soil was al-Iraqi that Laith Alkhouri said to us that he needed assistance migrating next door. "The moment that ISIS expanded into Syria, al-Iraqi went in. There is no way he went on his own to Syria. He couldn't navigate the place by himself. He led ISIS in Aleppo and Latakia, and he must be the group's top guy for security in Deir Ezzor. He's leading much of ISIS's current efforts against other Syrian rebel factions."

Another graduate of both Bucca and the Baath regime was Fadel Ahmed Abdullah al-Hiyali (also known as Abu Muslim al-Turkmani or Haji Mutazz). In December 2014 General Martin Dempsey, the chairman of the Joint Chiefs of Staff, claimed that al-Turkmani was killed by US air strikes, though jihadists say that it was in November. Prior to that, al-Turkmani was thought to have occupied a position possibly equal to that of al-Anbari in the ISIS hierarchy. A former lieutenant colonel in Iraq's Special Forces, he was apparently one of many victims of the disbandment of the Iraqi army in 2003 by Paul Bremer, the American envoy who ran Iraq after the war. Al-Turkmani linked up with another Sunni insurgent group before joining AQI.

Baghdad is said to have handpicked al-Suweidawi and al-Turkmani during their detention at Camp Bucca.

In some cases, the devil's rejects were also Bremer's and al-Maliki's. The *New York Times* reported in August 2014 that after Mosul fell, an unnamed former general in Saddam's army called to apply to the Iraqi Security Forces. His application was refused. Now a member of ISIS, he has reportedly told the army that wouldn't have him, "We will reach you soon, and I will chop you into pieces."

"The Baathists originally said that their return to power was going to be based on Islam," Harvey told us. "That's what Saddam's letters and his guidance said." Michael Pregent, a former US military intelligence officer who advised the Kurdish peshmerga in Iraq, argues that ISIS's attempt to mask or elide the curricula vitae of its top commanders is part of its war strategy. "They can't use their old affiliation as a recruitment tool to get people to come over and fight. A return to Baathism isn't a great selling point, especially when you claim to be committed to Baathism's defeat in Syria. It's like saying that every Army Ranger or Special Forces soldier suddenly became a Branch Davidian."

FROM TBILISI TO ALEPPO

There is one prominent exception to al-Baghdadi's preference for Iraqis over foreign mujahidin in positions of influence in ISIS. Known internationally as the "red-bearded jihadist," Abu Omar al-Shishani, or Tarkhan Batirashvili, as he was born, is an ethnic Chechen in his late twenties from the Pankisi Gorge region of Georgia who actually served in the US-trained Georgian army as a military intelligence officer. He fought in the 2008 Russo-Georgian War but was later diagnosed with tuberculosis, according to his father, Teimuraz, and so was dismissed from the army.

The Batirashvili men were all Christian, but Teimuraz's sons became radical Muslims. Al-Shishani even hung up the phone when told that his father hadn't converted to Islam.

He was arrested for arms possession and served time in a Georgian prison, where his evolution into a hard-core Salafist may have taken place. Released in 2010 as part of Georgia's general amnesty for prisoners, al-Shishani traveled sometime thereafter to Turkey, and then crossed into Syria. "Now he says he left because of his faith, but I know he did it because we were poor," Teimuraz told the BBC.

The Chechen first emerged in Syria in 2012 as the head of his own al-Qaeda–inspired jihadist cell, Jaysh Al-Mujahireen Wal-Ansar (the Army of Emigrants and Partisans), which consisted mainly of Muslims from the former Soviet Union. Russia's domestic security service, the FSB, has reckoned that as many as five hundred Russian nationals are fighting in Syria, with hundreds more from other ex-Soviet countries, a statistic that can't be independently confirmed. However, it bears noting that Russia factors prominently into ISIS's propaganda as an enemy nation, no doubt owing to its warrior class from the Caucasus and desire to recruit more.

Serially reported since as having been killed in combat—typically at the hands of Kurdish militias—he has now even earned the special attention of Ramzan Kadyrov, Vladimir Putin's handpicked warlord-president of Chechnya. In November 2014 Kadyrov announced one of the many alleged deaths of al-Shishani, the "enemy of Islam," on his favorite social media platform, Instagram, before deleting the announcement. This prompted speculation that the Chechen may have actually been killed in Syria and that Kadyrov's obituary was the FSB's way of confirming the news. Whatever the case, the Georgian's main function for ISIS seems to be as its celebrated Patton of the *muhajireen*.

Chechens, as a rule, are viewed by others ISIS jihadists as the most formidable warriors, owing to decades of experience fighting a grueling insurgency against the Russian army. "Shishani is the most visible commander, even while ISIS's command-and-control is still being directed by Baghdadi and former Baathists," according to Chris Harmer, an analyst at the Institute for the Study of War. "The Chechens stand apart from the other foreign jihadists. If I'm in the ISIS Military Council, I'm not going to take a guy who has experience fighting the Russians and turn him into a suicide bomber. I'm going to make him a platoon commander."

For more than a year, al-Shishani's genius as a military strategist was heralded and taken as the received wisdom among observers of the Syrian conflict after the Army of Emigrants and Partisans played a decisive role in sacking the Menagh air base in Aleppo, an installation that had been besieged for months by rebels of all sorts, including ISIS. Some of them even made impressive incursions inside the base only to then be beaten back by Syrian soldiers. Menagh finally fell after al-Shishani dispatched two foreign suicide bombers (one was reportedly a Saudi) who detonated a VBIED in an armored car they drove right up to the base's command center. Largely a morale boost to the anti-Assad cause, the Menagh operation was generously credited by other rebels as a major ISIS victory over the regime.

Lately, this heroic portrayal has come in for revisionist scrutiny by al-Shishani's former comrades who fought alongside him and say his legend is tabloid embroidery. As Radio Free Europe / Radio Liberty reported in November 2014, another Chechen jihadist named Khalid Shishani believes that his namesake is actually a lousy field commander. "Umar Shishani is a person who is absolutely useless in military terms," Khalid wrote in a statement posted to Russian jihadist forums. "He lacks knowledge of military tactics—and that's putting it nicely. Take note that it's only the infidel (i.e., the Western) mass media that has written about Umar Shishani's military genius. They have greatly inflated his identity and presented him as a genius military specialist, which is the complete opposite of the real picture. This person only knows how to send mujahedin as cannon fodder, and that's it."

Even if we attribute this to sour grapes or an intramural falling-out, it must be said that al-Shishani's reputation has been better served by the *Daily Mail* than by the Salafist-Jihadist cognoscenti. Alkhouri said that he's the butt of innumerable jokes in online jihadists forums because his knowledge of Islam is "shit," and his spoken Arabic is even worse.

THE MANAGEMENT OF HYPE

The transformation of foreign fighters into contemporary Saladins is actually a main plank of jihadist recruitment, going back to al-Zarqawi's days. After all, even the Jordanian founder of AQI had come off as Gomer Pyle with an assault rifle until his tech department edited him into every inch the emir. "Look at who these foreign fighters are, first of all," Richard, the ex-counterterrorist, said. "In most cases, they're adventurers who don't have a pot to piss in back home, whether that's Belgium, Manchester, Algeria, Yemen or, OK, Georgia. They got hopped up through social media or proselytizing outside the mosque and went off to fight jihad. These are the same guys militaries around the world have been counting on forever to be privates or infantrymen. They're knucklehead nineteen-year-olds looking to do something in their life because they don't have shit to do back in Belgium."

Western sensationalism has perversely contributed to the lure or glamour of ISIS as much as it has to its lurid appeal to the young and disaffected. Stories about pretty, middle-class teenage Austrian girls going to off to fight with and marry the takfiris—and copycats who are stopped en route before they can reach Syria—continue to draw headlines in the manner that Charles Manson's latest nuptials do. People are fascinated by the psychopathic spectacle of ISIS, and especially by those they see as "like them" but who are so drawn to it that they abandon seemingly comfortable lives in the West to jihadism.

Scott Atran, an anthropologist at the University of Michigan, has made a close study of the psychological and social motivations behind jihadism and argues that ISIS is really no different from the revolutionary-romantic movements that have reveled in bloodshed throughout history. "You can't inspire people to kill people and harm others without moral virtue," he told us. "It's very much like the French Revolution. When Robespierre introduced the terror as a tool of democracy—they were quite ostentatious about it."

Who would join ISIS? In 1940 George Orwell wrote an essay in which he asked a similar question of a book advocating what he summarized as a "horrible brainless empire in which, essentially, nothing ever happens except the training of young men for war and the endless breeding of fresh cannon-fodder." How could such a "monstrous vision" be put across when liberal democracy was meant to have ended such barbarism, he wondered? And why was a nation flinging itself at the feet of a man who offered "struggle, danger and death" where other forms of government were offering a "good time"? Orwell was reviewing *Mein Kampf*.

9

REVOLUTION BETRAYED
JIHAD COMES TO SYRIA

On January 31, 2011, Bashar al-Assad gave an interview to the *Wall Street Journal*. Reflecting on the revolutions that had swept Tunisia, Egypt, and Libya, he was in a boastful mood about the chances of a similar upheaval coming to his own country. "Syria is stable," he proclaimed. "Why? Because you have to be very closely linked to the beliefs of the people. This is the core issue." Al-Assad was right: it was the core issue.

Just three days before his interview took place, soldiers from his regime had dispersed a candlelight vigil organized in solidarity with the Egyptian protestors in Bab Touma, a Christian quarter in Damascus's Old City. Then, on February 17, a spontaneous protest erupted in the souk in the capital's neighborhood of al-Hariqa after a police officer insulted the son of a local merchant. Although the protest was carefully directed against the behavior of the police officer, the slogan transcended a single crime: "The Syrian people will not be humiliated." That demonstration came to an end after Syria's Interior Minister arrived on the scene to address the angry crowd and apologize. It was too late. More demonstrations erupted and spread against the atrocities being committed by Gaddafi in Libya and, implicitly, by the dynastic dictator at home who had just described his reign as unimpeachable.

"THE PEOPLE WANT THE FALL OF THE REGIME"

A reform movement became a full-fledged revolution after a hinge incident in the city of Deraa. Fifteen schoolboys, some as young as ten years old, were arrested by the regime's security forces under the supervision of al-Assad's cousin, General Atef Najib, for scrawling pro-democracy graffiti on their school's walls. Some of the slogans were adopted from TV broadcasts about other countries, but one especially creative phrase, which rhymes in Arabic, ran, "It's your turn, Doctor," referring to al-Assad's ophthalmology degree. A common account of what followed claims that when the families of detainees told Najib that these were their only children, he replied: "Send us your wives, and we will make you new children."

Similar protests soon broke out in Damascus, Homs, Baniyas, and then across all of Syria. The response was widespread state violence. Many peaceful demonstrators and activists were shot by soldiers, riot police, Mukhabarat, and pro–al-Assad militiamen. Others were arrested and hauled off to any number of security prisons. As documented by Human Rights Watch, the secret police used a broad array of torture against their captives, including pipe beatings, whippings, electrocutions, acid burns, fingernail extractions, bastinados, and mock executions. Detainees of all genders and ages were also raped. One woman held at the Palestine Branch of Military Intelligence in Damascus, one of the most feared Mukhabarat prisons in Syria, told the BBC what happened to a fellow female prisoner. "He inserted a rat in her vagina. She was screaming. Afterwards we saw blood on the floor. He told her: 'Is this good enough for you?' They were mocking her. It was obvious she was in agony. We could see her. After that she no longer moved."

General Najib's threat had not been idle, as rape was systematically used by the al-Assad regime from the early days of the uprising. According to Farha Barazi, a Virginia-based human rights campaigner, many rapes resulted in unwanted pregnancies, with Syrian gynecologists seeing victims as young as eleven. In April 2012 Barazi recounted to these authors the story of "Salma," a young girl from Baba Amr, Homs, whose house was raided by the *shabiha*, mercenary gangs loyal to al-Assad. "She told them, 'Please, please—don't you have sisters? Don't you have mothers? Just leave me, please not in front of my dad.'" The shabiha tied Salma's father to a chair in his own house and forced him to watch as three or four men raped his daughter. "They made him keep his eyes open and watch," Barazi said. "We have documented eleven cases so far of women needing abortions because they were raped. We had to move them all from either Baba Amr or Idlib to Aleppo, where it was safer to perform this procedure. They are all safe now, but when I called some of them, they were in hysterics. All have suffered severe psychological trauma because of what they've gone through." Since Barazi's interview almost three years ago, those documented cases have skyrocketed. Close to 200,000 people have been killed in Syria, and another 150,000 are still detained in regime prisons, according to "Caesar," a code-named Syrian military police photographer who defected and smuggled out of the country some fifty thousand photographs depicting horrific detainee atrocities. "What is going on in Syria is a genocidal massacre that is being led by the worst of all the terrorists, Bashar al-Assad," Caesar testified before the US Congress in July 2014. Stephen Rapp, the State Department's ambassador-at-large for war crimes, has said that his disclosures constitute "solid evidence of the kind of machinery of cruel death that we haven't seen frankly since the Nazis."

"ASSAD, OR WE BURN THE COUNTRY"

In his epic poem "Child of Europe," which deals in a series of ironic couplets about the intellectual and moral depravities of totalitarianism, Czeslaw Milosz offered this apostrophe to the offspring of the twentieth century: "Learn to predict a fire with unerring precision / Then burn the house down to fulfill the prediction." Al-Assad resorted to much the same logic when faced with months of protests calling for his ouster.

From the outset, he had portrayed his opponents, even those who were only calling for modest economic reforms, as al-Qaeda terrorists, hirelings of the United States, Saudi Arabia, Qatar, and Israel—surely one of the most elaborate coalitions of the willing in modern history. The goal of this silly-seeming but consistent propaganda and disinformation campaign was simple. As we've seen, al-Assad was always desperate to win the attention and cooperation of the West, even while suborning terrorism against it. Faced with revolution, and blaming the West for the very crimes he himself had long committed, he sough to ensure his political longevity through self-fulfilling prophecy. His regime undertook several measures to bring violent Islamism home to Syria. It was no coincidence that one of the favored slogans of his loyalists was "Assad or we burn the country."

Qusai Zakarya is a Palestinian refugee who lived in the Damascus suburb of Moadamiyeh and survived both the regime's August 2013 chemical weapon attack and a months-long starvation campaign imposed on his town before he was able to leave Syria under complicated circumstances. "From the beginning, if you were Sunni, and especially if you were Palestinian, you were treated as something less than human by Bashar's forces," Zakarya told us. "'There is no god but Bashar,' the shabiha would say as they kicked protestors or pulled the hair from their head or beards. This was very deliberate. It was also genius."

What Zakarya meant was that the verbal, psychological, and corporal abuse unleashed on Sunnis was *designed* to radicalize them and push them to acts of extremism. "Assad used a lot of the Alawite forces to repress the opposition in key areas," said Shiraz Maher, an expert on radicalization (and a former Islamist himself) at King's College in London. "It was physical torture mixed with a campaign to mock the core aspects of Sunni belief. That's what caught the attention and anger all around the world, above and beyond what drew the average guy in the Midwest to pay attention to what was happening in Syria. Assad set the Sunni Muslim world on fire. This is why the foreign fighter trend started from the Gulf and North Africa." Lighting this fuse proved remarkably easy after decades of dictatorial misrule.

Sectarianism in Syria, as in Iraq, long predated civil war and was as much the by-product of a minority sect lording it over a restive majority as it was of an antique dispute among Muslims about the lineage of the Prophet in the seventh century. In this case, it was the minority Alawites, a mostly cultural offshoot of the Shia, who constitute between 8 percent and 15 percent of the population in Syria, ruling over the Sunnis, who constitute close to 75 percent. As in Saddam's Iraq, the majority sect was also well represented in all levels of government; for instance, al-Assad's wife, Asma al-Assad, is a Sunni, as have been several high-ranking regime security and military officials. And though it was always the case that minorities were represented in the early protest movement, demography in Syria proved revolutionary destiny: Sunnis were viewed as, and most often were, the ones standing up to the regime in number. The expectation of this contingency had created a republic of fear and paranoia in Assadist Syria.

In 2010 Nibras Kazimi published an incredibly prescient study titled *Syria Through Jihadist Eyes: A Perfect Enemy*, which featured a number of telling vignettes, all drawn from his many interviews with Syrians of various religious, ethnic, and socioeconomic backgrounds in the country. Kazimi met a "Damascus-born plastic surgeon," for instance, whose father was a high-ranking Alawite officer in the Syrian Arab Army and had been a personal friend of Hafez al-Assad. The surgeon was exhibited in a photograph with Hasan Nasrallah, the leader of Lebanese Hezbollah. As one of the beneficiaries of Assadism, this man ought to have been, writes Kazimi, "the portrait of an assimilated upper middle-class [Alawite], confident of his standing in Syrian society. But he isn't. When he drives his late-model Volvo, he keeps a submachine gun handy on the passenger's seat. He said, 'Do you know the Sunnis have a saying, *mal'oon baba Hassan* ('Cursed is Baba Hassan')? Do you know who Baba Hassan is? He's Ali bin Abi Taleb, the father of Hassan and the first of the twelve Shia Imams. They hate us. That is who they are. . . . If given the chance, they will massacre us." Out of such societal dysfunction, a counterrevolutionary strategy was born.

"The sectarianism was carefully manufactured by Assad from the get-go as a tool of his suppression," Maher said. "'This is not a peaceful uprising, it's a sectarian one, the Sunnis are rising up and will kill all the minorities.' This was the original line, and it tried to do two things. First, peel off the rest of Syria from the Sunnis who were rebelling so that Alawite or Christian dissidents wouldn't join the uprising, even though some of them did. Second, provoke concern in the international community about what was taking place—namely, that minorities were all going to be slaughtered by terrorists."

The shabiha were the main protagonists in furthering this agenda. Named "ghosts" after the Mercedes Shahab cars in which they used to smuggle everything from cigarettes and drugs to food and weapons into Syria's gray market economy in the years before the revolution, these muscle-bound thugs, most of whom were Alawites, were enlisted by Damascus to commit some of the worst crimes against humanity. According to one who was detained by rebels in 2012, each *shabih* was paid $460 per month, plus another $150 bonus for every person he killed or captured. "We love

Assad because the government gave us all the power—if I wanted to take something, kill a person, or rape a girl I could," he bragged. In the Houla region of Homs, in May 2012, the shabiha embedded with Syrian army regulars and went house to house in the town of Taldou, following its sustained artillery bombardment, slitting the throats of more than one hundred people. Most of them were women and children. (The shabiha were readily identifiable, locals later testified, by their white sneakers; Syrian soldiers wore black boots.) Al-Assad blamed al-Qaeda for the massacre. However, an investigation by the United Nations found "reasonable basis to believe that the perpetrators . . .were aligned to the Government."

In an early awareness of what would later become al-Assad's main war strategy, State Department spokeswoman Victoria Nuland accused Iran of being an accomplice to the massacre. "The Iranians have clearly supplied support and training and advice to the Syrian army, but this shabiha thug force mirrors the same force that the Iranians use," Nuland said. "The Basij [a volunteer paramilitary originally built by the Iran's Revolutionary Guards to help fight in the Iran-Iraq War] and the shabiha are the same type of thing and clearly reflects the tactics and the techniques that the Iranians use for their own suppression of civil rights." Nuland noted that on the very same weekend that the Houla massacre had been carried out, the Quds Force Deputy Commander Esmail Ghani claimed credit for playing a "physical and non-physical" role in Syria's war.

SULEIMANI'S WAR

That role would only increase in the subsequent year when evidence emerged that the Quds Force and Lebanese Hezbollah were also training a more professionalized Basij guerrilla army, the so-called National Defense Force, and doing so in both Syria and Iran. With as many as one hundred thousand recruits, these irregulars have lately become one of the regime's main bulwarks in light of the successive failures of the Syrian army to beat back the rebels and reclaim territory on its own. Again, the legacy of Assadism bears on the current civil war: Many of the army's rank-and-file soldiers are Sunnis who have defected, deserted, or even been confined to barracks because their commanding (Alawite) officers fear that they might do so. Other infantrymen have been killed by rebels in three years of attritional war.

"The Syrian army couldn't handle this three-year crisis because any army would be fatigued," IRGC operative Sayyed Hassan Entezari said by way of accounting for the genesis and necessity of the National Defense Force. "Iran came and said why don't you form popular support for yourself and ask your people for help. . . .Our boys went to one of the biggest Alawite regions. They told the head of one of the major tribes to call upon his youth to take up arms and help the regime." Each brigade of the National Defense Force is supervised by an IRGC officer who acts the part of an embedded commissar ensuring ideological discipline.

Reuters conducted interviews with several cadets of this IRGC program in April 2013. All were from Homs and most were Alawites, although some hailed from other minority sects. One interviewee, Samer, was one of the rare Christians who had undergone training in Iran. He told the news agency: "The Iranians kept telling us that this war is not against Sunnis but for the sake of Syria. But the Alawites on the course kept saying they want to kill the Sunnis and rape their women in revenge."

The camp at which Samer must have trained is called Amir Al-Momenin (Commander of the Faithful), located about fifteen miles outside of Tehran; it's where the Quds Force's ballistic missiles are housed. According to an Iranian military officer who spoke to the *Wall Street Journal* in September 2013, the trainees "are told that the war in Syria is akin to [an] epic battle for Shiite Islam, and if they die they will be martyrs of the highest rank."

Unsurprisingly, the National Defense Force has already been implicated in anti-Sunni pogroms, one having taken place in the town of al-Bayda and a few neighborhoods in the city of Baniyas, in the coastal province of Tartous. In May 2013 eyewitnesses interviewed by Human Rights Watch testified that "government and pro-government forces entered homes, separated men from women and young children, rounded up the men of each neighborhood in one spot, and executed them by shooting them at close range. . . . In many cases, the pro-government forces burnt the bodies of those they had just shot."

Although al-Bayda and Baniyas are home to a minority Christian population, all the Christian witnesses who spoke to the NGO said that pro-regime forces "only killed Sunnis and burned Sunni homes." The regime, meanwhile, claimed that it had killed "terrorists."

Iran's involvement in Syria has strongly mirrored its involvement in US-occupied Iraq, with one stark and ironic exception: now *it* appears to be the occupying military force, desperately trying to hold together a shambolic and undisciplined native army. Suleimani's militias have taken on more and more military responsibility as al-Assad's conventional forces have deteriorated, died, or fled. This has resulted in high-profile Iranian fatalities, most famously that of senior Quds Force Commander Hassan Shater, who was killed on a road that connected Damascus to Beirut. Notably, Tehran has relied only on operatives from its foreign intelligence arm of the IRGC to "assist and train" al-Assad's conventional army, but also ones from the IRGC's Ground Forces, men with extensive experience in suppressing ethnically driven insurgencies, such as among Azerbaijanis in Iran's West Azerbaijan province. Several members of IRGC Ground Forces, including a brigade commander, were among forty-eight Iranians captured by Syrian rebels and subsequently released in January 2013 as part of a prisoner swap.

A report published by the Institute for the Study of War found that in one interesting respect, Iran's counterinsurgency tactics in Syria may consciously be replicating America's in Iraq. In Homs, the city known as the "birthplace of the revolution," to which the Syrian army laid merciless siege in 2012, once the rebels were expelled, the regime constructed a ten-foot-high concrete wall redolent of the one US forces had constructed around Sadr City in 2008. "Iranian observers working with proxies in Sadr City at that time would have seen the effectiveness of the campaign firsthand and could have advised the Assad regime to adopt a similar approach," the report concluded.

"Syria is occupied by the Iranian regime," former Syrian prime minister Riyad Hijab declared after his defection in August 2012. "The person who runs the country is not Bashar al-Assad but Qassem Soleimani, the head of Iranian regime's Quds Force."

As early as May 2011, Suleimani and his deputy, Mohsen Chizari—the same operative who had been detained by JSOC in 2006 after attending a meeting at SCIRI headquarters—were sanctioned by the US government for their "complicity . . .in the human rights abuses and repression of the Syrian people." Suleimani was designated specifically as the "conduit for Iranian material support" to Syria's General Intelligence Directorate. Such support, as later came to light, included the trafficking of arms, munitions, and Quds Force personnel in civilian and military airliners across Iraq's airspace to Damascus, prompting several demarches from Washington to Baghdad, all met with denials by the al-Maliki government that any such sky corridor existed. (In 2012, when the Iraqis stopped denying it, they claimed it was "humanitarian aid" and that the United States had failed to provide any evidence of weapons being transferred.) According to US intelligence, Suleimani's helpmeet in smuggling men and arms to Syria via Iraq is Hadi al-Amiri, the head of the Badr Corps, which al-Zarqawi made a lightning rod for AQI's Sunni recruitment in 2004. By 2013 al-Amiri was Iraq's Transportation Minister.

This may account for why the "spillover" of one country's war into another country wasn't merely confined to movement of Sunni jihadists. In January 2014 the Meir Amit Intelligence and Terrorist Information Center in Israel calculated that there were actually more foreign Shia fighters helping Assad than there were foreign Sunni fighters trying to overthrow him.

Jaafar Athab, a member of Asa'ib Ahl al-Haq, the group responsible for killing five American servicemen in Karbala in 2007, was killed in Syria in 2012, whereupon his body was brought back to Baghdad and given a funeral in Tahrir Square under the supervision of the Iraqi Security Forces. Kata'ib Hezbollah has also lost Shia militiamen in Syria. Ditto Muqtada al-Sadr's Mahdi Army, which formed a Shia-Alawite Special Group made up of "[five hundred] Iraqi, Syrian, and . . .other nationalities" called the Abu al-Fadhal al-Abbas brigade. Phillip Smyth, an expert on the Special Groups, documented in August 2013 how the Badr Corps's own Facebook page had announced a 1,500-strong presence in Syria and public funerals for its members slain in Iraq. Most of these fighters couched their participation in al-Assad's war in strictly defensive language; they were going off, they said, to "protect holy shrines." Though it is true many Shia-Alawite militants were deployed to religious sites, notably the Sayyida Zeinab mosque in the Damascus suburbs, this custodianship of sacred architecture became a sectarian euphemism or code for what was, in effect, Shia Islamist holy war—or counterinsurgency à la Suleimani.

Iran has even sent thousands of Afghani refugees to fight on al-Assad's behalf, offering them residency rights and as much as $500 per month. Others are allegedly ex-Taliban fighters who became Iranian mercenaries to fight "against those who are being assisted by Americans in Syria."

No IRGC-run subsidiary has been more integral to Assad's survival thus far than Lebanese Hezbollah, which was almost single-handedly responsible for expelling Syrian rebels from the town of al-Qusayr, which lies along a vital Syrian-Lebanese supply corridor. "Hezbollah is leading operations in Qusayr," one Party of God paramilitary confessed to NOW Lebanon. "The Syrian army is only playing a secondary role, deploying after an area is completely 'cleaned' and secured."

Of course, what he meant by "clean[ing]" areas is more accurately described as ethnic cleansing. "There have been obvious examples of denominational cleansing in different areas in Homs," a Syrian activist named Abu Rami told the *Guardian* in July 2013. "It is . . .part of a major Iranian Shia plan, which is obvious through the involvement of Hezbollah and Iranian militias. And it's also part of Assad's personal Alawite state project."

The project alluded to was the supposed creation of an Alawite rump state on the Syrian coast. For a time, when it was still suffering territorial losses, the regime subtly put out indications that this would be its fallback plan if Damascus fell, a way to telegraph to the West that it would remain guarded of a vulnerable Alawite minority in the face of what it originally and consistently portrayed as the rebel cause: a Sunni supremacist plan for extermination.

BASHAR'S SECOND INTERVIEW

In marked contrast to his serene *Wall Street Journal* interview in 2011, al-Assad's first post-uprising interview with a Western newspaper was a forecast of Armageddon. "Syria is the hub now in this region," he told the *Sunday Telegraph*. "It is the fault line, and if you play with the ground you will cause an earthquake. . . . Do you want to see another Afghanistan, or tens of Afghanistans? Any problem in Syria will burn the whole region." The fire metaphor again. Absent, of course, from this apocalyptic forecast was any mention of whom the original arsonists was. But that was of little consequence, because it worked.

Not only did NATO and Washington rule out active military intervention in Syria in the form of a no-fly zone or the establishment of "safe areas" in parts of the country, but they were equally wary and dismissive of al-Assad's enemies, in a manner that can only have pleased al-Assad. When Hillary Clinton left government, she chastised President Obama for not collaborating with nationalist or secular rebels sooner—a supposed policy failure to which she attributed the rise of ISIS. But in February 2012, when she was still secretary of state, she told CBS: "We know al Qaeda—Zawahiri is supporting the opposition in Syria. Are we supporting al Qaeda in Syria? Hamas is now supporting the opposition. Are we supporting Hamas in Syria?" Not knowing who or what the opposition was would remain the public posture of the White House for years thereafter, until it solved this mystery and professed itself unimpressed with its discovery. "This idea that we could provide some light arms or even more sophisticated arms to what was essentially an opposition made up of former doctors, farmers, pharmacists, and so forth, and that they were going to be able to battle not only a well-armed state but also a well-armed state backed by Russia, backed by Iran, a battle-hardened Hezbollah, that was never in the cards," President Obama told the *New York Times* as late as August 2014, even after the CIA began arming and training a small number of rebels.

The president's assessment suffered from two problems, however. First, his characterization of the rebels was untrue. The Violations Documentation Center, a Syrian opposition source but one trusted for its empiricism, conducted a survey of rebel deaths in the war and found that doctors accounted for a statistically negligible 1 percent, while teachers and farmers even less than that. Soldiers, on the other hand, constituted the majority of fatalities, at 62 percent. As Ambassador Frederic Hof, Obama's former special adviser on Syria at the State Department, has reminded the president, Syria has a conscript army, meaning that most adult males have some prior military experience. Based on our reporting from Antakya, Turkey, we can attest a single refugee camp houses thousands of low- and mid-level defectors from the Syrian military.

Furthermore, the expectation that Syria's rebels could not defeat a battered and depleted Syrian army, even backed by Iranian proxies and Russian matériel, seemed odd given that the policy Obama ultimately adopted was to have them trained to defeat ISIS, the heirs to an insurgency that battered the most powerful army on earth in Iraq for nearly a decade. Given that these rebels' raison d'etre was fighting the regime, not ISIS, America's proxy counterinsurgents— Free Syrian JSOCs, basically—were bound to cause resentment and disaffection. "The Americans are using the lies to get information [about jihadists]," one rebel told *Newsweek* in February 2013. "If you ask any rebel in Syria right now, he will say America is our enemy." This was hyperbole, but became less so after al-Assad's sarin gas attack on rebels and civilians in Damascus in August 2013. When the United States failed to respond militarily, according to Obama's own "red line," many had had their fill of empty or broken promises. Not long after Obama inked a deal with Vladimir Putin to decommission Syria's chemical weapons program, scores of Western-backed rebels either quit the field, mutinied, or invited ISIS to raid their Syrian warehouses filled with US-sent aid and supplies.

THE JIHADISTS' AMNESTY

While rebel disillusionment with the United States and its true prerogatives in Syria took time to come about, al-Assad wasted little time guaranteeing that extremists dominated the insurgency. On May 31, 2011, only a few months into the uprising, he issued a general amnesty as part of his package of "reforms," mostly symbolic gestures aimed at placating the protest movement. In reality, the amnesty was more of a booby trap than a salve. Although meant to free all of Syria's "political prisoners," it was applied selectively—plenty of protestors and activists were kept in jail, while an untold number of Salafist-Jihadists were let out. Of these, many had not long ago been on rat lines to Iraq, only to return to Syria and be collared and locked up by the very Mukhabarat that had sent them there in the first place.

Muhammad Habash, the former Syrian parliamentarian, has said that the regime can only have known that at least some of the Islamists it was releasing would take up arms against the state. Three men did: Zahran Alloush, Hassan Abboud, and Ahmad Issa al-Sheikh, the current or former Salafist leaders of the best-organized rebel brigades in Syria. There's a famous photograph of them standing in a row, all smiles, not long after being decreed free men by al-Assad. Future ISIS members were also amnestied, including Awwad al-Mahklaf, who is now a local emir in Raqqa, and Abu al-Ahir al-Absi, who served time in Sednaya prison in 2007 for membership in al-Qaeda.

In August 2012, after his brother Firas was killed near the Turkish border, al-Absi took charge of the Mujahideen Shura Council, a group that Firas had started. As of mid-July 2014, according to the US State Department, al-Absi became ISIS's provincial leader for Homs, in the Aleppo region.

Habash, as mentioned earlier, had been in charge of the deradicalization program at Sednaya in 2008 after proposing himself for the role to Syria's National Security Bureau. "Salafism could have been controlled or reformed," he told us. "The regime drove Salafists and Sufis to violence. Ideology was part of the reason, but let me tell you: if Gandhi spent three months in Syria, he would be a jihadi extremist."

Prisons in Syria are bywords for Islamization—terrorist universities in the heart of the Middle East, albeit where the faculty often encourage their students to learn. A revealing anecdote was relayed to the authors by Fawaz Tello, a longtime Syrian dissident who was arrested by the regime on September 11, 2001, when, understandably, the world's attention was diverted elsewhere. He had been an activist associated with the Damascus Declaration, a pro-reform political movement that enjoyed a brief flowering in the initial days of the dauphin's "reformist" presidency, only to be summarily crushed thereafter. Tello was sent to Adra prison, northeast of Damascus, where he made the acquaintance of Nadeem Baloosh. "He was a young man from Latakia," Tello said. "He had been in Turkey, and when he returned to Syria, Turkish intelligence informed the Mukhabarat and they arrested him. He spent more than a year in Adra." Baloosh was in a neighboring cell to Tello's, and during that time, the two had discussions at night, "shouting" through the doors. "I found that there was nothing compatible with this man. He had very extremist views. But he was also talking to other Islamists in the other cells and he was spreading his ideology. He hadn't been a member of al-Qaeda, nor had he attended any military training camps. He was just a Salafist, but nonviolent. A lot of people put into prison were like this. During their time in the jail, it was as if they were attending jihadist college—including Baloosh."

After Tello was released from Adra, Baloosh was transferred to Sednaya where, in 2008, he became one of six ringleaders of a notorious prison riot, the events and aftermath of which have been rendered somewhat opaquely, although at least twenty-five people were killed and ninety more were injured. "Directly after he and the others took over the prison, they executed a handful of inmates," Tello recounted, "claiming they were regime informants. Baloosh was personally responsible for executing one of these inmates. His victim wasn't an informant, he just didn't agree with Baloosh's ideology."

When the regime finally regained control of Sednaya, it executed the six ringleaders of the riot—except Nadeem Baloosh. "He received no death sentence and he was released in 2010, well in advance of completing his original sentence, which was supposed to have lasted until 2015. He returned to Latakia and opened up a shop."

In the early days of the Syrian uprising, Baloosh joined the peaceful demonstrations in Latakia, the coastal province whence the al-Assad family claims its ancestry. However, he was kicked out by other activists because of his viciously sectarian slogans against the Alawites—these, in the Alawite heartland of Syria. "They didn't accept him. Less than a year later, maybe nine months, some rebels took up arms against the regime in Latakia. They ran to the mountains and founded battalions. Baloosh was one of them. Nobody was following him, but he went to the mountains and established his own battalion. His battalion then joined Jabhat al-Nusra," Tello said, referring to the al-Qaeda franchise in Syria.

Although Baloosh was released from Sednaya before the protest movement began, his story generally tracks with what foreign and Syrian officials have said in the past few years about the makeup of the country's now-numerous terrorist cells. For instance, in January 2014, Major General Fayez Dwairi, a former Jordanian military intelligence officer who helped run the kingdom's Syria crisis portfolio, told the Abu Dhabi–based newspaper the *National*, "Many of the people who established Jabhat Al Nusra were captured by the regime in 2008 and were in prison. When the revolution started they were released on the advice of Syrian intelligence officers, who told Assad 'they will do a good job for us. There are many disadvantages to letting them out, but there are more advantages because we will convince the world that we are facing Islamic terrorism.'"

In an even more noteworthy example, a twelve-year veteran of Syria's own Military Intelligence Directorate told the same newspaper that al-Assad's general amnesty in 2011 was designed to sow terrorism in Syria for propaganda value. "The regime did not just open the door to the prisons and let these extremists out, it facilitated them in their work, in their creation of armed brigades," the intelligence officer, an Alawite who defected from his unit in northern Syria in the summer of 2011, told the *National*. "This is not something I heard rumours about, I actually heard the orders, I have seen it happening. These orders came down from [Military Intelligence] headquarters [in] Damascus." The regime also made an abundance of weapons available to these extremists in Idlib and Deraa, the officer added.

Nawaz Fares was the former Syrian ambassador to Iraq, a country which, as we examined in a previous chapter, al-Assad was intent on destabilizing with terrorism up until late 2009. Fares defected in July 2012 and told the press that Damascus was still playing with jihadist fire well into the revolution. Fares was in a position to know firsthand how this collaboration had worked; before moving to the Syrian embassy in Baghdad, and after the toppling of Saddam, he had served as a regime security chief as well as a provincial governor near the Syrian-Iraqi border. He recalled to the *Sunday Telegraph* how he "was given verbal commandments that any civil servant that wanted to go [to Iraq] would have his trip facilitated, and that his absence would not be noted." He also said that he knew several regime "liaison officers" who were coordinating with al-Qaeda operatives up until the moment of his defection—the summer of 2012. More intriguingly, Fares claimed, all the large-scale terrorist attacks that had occurred in Syria, beginning in late 2011, were "perpetrated by al-Qaeda through cooperation with the security forces," including an especially devastating one that had targeted a military intelligence building in a Damascus suburb in May 2012.

Are such allegations invented or politically motivated? Perhaps, though in the case of the Alawite intelligence officer, it bears mentioning that he told the *National* that he still preferred al-Assad's rule to the victory of a radicalized opposition. Whatever the truth, these allegation are founded on the plausible premise of proven past collusion between Damascus and AQI, which extended almost to

2010. So if the regime categorically terminated its relationship with jihadists in the yearlong space between the bombings in Baghdad and the outbreak of unrest in Deraa, then it is one of the most dramatic recipients of blowback in modern history.

HOW ISI CAME TO SYRIA

A few months before the last American GI left Iraq, Abu Bakr al-Baghdadi dispatched a handful of operatives into Syria. According to journalist Rania Abouzeid, who has embedded with jihadists in Syria, eight men crossed into the country's northeastern province of Hasaka in August 2011, during Ramadan. Among those making the journey was Abu Mohammed al-Jolani, a Syrian from Damascus who had fought with ISI and was about to redirect his attention against the regime that had likely once facilitated his traffic in the opposite direction.

Although it's been rumored that al-Jolani, who's in his early thirties, had also been released from Sednaya under the general amnesty, there's no hard evidence to substantiate that claim. Major General Dwairi told the *National* that al-Jolani was in regime custody at one point, but he did not specify the time or the prison. Al-Jolani's first point of contact in Hasaka, Abouzeid reported, was a former Sednaya inmate who hosted the ISI cohort, consisting as it did of "several Syrians, a Saudi, and a Jordanian," during their first night in Syria. (What has been established with certainty is that al-Jolani had been a detainee at Camp Bucca, where he was misidentified by US forces as an Iraqi Kurd from Mosul.)

Al-Jolani's cell allegedly waged a series of car bombings in Damascus targeting the security services and the army in late 2011, but it didn't claim credit for them until January 23, 2012, when Jabhat al-Nusra declared its formation as a group.

Al-Jolani also took care to hide his organizational ties to ISI and AQI, so much so that even members of his own cell weren't quite sure what Jabhat al-Nusra was getting up to or how it had carried out its daring attacks. Christoph Reuter, a correspondent for the German weekly *Der Spiegel*, who has reported extensively in Syria, told us: "The first real al-Nusra groups emerged in July 2012 in Aleppo. When we talked to one of them, asking them, 'Oh, so, you are al-Nusra?,' they said, 'Yes, yes yes!' 'So how did you blow up the security building in Damascus?' 'No clue,' they conceded after a while. 'We took the name, because it is a great name, and we get money from the Gulf with it.'"

Al-Jolani, in other words, spent close to six months building— or reconstituting—a clandestine jihadist network in Syria before he debuted it as a strictly homegrown affair. This was incredibly savvy, as it turned out, because al-Nusra not only proved to be one of the most formidable anti-Assad insurgencies in the civil war, but its relative "moderation" in its engagement with local communities earned it the respect and approval of even non-Islamists. Al-Nusra, for instance, did not declare war on Syria's minorities, as ISIS later did. In some cases, it even protected churches to show Christians that it was very much part of the social and religious mosaic of Syria, not a foreign takfiri group. In this, analysts say, al-Jolani conformed to al-Zawahiri's plan of action following bin Laden's assassination in May 2011. "Zawahiri was strictly against targeting other religious groups or sects such as Shia, Yazidis, Hindus, Christians, and Buddhists unless they targeted Sunnis first," Laith Alkhouri said. "This owed to the enormous negative backlash against al-Qaeda in Iraq from the time of Zarqawi and Masri and Baghdadi. Zawahiri also urged jihadi groups to reach out to the Muslim public, people who he claimed had been absent from true Islamic teaching in Syria, Lebanon, and North Africa. The goal was to unify people around the concept of tawhid, or monotheism."

Takfirism as a binding social contract for al-Qaeda had failed in Iraq, thanks to US and tribal efforts. Al-Nusra was thus the vehicle by which al-Zawahiri hoped to refurbish in Syria the damaged reputation his franchise had incurred next door. Al-Jolani later explained to Al Jazeera the origins of al-Nusra as the belated realization of a long-held ambition of al-Qaeda, to help free the Syrian people from a tyrannical regime:

"Nobody can ignore the significance of the Levant," he said. "It is the land of conflict, ancient and modern. . . .When the [Syrian] uprising started, one of the leaders of [the] Islamic State in Iraq asked us what to do. We said let's begin working there. . . .The regime was grossly oppressive and people were far away from the idea of picking up arms against it or even accepting the path we are taking and unable to beat the consequences of any confrontation with this regime. So this uprising removed many of the setbacks and paved the way for us to enter this blessed land. . . .We asked for [permission to found Jabhat al-Nusra], but this idea was in the mind of the al-Qaeda leadership for a while."

As commander of al-Nusra, al-Jolani personally oversaw his group's operations all over the country, in some cases posing as a decoy representative dispatched by the real al-Jolani to test the mettle of his rank and file. (As in Camp Bucca, AQI resorted to counterintelligence feints not only to fool its enemies but also to trick its own recruits.)

Al-Zawahiri issued two communiqués in early 2012, implicitly certifying al-Jolani's endeavor without ever acknowledging it. In the second communiqué, released on February 11, the Egyptian "appeal[ed] to every Muslim and every noble, free man in Turkey, Iraq, Jordan, and Lebanon to come to support his brothers in Syria with all that he possesses with himself, his wealth, his opinion, and information." Al-Zawahiri excoriated the al-Assad regime for keeping "the splendor of the Ummah's youth in its prisons, torturing and killing them. It has protected the Israeli borders [for] about forty years, participated with America in the war against Islam in the name of terrorism, shed the blood of Muslims in horrible massacres in Hama, Homs, Jisr al-Shughur and Daraa, for consecutive decades, and includes a group of thieving robbers, who are looting the wealth and resources of Syria using iron and fire."

Not about to let another good war go to waste, al-Zawahiri was once against channeling the Services Bureau era, and his dead boss, in issuing a global casting call for mujahidin.

10

CONVERTS AND
"FIVE-STAR JIHADISTS"
PROFILES OF ISIS FIGHTERS

For this book we conducted interviews with dozens of ISIS associates who operate inside Syria and Iraq in a range of sectors, including religious clerics, fighters, provincial emirs, security officials, and sympathizers, and we found that what draws people to ISIS could easily bring them to any number of cults or totalitarian movements, even those ideologically contradictory to Salafist Jihadism. Far from homogenous, the organization spans an array of backgrounds and belief systems, from godless opportunists to war profiteers to pragmatic tribesmen to committed takfiris.

THE POWER OF PERSUASION

In October 2014 ISIS's security squad arrested Mothanna Abdulsattar, a well-spoken nineteen-year-old media activist working for the Free Syrian Army, around two months after it assumed control of his region in eastern Syria. He was taken for an interrogation at a nearby jihadist base amid threats to his life, the fate of which, he found out, could be determined by his professional affiliation. Working for the Syrian opposition or Saudi media arms meant death. "If you are working for Orient or Al-Arabiya, we'll chop your head off," Abdulsattar was told. Working for Qatar's Al Jazeera, according to the conversation between Abdulsattar and the ISIS members, was evidently less of a problem. Abdulsattar told us that he was relieved when a smiling, respectful older jihadist stepped in to save him from an ISIS commissar's line of questioning.

"Abu Hamza was quiet and respectful," Abdulsattar remembered, referring to Abu Hamza al-Shami, a senior religious cleric in ISIS from the township of Minbij in eastern Aleppo. "Even his face makes you comfortable. He began by talking about the FSA, and why ISIS was fighting it. He said because they accept ungodly laws and receive funding from America, and God said: 'Whoever aligns with them, he's one of them.' He then talked about al-Dawla. He asked me, 'Why aren't you pledging allegiance? The Prophet said that those who die without having bayat to someone—their death will be a *jahiliyyah* [un-Islamic] death.' Honestly, when I heard that, I was shocked to my core. For the first time, I realized, the hadith is true."

But Abdulsattar still wasn't ready to pledge allegiance to Abu Bakr al-Baghdadi. So Abu Hamza smiled and asked him to take his time. A week or so later, Abdulsattar decided to commit.

He spoke with gusto about his journey into ISIS, downplaying the eight hours he spent in its custody as more of a rite of passage than a life-or-death grilling. Abdulsatter said that he was ultimately swayed by ISIS's "intellectualism and the way it spreads religion and fights injustice."

A great number of ISIS members who were interviewed for this book echoed similar sentiments—and hyperbolic appraisals— of the terror army, which has mastered how to break down the psyches of those it wishes to recruit, and then build them back up again in its own image. Abdulsattar's reference to "intellectualism" may seem bizarre or even grotesque to a Western observer, but it refers to ISIS's carefully elaborated ideological narrative, a potent blend of Islamic hermeneutics, history, and politics.

What he described was no different from the total moral and intellectual immersion explained by Communists who later abandoned their faith in Marxism-Leninism. "We have thrown overboard all conventions, our sole guiding principle is that of consequent logic; we are sailing without ethical ballast," Arthur Koestler's Rubashov remembers in *Darkness at Noon* after facing his own interrogation by Party commissars. Minutes later, Rubashov is shot by the very dictatorship to which he had given his life for forty years.

"When you listen to the clerics of the al-Dawla," Abdulsatter said, "you are shocked that most of our Islamic societies have deviated from the true religion. They follow a religion that was invented two decades ago, or less. Most of our societies that claim to be Muslim, their religion is full of impurities, 90 percent of it is bida'a [religious innovation]. Take *shirk* for example: we associate in our worship things other than God, and we don't even realize it. Omens, for example. When we adjust our posture in front of other people inside a mosque, that is *riya'* [ostentation]." ISIS offered Abdulsattar something he could not find under Assadism or the Free Syrian Army. It offered him "purified" Islam.

"When you meet a cleric or a foreigner with ISIS, and he sits with you for two hours, believe me you will be convinced," he continued. "I don't know, they have a strange way of persuading people. When they control an area, they enforce religion by force, you have to pray whether you like it or not. We were all oblivious to the most important obligation in Islam—jihad. They shed light on jihad. Every time you watch a video by them, you are going to have a strange feeling that pushes you toward jihad."

Even those victimized or persecuted by ISIS attest to the group's "power of persuasion."

Abu Bilal al-Layli had been in charge of funding the FSA in his hometown, Albu Layl in Deir Ezzor. When ISIS arrived, he left for Turkey. The jihadists burned down his house and put him on its wanted list. He sees them as a band of illiterate thugs who hold a twisted understanding of religion, but he nonetheless admires their ability to persuade the young and the old, particularly those with little religious background. "ISIS used money and talk of justice and war against thieves to lure people. For some, it worked. In our areas, you see people longing for Islam and wanting someone to fight . . .*haramiya* [thieves]. They bought into the 'Islamic State' idea, thinking that the jihadists were honest. Those who joined Daesh hardly memorized a few Quranic verses. They had no religious base. They were simply lured by the power of persuasion."

THE NOVICE

Hamza Mahmoud was a fifteen-year-old boy from a well-to-do family in Qamishli, in northern Syria. Hamza's parents learned that he joined ISIS after he started to disappear from their home for long stretches in the summer of 2014. After many failed attempts to prevent him from returning to the group, one of his brothers said, Hamza's father deliberately broke one of Hamza's legs. Once it healed, he left his family home again and severed direct communication with his parents. According to his brother, Omar, Hamza refused to speak to his family lest his mother's cries or his father's admonitions influence his decision to remain with ISIS. He would only communicate with his brothers, who were outside the country.

During a Skype conversation organized for the authors, Omar haplessly tried to persuade Hamza to quit ISIS and return home. "Hamza, this is not right, you're still young, this is a misguided group," Omar told him. "Nothing in Islam calls for slaughter and violence." Hamza responded, in mechanical but classical Arabic, by citing hadith and verses to validate acts carried out by his new masters. Also, he insisted, the common portrayal of ISIS was biased and wrong. "Don't believe everything you hear in media," Hamza said. "The brothers are true Muslims. They are doing nothing but the right thing. If you see what I see and hear what I hear, you will know."

Omar then told Hamza that Syria has people from various sects and religions who have lived side by side for centuries. Hamza was particularly shocked when his brother added that among his friends who were living in the same residence were Alawites and Yazidis. "You have Yazidis next to you?" Hamza answered. "Kill them and get closer to God."

THE KURD

The idea that a Kurd would join ISIS seems counterintuitive, given that the organization's upper cadres are replete with former Saddamists from the Baathist regime that was responsible for a genocidal campaign against the Kurds. More recently, ISIS has targeted Kurdish villages and towns, such as Kobane, on the Syrian-Turkish border, and besieged Erbil, the capital of Iraq's Kurdistan Regional Government, before having its advance halted by US air strikes in August 2014. Kurdish militias in Syria and Iraq, including the Iraqi peshmerga and the People's Protection Units (YPG), are considered secularists and Marxists, respectively, and therefore marked for death. And whereas other Sunni insurgencies with strong Baathist composition—particularly al-Douri's Naqshbandi Army—have tried and mostly failed to recruit Kurds, not only has ISIS succeeded, it has found remarkable success in the very site of Saddam's genocide, the Iraqi city of Halabja.

ISIS's spokesman, Abu Muhammad al-Adnani, has justified

the campaign against the largest stateless people of the Middle East in the following terms: "Our war with Kurds is a religious war. It is not a nationalistic war—we seek the refuge of Allah. We do not fight Kurds because they are Kurds. Rather, we fight the disbelievers amongst them, the allies of the crusaders and Jews in their war against the Muslims. . . .The Muslim Kurds in the ranks of the Islamic State are many. They are the toughest of fighters against the disbelievers amongst their people." Emphasizing the point, and also driving the wedge among Kurds deeper, in October 2014, one of ISIS's "Muslim Kurds," Abu Khattab al-Kurdi, was reportedly leading the jihadists' battle against the YPG in Kobane. He was joined by other Kurds from Hasaka, Aleppo, and northern Raqqa.

Why are Kurds joining ISIS? Hussain Jummo, the political editor at the Dubai-based *Al Bayan* newspaper, and a prominent analyst of Kurd politics, offers the most plausible explanation. After Saddam's Halabja massacre, many families in the town were left impoverished as others built new homes and carried on with their lives as before. Charities that were started and meant to tend to the victims of the chemical attacks were mainly Salafist in orientation, and organized and funded by Gulf state sponsors, including Kuwait's Society of the Revival of Islamic Heritage, which has been accused by the United States of bankrolling al-Qaeda. So after decades of proselytization in the Kurdish regions of the Middle East, Halabja became the epicenter of Kurdish Islamism. (Recall, too, that al-Zarqawi's first landing point in Iraq was via Ansar al-Islam, the al-Qaeda affiliate, in the mountains of northern Kurdistan.)

In Syria the Kurdish turn to ISIS has been less common, although not unheard of. Syrian Kurds are predominately secular or Sufi from the Khaznawi order, named after the family that inaugurated it. However, we spoke with two Kurds from Aleppo and Hasaka who said they were driven to ISIS because of the organization's pan-Sunni, rather than pan-Arab, philosophy. A Kurdish ISIS member from Hasaka relayed a conversation to the authors he had with an ISIS recruiter shortly before he joined. The recruiter told him that Jabhàt al-Nusra, which had by then split from ISIS, was essentially an "Arab" organization, rather than an Islamic one. ISIS was actually blind to ethnicity, he said, and attended only to true faith.

In much the same vein, ISIS has also attracted large numbers from the Turkomen minority, which has suffered a large share of discrimination and repression under despotic Arab regimes. Turkomen ISIS members have been key to the rise of the organization in Mosul and the areas outlying it. Al-Baghdadi's deputy, Abu Muslim al-Turkmani, who was reportedly killed in December 2014, is Turkomen.

THE SEDNAYA ULTRAS

A particular breed of takfiris dominates ISIS's mid- and upper echelons, subscribing to a narrow set of doctrinal tenets at odds with the more expansive and welcoming ideology described previously. Abu al-Athir al-Absi, the former Sednaya prisoner who was released under al-Assad's general amnesty, is the perfect case study in this category.

Al-Absi formed a group, Usud al-Sunna ("Sunni Lions"), in Aleppo's countryside soon after he was released; he then became instrumental in rallying support for ISIS after its split from Nusra in 2013. Al-Absi took a hard line against other Islamist and jihadist groups many months before ISIS was formed—a position that many say was an extension of the ideological conflict among jihadists at Sednaya prison (although that may also be linked to the fact that al-Absi holds many of the groups responsible for the death of his brother Firas).

According to Wael Essam, who met al-Absi after the Syrian uprising started, the jihadist has considered many of his fellow former inmates at Sednaya to be kuffar, including those who now lead rival

Islamist brigades and battalions in Syria. Why? Because they refused to pronounce as nonbelievers the *taghut* (tyrannical or false) Muslim rulers in the Middle East and the majority of Muslims in the region. Also, al-Absi explained, these Islamists acceded to the surrender of Sednaya to the Syrian authorities after the bloody 2008 riot.

Al-Absi and his cohort were outliers among Salafists at Sednaya. Few of the inmates shared their ultraist ideology or joined them in defying the regime even after it had amassed soldiers from the 4th Armored Division outside their ward.

The tensions between ISIS and other jihadist and Islamist groups in the Syrian Civil War can be viewed as the resumption of an argument that took place behind bars in the preceding years. Abu Adnan, a security official in ISIS, told us that most of the rebel Islamist brigades and battalions were formed as insurgent reunions within the various prison wards. "They did not just come together," he said. "These men all knew each other, and the factions that were formed later already had the personnel and ideological infrastructure in place. The personality conflicts and political differences continued."

Abu Bakr al-Baghdadi visited Syria in late 2012. Al-Absi was one of his staunchest defenders and one of the loudest proponents of the declaration of an Islamic caliphate, helping al-Baghdadi secure the allegiance of various al-Nusra fighters and other jihadists and militants then part of rival insurgencies in Syria.

THE FENCE-SITTERS

Another category of ISIS recruits consists of those who already held Islamist or jihadist views but had limited themselves to only orbiting takfiri ideology. The final gravitational pull, so to speak, differed depending on circumstance. Some joined for the simple reason that

ISIS overran their territories and became the only Islamist faction available to join. Others were simply impressed with ISIS's military prowess in campaigns against rival rebel factions. Still others fell out with their original insurgencies and found ISIS more organized, disciplined, and able-bodied.

For what might be called "extra-mile extremists," the conversion experience is hardly as sweeping or comprehensive as it was for men like Abdulsatter. They have tended to trickle into ISIS from the rank and file of the Islamic Front and Islamist-leaning groups in Iraq and Syria as a result of leadership disputes, or the abortive Syrian Sahwa that erupted in late December 2013.

The trend of defections to ISIS was most conspicuous in September 2014. It was that month that a dozen Islamist factions, including al-Nusra, issued a joint statement disavowing the Western-backed Syrian National Coalition, the political arm of the opposition, and called for unity under "an Islamic framework." In October seven Islamist groups then formed the Islamic Front and issued a statement rejecting democracy in favor of an Islamic shura-based system.

Over that period, ISIS made significant gains at the ideological level. Many Islamists struggled to reconcile warring against a fellow Salafist group—a position shared by many ordinary Syrians, who believed that any diversion from the main conflict against the al-Assad regime and its Iranian proxies amounted to treason. Younger members of the Islamic Front in particular held more religiously reactionary beliefs and subscribed more ardently to the jihadist discourse of establishing an Islamic state. Some Islamic Front commanders, in fact, provided protection to ISIS convoys or simply refused to turn their guns on them. The disunity only benefited ISIS.

Liwa Dawud, once the most powerful subfaction within the

Islamic Front brigade known as Suqour al-Sham (Falcons of the Levant), saw around one thousand of its own jump ship to ISIS in July 2014.

Increasingly, fighters from the Islamic Front and al-Nusra have migrated to ISIS as the franchise has expanded farther into both Syria and Iraq.

ISIS benefits from the absence of a "Syrian" jihadist discourse to keep pace with the intensifying violence in a war-ravaged nation, which, by August 2014, had seen close to two hundred thousand killed. Established Syrian Islamists, especially the Muslim Brotherhood, have steered away from adopting such a discourse and have instead presented themselves as part of the mainstream pro-democracy movement, even though they financially and politically backed rebel Islamist factions. Even al-Nusra, to some extent, positioned itself as a "nationalist" outcropping without international ambitions. This hypocrisy meant that ISIS more or less had a monopoly on the global Salafist-Jihadist narrative, and its intoxicating vision of world conquest.

THE POLITICKERS

As it happens, the closer ISIS came to realizing its territorial ambitions, the less religion played a part in driving people to join the organization. Those who say they are adherents of ISIS as a strictly *political* project make up a weighty percentage of its lower cadres and support base.

For people in this category, ISIS is the only option on offer for Sunni Muslims who have been dealt a dismal hand in the past decade—first losing control of Iraq and now suffering nationwide atrocities, which many equate to genocide, in Syria. They view the struggle in the Middle East as one between Sunnis and an Iranian-led coalition, and they justify ultraviolence as a necessary tool to counterbalance or deter Shia hegemony. This category often includes the highly educated.

One example is Saleh al-Awad, a secular lawyer from Jarablous, Hasaka, who was a staunch critic of ISIS before deciding that it was the only bulwark against Kurdish expansionism in his region. Saleh took part in the peaceful protest movement against al-Assad and was an advocate of democratic change in Syria. "We're tired, every day they [ISIS] cut off four or five heads in our town," he told us before his conversion experience took place. A few months following that exchange—around the time that ISIS started besieging Kobane—Saleh said he joined the head-loppers.

A large number of Arabs in Hasaka share views similar to his own. One influential resident of the province said that "thousands" would join ISIS tomorrow if it invaded the city and provincial capital of Hasaka because of fears of what might happen to them under Kurdish domination.

A similar dynamic exists in mixed communities near Baghdad, such as Baqubah, and in Homs and Hama, where sectarian tensions shape people's political orientations.

A dozen ISIS-affiliated Arabs who conform to this political category might even be described as secular or agnostic (many said they don't pray or attend mosque) and expressed deep objections to us about the atrocities being committed by ISIS. Nevertheless, they see it as the only armed group capable of striking against the "anti-Sunni" regimes and militias in Syria, Iraq, and beyond. By way of justification, Salim told us that violence has always been part of Islamic history and always precedes the establishment of strong Islamic empires, including the Ummayads, Abbasids, and the second Ummayad kingdom in modern Spain.

This sense of dejection, or injustice, felt by many Sunnis who now identify as a persecuted and embattled community is known in Arabic as *madhloumiya*, a concept historically associated with the Shia, for whom suffering is integral to their religious discourse. Equally paradoxical is that even where Sunnis are in the majority, they have taken to behaving as an insecure minority. The Shia in these areas, by contrast, appear more decisive, confident, and well organized, no doubt thanks to Iranian patronage and the militia-ization of their communities by Qassem Suleimani's Quds Force. Shia militants, as we've seen, are crossing national boundaries as much as their Sunni counterparts to participate in a holy war.

Sunnis feel under assault—from al-Assad, Khamenei, and, up until recently, al-Maliki—and devoid of any committed or credible political stewards. Their religious and political powerhouses, meanwhile, are perceived as complicit, politically emasculated, discredited, or silent: the Gulf Arab states, which either have Sunni majorities or Sunni-led governments, have been reduced to begging the United States for intervention.

ISIS has exploited this sense of sectarian grievance and vulnerability with devious aplomb. As al-Zarqawi could point to the Badr Corps in 2004, al-Baghdadi can now point to anti-Sunni atrocities being committed by the National Defense Force, Asa'ib Ahl al-Haq, Lebanese Hezbollah, Kata'ib Hezbollah or, indeed, the Badr Corps in Syria and/or Iraq, and offer them up as proof that Sunnis have no hope but the caliphate.

PRAGMATISTS

In areas fully controlled by ISIS, pragmatists support the group because it is effective in terms of governance and delivery of basic services such as sanitation and food delivery (although this may be coming to an end). ISIS has established a semblance of order in these "governed" territories, and people view the alternatives—al-Assad, the Iraqi government, or other militias—as far worse. For those weary of years of civil war, the ability to live without crime and lawlessness trumps whatever draconian rules ISIS has put into place. Members of this category sometimes keep their distance from ISIS, to avoid trouble, while others actually seek out areas where ISIS is said not to be committing atrocities.

Abu Jasim, a cleric who joined ISIS after it overran his home in eastern Syria in the summer of 2014, said that he would deliberately avoid details of what ISIS did or didn't do. "I see them leaving people alone if nobody messes with them," Abu Jasim told us. "All I do is to teach people their religion, and I hope to get rewarded by God for what I do."

THE OPPORTUNISTS

There are also those who were drawn to ISIS largely because of personal ambition. The opportunists tend to serve in the group's rank and file as well as its low-level command structures. They join to undermine a rival group, to move up the chain of a dominant military and political force, or simply to preempt ISIS's brutal justice for some past offense or crime they might have committed against the group.

Saddam al-Jamal, for example, was one of the most powerful FSA commanders in eastern Syria. After his prior rebel outfit, the Allahu Akbar Brigade, lost out to al-Nusra, which killed two of his brothers, al-Jamal pledged allegiance to ISIS. It apparently didn't matter that he had a reputation as a drug dealer.

Aamer al-Rafdan joined ISIS after it broke from al-Nusra, owing mainly to a dispute he had with the latter over oil revenues—also, a continuing rivalry between his tribe and the tribe that had been dominated by al-Nusra in Deir Ezzor. Al-Rafdan was later accused by al-Jolani's organization of stealing $5 million worth of cotton.

THE FOREIGN FIGHTERS

Outside Iraq and Syria, of course, the motivations for joining ISIS alter drastically and are almost always fed by serious misapprehensions of what is taking place in either country.

The radicalization expert Shiraz Maher has explained how digital apps or social media platforms such as Twitter, Facebook, and, in the ex-Soviet context, VKontakte (Russia's answer to Facebook) have revolutionized jihadist agitprop. Much of the online chatter among Western-born ISIS recruits sounds more like a satire of the group than an earnest commitment to it: "Does the Islamic State sell hair gel and Nutella in Raqqa?" "Should I bring an iPad to let Mom and Dad know that I arrived safely in caliphate?" "I was told there'd be *Grand Theft Auto V.*"

In an article for the *New Statesman*, Maher observed that, "During the Iraq War, sympathisers of al-Qaeda needed access to password-protected forums, where they could learn about events on the ground. These forums were not easy to find and access was harder to gain. Crucially, most of the conversations were in Arabic, a language alien to most British Muslims." Now every British Muslim who goes off to fight in Syria or Iraq becomes a virtual wrangler or recruitment officer for more of his own kind. One example was Mehdi Hassan, a twenty-year-old from Portsmouth who went off to join ISIS and died fighting in the battle of Kobane in November 2014. Hasan had actually enlisted along with several friends from Portsmouth, all of whom were drawn to the dazzling images of ISIS's martial triumphs and its whitewashed depiction of life under takfiri rule. They were known as the "Pompey lads," and, as Maher wrote, "Of the men he travelled with, only one is still fighting: three are dead and another is in prison in the UK."

In December 2013 Maher's ICSR calculated that the number of foreign fighters enjoined with the Syrian opposition was "up to

11,000 . . .from 74 nations." Most of them signed up with ISIS or other jihadist groups, with few going to join mainstream FSA factions. Western Europe, the study found, accounted for 18 percent of the total, with France leading among nations as the number one donor country for jihadists, followed closely by Britain. That number only grew, particularly in light of the US coalition war against ISIS; by September 2014 the CIA calculated fifteen thousand foreign fighters in Syria, two thousand of whom were Westerners. However, the predominant emigration trend has always been from the Middle East and North Africa, with Saudi Arabia, Libya, and Tunisia being the highest feeder countries of foreign Sunni militants.

Missionary jihadists who were driven by civilian suffering, according to Maher, constituted a plurality of Britons who joined ISIS. They saw jihad as an obligation to defend women and children as the war dragged on in Syria, Maher told us.

Inside Syria, a similar trend—of fighters drifting to extremist groups—existed since mid-2012, when reports of civilians being slaughtered by pro-Assad militias became international news.

The impact of those massacres on the psyche of anti-regime Syrians was also immense. Those conscious of their own radicalization typically point to the Houla and al-Bayda and similar massacres as the reason for their turn to Islamist and jihadist rebel factions closer to the end of 2012. However, native Syrians tended to enlist with homegrown extremist factions rather than the more foreigner-friendly ISIS. Even still, ISIS benefited from the Assadist massacres in another respect: for one, the gruesome manner in which they were carried out helped create some level of tolerance for beheadings, which was accepted by many Syrians as retribution against the regime and its Iranian-built militias.

The most notorious regime massacres typically occurred in areas where Alawite, Sunni, and Ismaili (another Shia offshoot) villages and hamlets adjoined one another, the better to encourage sectarian reprisal bloodlettings. They also followed a pattern of assault: a village would be shelled overnight by the Syrian Arab Army, and the next morning, militiamen from nearby would storm it. Armed with knives and light weapons, they would go on killing sprees, slaughtering men, women, and children. The killing was portrayed as systematic and driven by sectarian vigilantism. Videos of torture also showed shabiha or popular committees, the precursors to the National Defense Force, taunting Sunni symbols and forcing victims to affirm al-Assad's divinity and make other sacrilegious statements.

Maher notes a second category of foreign fighters: martyrdom-seekers, who want nothing more than to carry out a suicide operation and thus be lionized in the annals of jihadism. For many foreign fighters from the Gulf states, the glorification of suicide bombers has been a constant on jihadist chat forums and websites since AQI got started. Saudi nationals often point to the fact that many Saudis carry out these self-immolations to argue that ISIS leaders discriminate against their compatriots by sending them to their deaths, whereas Iraqis hoard all the leadership positions in the organization for themselves.

The final factor leading foreign fighters to ISIS, according to Maher, is pure adventurism. Adrenaline junkies tend to be non-practicing Muslims and are often drug users or addicts, or involved in criminality and gang violence back home—much as al-Zarqawi himself was in Jordan before discovering the mosque. Going off to fight in Syria represents just another rush for these types.

AFTER MOSUL

Many interviewees from other Arab countries admitted they had not been following developments in Iraq and Syria closely before they started supporting ISIS. That changed after the fall of Mosul. One Egyptian Islamist, for instance, told us that he was not sure which factions in Syria or Iraq were good or bad, but after ISIS stormed through Ninewah, he began conducting "research" and found that the establishment of the caliphate was "consistent with" stories foretold by Prophet Muhammad. Scott Atran, the anthropologist at the University of Michigan, relayed a similar anecdote. "I remember talking with an imam in Spain who said, 'We always rejected violence, but Abu Bakr al-Baghdadi put us on the map. The caliphate doesn't have to be violent. It can be just like the European Union!'"

Detachment from the mundane realities of ISIS has made many Arabs susceptible to its self-aggrandizing portrayal as a God-anointed Sunni resistance movement inspired by early Islamic history and fundamentals. In order to control this self-presentation, ISIS has resorted to a sophisticated tool kit of propaganda and disinformation.

11

FROM TWITTER
TO *DABIQ*
RECRUITING THE NEW MUJAHIDIN

"DON'T HEAR ABOUT US, HEAR FROM US"

A theme that recurs in our conversations with ISIS members is how the organization has improved on the mistakes of its jihadist forebears by not allowing detractors in the foreign press to shape popular perceptions about it. "Don't hear about us, hear from us" is a phrase that has come up repeatedly in the course of our interviews with ISIS recruits.

Slightly overstating the power of social media in the terror army's ascendance was Iraq's former national security adviser Mowaffak al-Rubaie, who told Al Jazeera that it was more or less Twitter and Facebook that caused thirty thousand Iraqi Security Forces soldiers to drop their weapons, eschew their uniforms, and leave Mosul free for the jihadists' taking.

Overstating though he may have been, al-Rubaie did have a point. Two weeks before the fall of the city, ISIS had released one of its most popular videos to date, titled *Saleel al-Sawarim*, or *Clanging of the Swords*. A characteristic example of "jihadist pornography," it demonstrated ISIS's peerless ability to produce sleek, hour-long propaganda and recruitment films, featuring the very kind of content that Western politicians and diplomats have hoped will *dissuade* people's attraction to the group.

A preacher brandishing a machete proclaims the Islamic State and warns the kuffar and Jews of Jerusalem that the jihadists are coming for them. He then leads the tearing up of passports.

In scenes we see so-called Rafidah Hunters drive by other cars on a road, blasting their guns at what they say are Shia soldiers headed to join their "Safavid" Iraqi army units. Inside the perforated vehicles are the bloodied corpses of young boys in civilian clothing; any who stir are fired upon. In another scene, ISIS shoots a man running away from them. He is injured but still alive and tells them, "I'm a driver." The film then splices the image of him lying on the ground with his official Iraqi army photograph. He is killed.

A mosque in Anbar shows ISIS taking what look to be applications from unarmed civilians. The narrator explains that if you were formerly a member of the Anbar Awakening Councils, or Sunni politicians aligned with the Iraqi government, you are entitled to "repent and stop waging war against the mujahidin." If you do, you'll be granted "clemency" and all your past crimes against ISIS will be forgotten—but this must happen before ISIS gets "a hold of you." Likewise, any Sunni soldiers or policemen or agents of the Mukhbarat are encouraged to quit and turn in their weapons. "You carried your weapons and stood with those rafida, fighting your sons," one masked ISIS fighter tells a gathered assembly inside the mosque. "We are your sons, we are your brothers. We can protect your religion and your honor."

Clanging of the Swords also exhibits ISIS's supposed omnipresence and its cloak-and-dagger tradecraft in reaching its enemies.

Its agents dress in Iraqi Security Forces uniforms and raid the home of an Awakening commander. They are the "Sahwat Hunt-ers." When the commander is grabbed, he says he must call the army to verify these men's identities because he is afraid they're really from ISIS.

In the very next scene, two young boys, the sons of a Sahwa commander, are digging a giant pit in the dirt. They explain that their father convinced them to work with the Iraqi government. Then it's their father's turn to dig. When he falters, the mujahidin taunt him: "You didn't get tired when you set out to become a commander in the Sahwa and were working at the checkpoints." He addresses the camera, advising everyone in the Awakening to repent. "I am now digging my own grave," he says.

A counterterrorism official from Samarra is interrogated in his living room. Then he is led into his bedroom as an ISIS fighter, also dressed as an Iraqi soldier, pulls his security uniforms out from his wardrobe. The man is blindfolded with a scarf. Then he is beheaded.

Not quite at the level of a Leni Riefenstahl film, *The Clanging of the Swords* more than adequately conveys its message to its target audience. The video debuted just as rebel groups in eastern Syria and Aleppo—sahwats of a more recent vintage—were battling ISIS. None of these factions had anything comparable to present to their militants or to outsiders suggesting a like prowess or unity of purpose. For Iraqis, if you were Shia in an ISIS-infiltrated area, you were doubtless terrified. If you were Sunni, why bother turning up for work as a soldier or policeman or elected councilman if a simple pledge of allegiance meant keeping your head for the foreseeable future? ISIS claimed to be unstoppable and indomitable. Many believed it.

TWEETING THE CALIPHATE

Clanging of the Swords was posted on YouTube several times (although it was taken down just as often), and on file-sharing sites such as archive.org and justpaste.it and heavily promoted by ISIS members and "fanboys" (groupies or unaffiliated enthusiasts) on Twitter and Facebook. This not only maximized its viewership through crowd-sourcing, it also helped drown out antagonists and critics. "Everybody should know that we are not who they think we are," an ISIS media activist in Aleppo told us in what has become a common refrain. "We have engineers, we have doctors, we have excellent media activists. We are not *tanzim* [an organization], we are a state."

Such triumphalism to one side, ISIS's propaganda suffers from the same inborn deficiency of all cultish or messianic messaging: the creation of false expectations, which inevitably leads to anti-climax and disillusionment. As Shiraz Maher put it, describing the general condition of war under less fanatical circumstances, "A lot of foreign jihadists get to Syria and after a few days or weeks start to complain about the downtime and boredom. The videos over-dramatize the experience for them."

We found that one of the less scrutinized social media tools used by ISIS is Zello, an encrypted application for smartphones and computers that allows users to establish channels to share audio messages. Often used by pro-democracy activists in the Middle East to hide from an authoritarian government's scrutiny, Zello has lately been repurposed by ISIS as a simple how-to guide for making bayat to al-Baghdadi, thanks to a prominent pro-ISIS user, Ansar al-Dawla al-Islamiya. The application essentially turns mobile phones into walkie-talkies, through which anyone curious about ISIS or seeking to join up can listen to sermons by affiliated clerics, simulcast as Christian revivals might be.

Incredibly user-friendly, Zello is quite popular among ISIS's younger audiences. According to Ahmed Ahmed, a Syrian journalist from Sahl al-Ghab, Hama, two young boys from his village joined ISIS after listening to sermons through Zello. Mohammed, a fourteen-year-old who worked in southern Turkey, disappeared at the Bab al-Hawa border crossing in October 2014. Answering a call for help from Mohammed's father, Ahmed composed a Facebook post asking his friends and followers for any information about the boy. An hour later, Ahmed told us, Mohammed called his parents from the Iraqi border and said, "I am with the brothers."

Mohammed's father was shocked to hear the news and later told Ahmed that his son would regularly listen to ISIS sermons through Zello. "His father warned him about them and told him that they were liars. But the boy would respond that he just wanted to hear what they were saying. The majority of young people join ISIS after they listen to their preaching."

ISIS also has offline means for brainwashing youth. In May 2014 it abducted around 153 schoolchildren between the ages of thirteen and fourteen in Minbij as they traveled back to their hometown of Kobane, after having sat for exams in Aleppo. ISIS put the children in a Sharia training camp and kept them hostage for months, releasing them the following September. According to two journalists from Hama close to the families of a few of those abducted, some of the children voluntarily chose to stay on and become members of ISIS even after being offered the opportunity to return to their families.

A relative of one such recruit spoke of how his cousin refused to return with his mother despite contrary advice from a local ISIS emir. The mother had told the emir that the boy, Ahmed Hemak, was her only son and that her husband was dead, which, according to Islamic teachings, ought to have compelled the boy to remain with his mother. But the child had become a dogged convert and had no wish to abandon the movement.

END TIMES

In much of its public discourse, ISIS relies on Islamic eschatology for legitimacy and mobilization. A hadith attributed to the Prophet

Muhammad about an end-of-days battle between Muslims and Christians in Dabiq, a town in rural Aleppo, is a frequent reference point—so pervasive that ISIS's propaganda magazine is named for it. In the videos, this hadith is recited by al-Zarqawi as an ISIS jihadist marches, in slow motion, holding up a black flag: "The spark has been lit here in Iraq and its heat will continue to intensify, by Allah's permission, until it burns the crusader army in Dabiq." It also opens every issue of *Dabiq* as a motto tantamount to "All the news fit to print."

Much like its Baathist forerunners, ISIS has managed to turn outsider or enemy opinion of it into part of its world-historical struggle. For instance, the announcement in August 2014 of an international coalition to fight ISIS in Syria was hailed as a sign that the Islamic prophecy was nigh, especially as it followed the declaration of a caliphate, another event foretold by the Prophet. According to a famous hadith, Muhammad explained to his followers that after him, a caliphate modeled on prophethood would be established, and that would then be followed by a coercive kingdom and tyrannical rule. Finally, another caliphate modeled on prophethood would be established. Both Islamist and jihadist organizations often used this hadith to mean that a caliphate will replace the tyrannical regimes in the Arab world.

ISIS employs Islamic symbolism to animate its fighters and draw sympathy from Muslims outside of its orbit. Al-Baghdadi claimed to be a descendent of Hussain, the grandson of the Prophet, which is a precondition set by many Islamic scholars for claiming legitimacy to rule Muslims. ISIS's use of lineage tales is particularly important in its arguments with fellow jihadists, for whom these genealogies are profoundly evocative and can mobilize Muslim youth around an imminent project. Frustration with the more gradualist approaches to building an Islamic state endorsed by, say, the Muslim Brotherhood sometimes leads Islamists to look at ISIS as an alternative. The fact that it has *already* announced the caliphate means that the hardest work has been done; Muslims can join and fight for its survival and expansion, even without traveling to Iraq and Syria.

Then there is the very land upon which the supposed caliphate has been founded. Al-Sham refers to both Damascus and Greater Syria (an ancient territory that encompasses most of the contemporary northern Levant, including the Turkish city of Antakya) and was described by the Prophet Muhammad as "blessed" and "the land of resurrection." Iraq and Syria were the cradles of the first Muslim empires, and the birthplaces of many of God's prophets, and the burial sites of many of the Prophet's companions. They are also sites for end times foretold by Muhammad. These symbols are used as ammunition for ISIS to promote its ideology and gain legitimacy among conservative Muslims, and are more effectively harnessed to audiences divorced from the day-to-day reality of ISIS control.

GLOSSY JIHAD

Dabiq's content, which we have cited throughout this book, explains ISIS's core mission and its behavior through an eschatological prism. The introduction of sex slavery, for example, was defended by the editors as one of the signs of "the Hour," meaning Judgment Day. According to a hadith, the apocalypse will come when a "slave gives birth to her master."

Abolishment of slavery, then, would make the realization of this prophecy impossible. So *Dabiq* concludes: "After this, it becomes clear where [ISIS spokesman] al-Adnani gets his inspiration from when saying, 'and so we promise you [O crusaders] by Allah's permission that this campaign will be your final campaign. It will be broken and defeated, just as all your previous campaigns were broken and defeated, except that this time we will raid you thereafter, and you will never raid us. We will conquer your Rome, break your crosses, and enslave your women, by the permission of Allah, the Exalted. This is His promise to us."

Many of the practices that ISIS has revived are intended as tocsins of Islamic prophecy, including the blowing up of shrines and the tossing of homosexuals from rooftops. One of ISIS's governors, Hussam Naji Allami, who was captured by Iraqi Security Forces in 2014, issued a fatwa ordering the demolition of shrines in Mosul on the premise that a hadith had called for it. In an interview with the Iraqi newspaper *Al-Sabah*, Allami said he issued the fatwa in response to criticism, namely from al-Qaeda, about the illegitimacy of ISIS, said not to be the foretold "caliphate modeled on the Prophet's methodology."

Whatever the perversion or barbarity, ISIS has a ready-made justification. The salability of its dark vision cannot be underestimated. Recently, the US State Department created a Twitter account called "Think Again Turn Away." It tweets photographs of ISIS atrocities and casualties and links to news stories describing them. It also engages with pro-ISIS accounts, in effect trolling them. Thus, in opposition to @OperationJihad, who wrote to no one in particular, quoting a jihadist anthem, "We have nothing to achieve in this world, except martyrdom, [i]n the mountains we will be buried and snow will be our shroud," the State Department rejoined: "Much more honorable to give a Syrian child a pair of boots than drive him from his home into snow w/your quest for death."

@OperationJihad didn't bother to reply.

Three days earlier, as the world was recovering from the terrorist slaughter of *Charlie Hebdo* journalists in Paris, ISIS or some contingent of its supporters appeared to have hacked the Twitter and YouTube accounts of CENTCOM, posting military documents and jihadist threats, including a menacing Tweet that read: "AMER-ICAN SOLDIERS, WE ARE COMING, WATCH YOUR BACK." Though the White House downplayed the incident as an act of "cybervandalism," less innocuous was one of the documents the "CyberCaliphate" hackers released: a spreadsheet titled "Retired Army General Officer Roster," which carried the names, retirement dates, and email addresses of US army generals. Posting such personal information on public platforms is known as doxxing.

Scott Atran is one of many analysts who believes that the US government hasn't adequately grasped the appeal of ISIS to those most susceptible to being drawn into it. "We keep hearing that the antidote is preaching moderate Islam. I tell people on the National Security Council, 'Don't you have kids? Does anything moderate appeal to them?'"

12

DIVORCE

AL-QAEDA SPLITS FROM ISIS

At the end of December 2014, ISIS released its sixth issue of *Dabiq*. The cover story promised a "testimony from within" al-Qaeda's home base of operations, the Waziristan region of southern Pakistan. Written by a man called Abu Jarir al-Shamali, a former associate of Abu Musab al-Zarqawi, the article was a more-in-sorrow-than-in-anger look at the degeneration of a once noble jihadist enterprise. Al-Shamali said he traveled to Waziristan after being released from an Iranian jail in 2010. He expected to find a proud Islamic emirate: "I had thought the mujahidin were the decision makers there and that the sharia laws were implemented by them there. But alas and sadly, the dominant law was the tribal laws." Children were attending the "secularist government" schools; paved roads indicated that Islamabad was still very much in control of the territory; and, women intermingled with men, "making the movement of the mujahid brothers difficult in the case of sudden military action." In short, al-Qaeda's emirate was a busted flush. Moreover, al-Shamali explained, the treachery of the mujahidin in Pakistan, principally Ayman al-Zawahiri and "his cronies who left from the arena of Waziristan carrying secret and private messages," had created a rift within ISI, which led to a civil war within a civil war in Syria. Jabhat al-Nusra was suddenly fighting ISIS.

AL-NUSRA AT WAR IN SYRIA

By August 2012 US intelligence estimated that al-Qaeda had roughly 200 operatives in Syria, a minority of the overall rebel formations battling the regime. But, as the Associated Press reported, their "units [were] spreading from city to city, with veterans of the Iraq insurgency employing their expertise in bomb-building to carry out more than two dozen attacks so far." And al-Zawahiri's exhortation had paid off because, as Daniel Benjamin, the State Department's top counterterrorism official said, "There is a larger group of foreign fighters . . .who are either in or headed to Syria," although he claimed that Western-backed rebel groups "assured us that they are being vigilant and want nothing to do with al-Qaeda or with violent extremists."

That vigilance would be severely tested as FSA brigades and battalions continued to complain about their lack of resources relative to the jihadists. At that point, the United States was sending "non-lethal aid" to the opposition in the form of walkie-talkies, night-vision goggles, and Meals Ready to Eat (MREs). FSA fighters had to rely on whatever weapons the military defectors in their midst took with them from the Syrian army, commandeered stocks from raided regime installations, and black-market purchases where the prices of even "light" arms such as Kalashnikovs, rocket-propelled grenade launchers, and ammunition had been inflated because of high demand. The rebels were also growing increasingly dependent on weapons purchased for them by Saudi Arabia and Qatar, two Gulf states with antagonistic agendas and a willingness to work with Islamist fighters deemed unsavory to the West.

A little-explored facet of the Syrian Civil War was how a highly competitive bidding war for arms by fighters naturally inclined toward nationalism or secularism accelerated their radicalization, or at least their show of *having been* radicalized. In a survey of the opposition carried out by the International Republican Institute (IRI) and Pechter Polls of Princeton in June 2012, rebels made their intentions for a post Assad Syria clear. The survey showed that 40 percent wanted a transitional government in Damascus, leading to elections; 36 percent said they wanted a constitutional assembly, as in postrevolutionary Tunisia, leading to elections. But that would slowly change, or at least appear to. In Antakya—which by the summer of 2011 had become a refugee hub, triage center, and a remote barracks for the rebels—we met with one mainstream FSA fighter who was recuperating from an injury caused by shrapnel. He drank alcohol and smoked marijuana and professed to want to see a democratic state emerge in the wake of Assadism. However, his battlefield photo showed a long-bearded Islamic militant redolent of the Chechen separatist warlord Shamil Basayev.

This rebel's brigade, he told us, was financed by the Muslim Brotherhood, and so he felt it necessary to play up his religiosity to ensure the subsidization of his men. Another rebel commander complained how he had to sell everything, from his family mining businesses in Hama to his wife's jewelry, to keep his small start-up battalion of a few hundred afloat, whereas jihadist leaders were turning up in safe houses throughout Syria with bags full of cash they were ready to dispense to their comrades to buy guns, bullets, and bombs. The eight-year-old arms and jihadist trafficking nexus in eastern Syrian and western Iraq was moving in the reverse direction.

On December 11, 2012, the US Treasury Department sanctioned al-Nusra as the Syrian arm of al-Qaeda, which it accused of seeking "to exploit the instability inside Syria for its own purposes, using tactics and espousing an ideology drawn from [al-Qaeda in Iraq] that the Syrian people broadly reject."

The designation failed to marginalize the jihadist cell. Instead, it rallied the opposition behind al-Nusra, not necessarily out of ideological sympathy but out of wartime exigency. Dr. Radwan Ziadeh, a Washington-based Syrian dissident who had belonged to the Syrian National Council, the first political vehicle for the opposition, called the decision misguided precisely because it seemed to certify the al-Assad regime's portrayal of the conflict—as a war against terror. Dissidents inside Syria saw it much the same way.

Having asked for the better part of a year for US military intervention in the form of a no-fly zone or arms for the FSA, activists chafed at America's blacklisting of one of the groups taking the fight most assiduously to their enemy. In December 2012, Syrians held one of their Friday demonstrations throughout the country. This one was titled "We are all Jabhat al-Nusra."

ISI OWNS AL-NUSRA

As it happens, the first al-Qaeda agent to confirm the Treasury Department's intelligence was none other than Abu Bakr al-Baghdadi, in an audio message publicized on April 8, 2013, more than a year after al-Nusra had established itself as one of the vanguard fighting forces. It was also a month after an array of rebel factions, led by Ahrar al-Sham and al-Nusra, took its first (and so far only) provincial capital away from Syrian soldiers in the eastern city of Raqqa, which was nicknamed the "hotel of the revolution" owing to the tripling of its population from internally displaced persons.

The fall of the city nearly coincided with the anniversary of another hinge moment in the history of the modern Middle East. It had been almost ten years to the day since US forces invaded Iraq in Operation Enduring Freedom. There was a grim symmetry between the two events. US Marines had famously helped local Iraqis raze a large statue of Saddam in Baghdad's Paradise Square, with one even briefly, controversially, covering the monument with the Stars and Stripes. Suddenly Islamists had just toppled a bronze statue of Hafez al-Assad and hoisted the Muslim *shahada*, the black flag with Arabic script reading, "There is no god but God, and Muhammad is His messenger," to a flagpole in another Arab metropolis ruled by Baathists. Within days, graffiti appeared on buildings in Raqqa, attributed to al-Nusra, warning that the punishment for theft was the loss of a hand. Pamphlets were distributed with images instructing women of the due modesty of dress expected of them. And while many residents had cheered the expulsion of the regime, not all welcomed their new masters or the divisive iconography they brought with them.

In the *New Yorker*, Rania Abouzeid reconstructed an intense debate had between Raqqans of all generations and an al-Nusra operative, who was handing out a leaflet explaining the necessity of replacing the Free Syrian flag—the pre-Baathist tricolor adopted by the opposition in the early months of the protest movement—with an Islamic one. Abu Noor, a man in his twenties, feared the shahada was an open invitation for the wrong kind of US intervention in Syria. "We will become a target for American drone attacks because of the flag—it's huge," he said. "They'll think we're extremist Muslims!" Abu Moayad, an older man who had helped smuggle ammunition to the rebels from Iraq, told al-Nusra that the flag denatured the first principles of the revolution: "We are not an Islamic emirate; we are part of Syria. This is a religious banner, not a country's flag."

ISI's seizure of Raqqa had happened by stealth, seemingly overnight, much as its insertion of al-Nusra into all of Syria. "When the situation in Syria reached that level in terms of bloodshed and violation of honor," al-Baghdadi declared on April 8, 2013, "and when the people of Syria asked for help and everyone abandoned them, we could not but come to their help so we appointed al-Jolani, who is one of our soldiers, along with a group of our sons, and we sent them from Iraq to Syria to meet our cells in Syria. We set plans for them and devised policies for them and we supported them with half of our treasury every month. We also provided them with men with long experience, foreigners and locals. . . .We did not announce it for security reasons and for people to know the truth about [ISI] away from media distortion, falsehood, and twisting."

Al-Baghdadi didn't just confine his message to confirming what was already widely assumed—he went further, announcing that al-Nusra and ISI were uniting into one cross-regional jihadist enterprise to be known as the Islamic State of Iraq and al-Sham (ISIS), which has alternatively been translated as the Islamic State of Iraq and the Levant (ISIL).

No thanks, came al-Jolani's reply, two days later.

Although respectful of his Iraq-based superior, whom he referred to as "honorable sheikh," al-Jolani said that he didn't approve of the merger, much less know about it beforehand. He thanked ISI for sharing its straitened operating budget with the Syrian franchise and confirmed al-Baghdadi's deputization of him to lead al-Nusra. However, al-Jolani left absolutely no doubt as to where his true loyalty lay—with Ayman al-Zawahiri, the "Sheikh of Jihad," to whom he publicly renewed his and al-Nusra's bayat.

What followed was a brief media intermission by al-Nusra and an attendant escalation in chatter by ISIS. Al-Nusra's official media network, al-Manara al-Bayda (the White Lighthouse), stopped producing material, while numerous videos began to appear from ISIS, fueling speculation that al-Baghdadi had triumphed over al-Jolani. It was only in late May–early June 2013 that al-Zawahiri, like an exhausted father trying to break up a fight between two unruly sons, intervened publicly.

In a communiqué published by Al Jazeera, he did his best to sound evenhanded in his judgment. Al-Baghdadi, he stated, was "wrong when he announced the Islamic State in Iraq and the Levant without asking permission or receiving advice from us and even without notifying us." But al-Jolani, too, was "wrong by announcing his rejection to the Islamic State in Iraq and the Levant, and by showing his links to al-Qaeda without having our permission or advice, even without notifying us." Al-Zawhiri thereby "dissolved" ISIS and ordered both ISI and al-Nusra back to its geographically delimited corners, one having control over Iraq, the other over Syria.

No doubt aware that this pronouncement wouldn't keep his two subordinates from restarting their argument, al-Zawahiri also hedged his bets. He appointed Abu Khalid al-Suri, al-Qaeda's "delegate" in Syria, to act as an on-the-ground arbiter of any further squabbles that might arise from his decree. Also, in the event that al-Nusra attacked ISI or vice versa, al-Zawahiri empowered al-Suri to "set up a Sharia justice court for giving a ruling on the case."

Al-Suri, who was killed in a suicide bombing in Aleppo in February 2014 (possibly at the hands of ISIS), was a veteran al-Qaeda agent, not to mention another beneficiary of al-Assad's general amnesty in 2011. He had helped found Harakat Ahrar al-Sham al-Islamiyya (the Islamic Movement of the Free Men of the Levant), one of the most powerful rebel groups in Syria today. Before his death, al-Suri was the linchpin of the long-standing operational alliance between al-Nusra and Ahrar al-Sham.

AL-ZAWAHIRI, DEFENDER OF SYKES-PICOT

Al-Zawahiri's suspicion that the crisis between his two field commanders would outlast his paternal intervention proved correct. Al-Baghdadi refused to abide by his edict and justified his defiance by claiming that al-Zawahiri, by insisting on a distinction between the lands of Syria and Iraq, was deferring to artificial state borders drawn up by Western imperial powers at the close of the First

World War, specifically the Sykes-Picot Agreement. That was no mild charge to level at the Sheikh of Jihad.

The brainchild of Sir Mark Sykes, the secretive twentieth-century compact between London and Paris had divided the remnants of the Ottoman Empire. "I should like to draw a line from the 'e' in Acre to the last 'k' in Kirkuk," Sykes told the British cabinet in December 1915. In reality, the Sykes-Picot Agreement was never implemented as it was originally envisaged: Mosul, for instance, was meant to fall to France's sphere of influence but in the end became part of the British mandate in Iraq. But despite being drawn along Ottoman boundaries more than one hundred years old, the pact has become a compelling complaint for successive generations of Baathists, Communists, pan-Arab nationalists, and Islamists. The agreement was, and still is, a synecdoche for conniving and duplicitous Western designs on the Middle East, so much so, in fact, that when ISIS stormed Mosul in June 2014 and bulldozed the berms dividing Iraq from Syria, it billed the act as both the physical and symbolic repudiation of Sykes-Picot. Implicitly, too, it was a rejection of al-Zawahiri's prescription for holy war. Al-Baghdadi's break with the Egyptian elder was therefore more than that of a lieutenant mutinying against a general. The ISIS emir was calling his boss a has-been and a sell-out.

The al-Nusra–ISIS rupture led directly to yet another transformation in the ranks of regional, not to say global, jihadism. The majority of foreign fighters in al-Nusra's ranks went over to ISIS, leaving the rump organization under al-Jolani heavily Syrian in constitution.

Inside Iraq, the dynamics and nature of ISIS changed as well. Al-Baghdadi had earnestly taken up the PR gambit inaugurated by al-Zarqawi, and then expanded by al-Masri and the first al-Baghdadi, and further Iraq-ized ISI, outfitting its upper echelons with former Saddamists. By incorporating al-Nusra's lower and middle cadres, al-Baghdadi thus found himself once again commanding a more internationalized terror army, one that spanned the Levant and Mesopotamia. Thus, by renouncing al-Qaeda, al-Baghdadi actually returned ISIS to a version of its earliest incarnation in Iraq.

THE SCHOOLTEACHER OF RAQQA

Souad Nawfal remembered when the anti-Assad protests gained traction in Raqqa. It was March 15, 2012, shortly after the death of Ali Babinsky, the first resident of the eastern province of Syria to be killed by regime forces. He was seventeen years old. "We buried him and then when we had a funeral and protest on his behalf, they fired on us and killed sixteen of our people."

She also remembered when she started protesting ISIS. "I started demonstrating because they took Father Paolo," she said, referring to the Italian Jesuit priest who for decades ran a parish north of Damascus and supported the Syrian revolution from its inception. After joining protests in Raqqa in late July, he was kidnapped by ISIS and has not been heard from since. "Paolo was my guest," Nawfal, a short, forty-year-old, hijab-wearing former schoolteacher told one of the authors during an interview in November 2013. "He used to come to break the fast at Ramadan in my house. He was coming to speak out against ISIS. He wanted to stop the killings and secrecy, all the stuff the regime does. He went in to speak to ISIS, but he never came out."

Nawfal became a hero to Syrian moderate activists, as well as a minor Internet celebrity for a four-minute video she made in which she lambasted ISIS for their draconian rule and religious obscurantism. The video is titled *The Woman in Pants* in reference to her refusal to adhere to ISIS's dress code for women. Nawfal said that she's spent the last two months protesting the new ideologues of her province, whom she sees not only as tarnishing Islam, but also as the mirror image of the very totalitarians she and her fellow activists wanted to be rid of in the first place. "They treat people horribly. They're exactly like Assad's regime. They scare people into submission."

Much like the Mukhabarat during the early days of the protest movement, ISIS has also banned civilians from taking photographs or making any recordings of provocative behavior in Raqqa. "ISIS would beat people in the street with leather. If anyone was going around taking 'illegal' pictures of this with a camera, they'd be taken into custody. In the month and a half I was protesting in front of the headquarters, no one would take my picture because they were scared."

The jihadi movement has succeeded, Nawfal believes, by preying upon the poverty, illiteracy, and wartime exigencies of this province to curry favor with the population. An especially effective tactic has been the brainwashing of Raqqa's children. "People that are poor and uneducated and not paying attention to what their kids are doing, their ten-year-olds will go out and then ISIS will promise the family food and money. They elevate these kids and call them 'sheikhs' and give them weapons and power, turn them into child soldiers. But these are ten-year-old boys who have never studied theology, and now they're sheikhs! I am worried that this is really ruining the idea of what Muslims are and what Islam is."

Nawfal became a daily fixture in front of ISIS's local headquarters, where she was cursed at, spit on, manhandled, and even run over. "I was standing out in front of this place, and there was an ISIS man with a long white beard who wanted to park his car there. But it's a huge area. He told me I had to move. I told him no. So he started swearing at me, berating me, but I still wouldn't move. So he hit me with the car twice. It wasn't that hard, but more for him to make a point."

She continued, "Every day they'd point a Kalashnikov at my head and threaten to shoot me. I'd tell them, 'Do it. If you kill me first, then the second bullet has to go to Bashar's head.' That'd irritate them."

Where her chutzpah may discombobulate the takfiris, the fact that she's both a small, middle-aged woman and more or less a solo act in defying them likely accounts for her survival and precarious freedom thus far. Nevertheless, she insists that she's narrowly escaped ISIS's distinct brand of social justice more than once, the last time after standing up for the rights of Raqqa's Christian community.

In late September ISIS attacked and burned two churches in the province, removing their crosses from the spires and replacing them with their black flag of global jihad. On September 25 it did this to the Sayidat al-Bishara Catholic Church, after which around two dozen people turned up at the site to protest. "I told them, 'What are you doing here? Go to the headquarters,'" Nawfal said. She led a march, and some of the protestors began following her, but by the time she reached the headquarters, she found that she was all by herself. Everyone had dropped out of the retinue out of fear. A day later, another church was stormed; Nawfal again went to demonstrate after she heard that people had been arrested. This time she carried a sign that read "Forgive me." The message was intended for her family, because she was certain that that day she'd either be killed or abducted. "First they tried to scare me away. They let off a bomb near me. I was there for ten minutes, and a sixteen-year-old member of ISIS came to me and called me an infidel and turned to the other ISIS men and said, 'Why are you letting her live?' He was about to kill me, but apparently he got orders for no one to talk to me.

"Five minutes later, a car came with guns and weapons. Somebody jumped out and started grabbing at my arm, hitting me on the shoulder. Another person was spitting at me, swearing at me. I thought I was finished at this point. I started to call the Syrian people around me. I shouted, 'Are you happy, Syrians? Look what they're doing to me. Look at your women, how they're getting raped, how they're getting attacked, and you're just sitting there, watching.'"

Nawfal said she'll only go outside to protest so long as no one on the street recognizes her. The minute an ISIS militant sees her, she leaves. She doesn't stay in one place anymore but moves from house to house, a fugitive in her own city. She doesn't believe the current situation will change in the near future. "If people have fear, Raqqa will not have freedom from ISIS. As long as ISIS continues to use the tactics of the regime, it's not going to become free."

Nawfal has since fled to Turkey.

SYRIA'S SAHWA

There are thousands more like Nawfal who have resisted ISIS locally in Raqqa and elsewhere. Abu Jarir al-Shamali's criticism of al-Qaeda's Waziristan operation—that the entire territory was more in thrall to Pashtun tribes than to the mujahidin—was of a piece with ISIS's obsession about sahwats, be they in Iraq or in Syria. Paradoxically, in trying to forestall an Awakening, it ended up precipitating one.

On July 11 2013, Kamal Hamami, a commander of the FSA's Supreme Military Council, was shot dead by ISIS gunmen at a checkpoint in Latakia. Although tensions following that incident ran high—"We are going to wipe the floor with them," one FSA commander told Reuters—the matter was swiftly hushed up, and Hamami's murder was referred to a Sharia court for "investigation." Similarly, when ISIS "accidentally" beheaded Mohammed Fares, a commander from Ahrar al-Sham, believing him to have been an Iraqi Shia militiaman (he allegedly muttered Shia mantras in his sleep), ISIS asked for "understanding and forgiveness" to preempt internecine war. Neither ISIS nor any mainstream or Islamist rebel group wanted to start a civil war within a civil war. And though many FSA rebels saw ISIS's draconian rule as a long-term danger for Syria, they also understood that Sahwa-come-too-soon would only benefit one man: Bashar al-Assad, who would then either sit back and watch the opposition devour itself, if not contribute to this self-cannibalization by helping ISIS attack the FSA.

That said, ISIS seemed intent on provoking a backlash. It kidnapped revered opposition activists, it terrorized civilians under its sway, it established monopolistic checkpoints that functioned more like chokepoints for rival factions. And it attacked Syrian rebels. On August 1, 2013, for instance, ISIS sent a car bomb to the base of Ahfad al-Rasoul (Grandsons of the Prophet) in Raqqa, killing thirty. ISIS then expelled the brigade from the city.

In late December 2013, the city of Maarat al-Numan, in Syria's Idlib province, staged a protest in favor of rebel unity against the al-Assad regime—and for the release of an FSA officer, Lieutenant Colonel Ahmad Saoud, who had been kidnapped days earlier by ISIS at a checkpoint. Curiously enough, Saoud, a defector from the Syrian army, had been traveling with a retinue to the Taftanaz air base in Idlib in order to parlay with ISIS and negotiate the release of military equipment—including antiaircraft missiles—that the latter had stolen from Fursan al-Haqq, an FSA faction. Saoud also represented the Idlib Military Council—a regional assembly representing all the rebel groups in the province—which had publicly demanded that ISIS free all its kidnapped civilians and pursue any civil or criminal complaints it had with rebels in the relevant Sharia courts. Saoud's own kidnapping, then, came in the midst of his trying to broker a compromise with ISIS. Maarat al-Numan's rally on his behalf had the intended effect: within hours of the protest action, ISIS released Saoud, making him the first FSA officer to leave its custody alive.

Then, on December 29, ISIS raided several dissident news organizations in Kafranbel, a city in the northwestern Idlib province, which had somehow managed, through two years of regime bombardment and the proliferation of jihadism, to retain the democratic principles of the original Syrian uprising. Among the buildings targeted was the Kafranbel Media Center run by the forty-one-year-old Raed Fares, an artist whose pro-revolutionary posters and slogans—all written in colloquial English and very often wittily allusive to Western popular culture—had helped make an Arab revolution intelligible to non-Arab audiences the world over. In one celebrated poster, the famous "king of the world" scene from the movie *Titanic* is reproduced, with Vladimir Putin cast as Leonardo DiCaprio and Bashar al-Assad as Kate Winslet. Lately, Fares had taken to comparing ISIS's depravity to the regime's, making them twin enemies of the Syrian people.

Hours earlier, before the ISIS raid, Fares's Media Center broadcast a radio program featuring Syrian women discussing their recent divorces. All too much for the takfiris, who abducted six of Fares's employees (they were released two hours later) and stole or smashed the center's computers and broadcasting equipment.

"The reason Kafranbel became important is because it's been persistently and consistently supporting the revolution in all of its aspects—whether it's the nonviolent revolution or the armed revolution or the humanitarian and civil society work," Fares told us. "The regime, when we would say something in opposition to them, they'd shell us. ISIS, when we made a drawing against them—the first in June of this year—they wanted to attack us, so they came and raided the Media Center. At the end of the day, they're both the same. They're both tyrants." (Not long after this interview, which took place as Fares was touring the United States, ISIS tried to assassinate him in Idlib. He was shot several times but recovered from his injuries.)

On New Year's Day 2014, ISIS finally overplayed its hand in Syria, killing Hussein al-Suleiman, or Abu Rayyan, a respected physician and commander in Ahrar al-Sham. Like Saoud, Abu Rayyan was abducted while heading to a negotiation meeting with ISIS. Abu Rayyan was locked up for twenty days and horribly tortured before being shot. Images of his mutilated corpse were then circulated on social media, outraging even those Ahrar

al-Sham supporters who had hitherto urged patience and reconciliation with ISIS. However, the brigade accused it of exceeding even the barbarity of the al-Assad's Mukhabarat and warned
that "if ISIS continues with its methodical avoiding of refraining
from . . .resorting to an independent judicial body, and its stalling
and ignoring in settling its injustices against others, the revolution
and the jihad will head for the quagmire of internal fighting, in
which the Syrian revolution will be the first loser."

On January 2 ISIS hit another FSA location, this time in
Atareb, Aleppo, driving even Islamist fighters into an alliance with
the FSA. The Islamic Front, which not a month earlier had commandeered an FSA warehouse full of weapons and supplies in the
Idlib village of Atmeh, declared solidarity with a fellow victim of
jihadist fanatics. "We hereby address the Islamic State of the re-
quirement to immediately withdraw from the city of al-Atareb,"
the Islamic Front stated in a press release, "and to end the killing
of the fighters based on false excuses and return all unfairly confiscated properties of weapons and bases to their rightful owners.
They must also accept the rule of God by agreeing to the judgments
of the independent religious courts to resolve the conflicts that arise
between them and the other factions. We remind ISIS that those
who originally liberated al-Atareb and the suburbs of Aleppo in
general are those whom you are now fighting."

By that point, Lieutenant Colonel Ahmad Saoud had joined with
a new rebel formation known as the Syrian Revolutionaries Front,
which claimed to have aggregated as many as twenty separate factions belonging to the Idlib Military Council. This new mainstream
front, Saoud told us, was founded with one purpose: "to fight [ISIS]."

The last group to join this budding Sahwa movement in northern Syria was the Army of the Mujahedeen, an alliance of eight
rebel brigades, all based in Aleppo. "We, the Army of the Mujahedeen," it declared, "pledge to defend ourselves and our honor,

wealth, and lands, and to fight [ISIS], which has violated the rule of God, until it announces its dissolution." The Army of the Mujahedeen gave ISIS a stark choice: either it could defect to the mainstream rebellion or it could surrender its arms and leave Syria.

What had begun as localized conflicts transformed into a massive armed campaign against ISIS led by the Islamic Front, the Syrian Revolutionaries Front, and the Army of the Mujahedeen, which swept ISIS from its territorial perches throughout much of northern Syria. This campaign coincided with an upsurge in popular anti-ISIS protests in Idlib and Aleppo, which ISIS tried to suppress by shooting the protestors.

As the FSA had feared, the al-Assad regime wasn't about to stay neutral in the internecine fight and intervened objectively on the side of ISIS. As the ground fighting continued, the Syrian Air Force took to bombing areas from which ISIS had just been expelled, hitting either FSA or Islamic Front targets, when it wasn't hitting civilians, and prompting further allegations among activists that ISIS was little more than a handmaid of the regime.

By January 4, following an FSA-issued 24-hour deadline for ISIS to surrender and abandon Syria, two hundred jihadists had been arrested. ISIS had executed civilians and rebels and resorted to car bombings and the shelling of rebel-held territories. In a desperate communiqué apparently suing for peace, ISIS issued three demands. All road blockades in cities and villages be lifted; no ISIS fighter be detained, insulted, or harmed; all ISIS detainees and foreign fighters from any other groups should be released immediately. If these demands were not met, then ISIS would issue a general order to withdraw from all the front-line positions against the regime—the clear implication being that it would return territory to al-Assad.

On January 5 the Islamic Front announced that it had been given no choice but to turn on its former ally; it had been "push[ed]" to battle, and while its charter was initially welcoming of foreign fighters offering assistance in the struggle against al-Assad, it would "not accept any group that claims to be a state." Atareb was retaken by the rebels, and the black flag of ISIS replaced with the Free Syrian tricolor. An activist for the Shaam News Network in Raqqa claimed that rebels had "liberat[ed] more than 80% of the Idlib countryside and 65% of Aleppo and its countryside." Another declared, "the presence of the State of Baghdadi is finished," in what would prove to be too optimistic a prediction.

By the end of the first week of January, al-Nusra was leading the charge against ISIS in its regional headquarters in Raqqa city, joined by Ahrar al-Sham. Some fifty Syrian hostages held by ISIS were released from Raqqa's answer to the DMV—which had been turned into a makeshift prison—as was one of many foreign journalists held captive by the group, the Turkish photographer Bunyamin Aygun, who'd been kidnapped the previous month. Two churches that had been burned or confiscated by ISIS were also "liberated" by al-Nusra, which declared its intent to restore them for Christian use.

A quaky truce brokered between ISIS, on the one hand, and al-Nusra and Ahrar al-Sham, on the other, appeared to lower the temperature a bit in the Aleppo suburbs, as did ISIS's withdrawal from strategic areas close to the Turkish border, including Atmeh and al-Dana.

Al-Jolani blamed ISIS for the week of fitna that shook northern Syria but urged the formation of independent legal councils for resolving disputes to accompany the cease-fire. He also said that "detainees will be exchanged between all parties . . .and roads will be opened for everyone."

Throughout the course of Syria's brief Sahwa—an Awakening that suddenly featured al-Qaeda's official franchise on the side of the sahwats—ISIS had raised a defiant slogan: "baqiyya wa tatamaddad" ("remaining and expanding"), promising to defeat this popular turn against it and reach the Arabian Peninsula. ISIS further bombed Ahrar al-Sham's base in Mayadeen, Deir Ezzor, near the Iraqi border, and its spokesman al-Adnani declared war on the rebels, threatening suicide attacks and car bombings against Syrians.

Amid the fitna, however, tensions and divisions within Islamist groups fighting ISIS began to appear. Abu Omar al-Shishani, then ISIS's commander in Aleppo, signed a truce with Abu Khalid al-Suri, al-Zawahiri's delegate in Syria, who was acting on behalf of Ahrar al-Sham and al-Nusra. For the moment, calm was restored between the jihadists.

THE AL-NUSRA–ISIS SPLIT

But the damage wrought on the al-Nusra–ISIS relationship was irreparable. On February 2, 2014, global al-Qaeda formally ended its association with ISIS, issuing a public statement: "ISIS is not a branch of the Qaidat al-Jihad [al-Qaida's official name] group, we have no organizational relationship with it, and the group is not responsible for its actions."

One of the jihadists who smuggled himself across the Iraqi-Syrian border with al-Jolani during Ramadan in 2011 was Abu Maria al-Qahtani. His real name is Maysara al-Juburi, and he's active on Twitter as a leading exponent for the al-Nusra worldview, particularly its ongoing family feud with ISIS, from which al-Qahtani defected after having served as a top commander. "The rumor is that he used to be a traffic cop before he became al-Nusra's military operative in Deir Ezzor," Laith Alkhouri told us. "He accused ISIS of destroying jihad in Iraq and Syria; he called the members 'deviants.'"

The lineaments of this divorce ran throughout the marriage. They were already discernible in that awkward first encounter between bin Laden and al-Zarqawi in Kandahar in 1999, and in

AQI's tempestuous eleven-year history. And though al-Nusra and ISIS have cooperated tactically since the split, allegedly even mulling some form of reconciliation in the face of coalition air strikes against both organizations in Syria, there is little chance that a broad rapprochement will occur. The latest issue of *Dabiq* makes plain that ISIS views al-Qaeda as a spent force in jihad, and itself as the inheritor of bin Laden's legacy. The differences are too deep and many by now, according to Alkhouri. "ISIS takes the super-rightist ultra-conservative route. It is legitimate to kill even those who you cannot otherwise repel their aggression. Jolani is one of those guys. Baghdadi is even rumored to have vowed to kill him. ISIS apostatizes Muslims who didn't know they committed some offense. So if you insulted the divine using a slang expression, they'll behead you even if you didn't know you insulted the divine."

Another major discrepancy is the chicken-or-egg one about Islamic state-building. For ISIS, theocratic legitimacy *follows* the seizure and administration of terrain. First you "liberate" the people, then you found a government. For al-Qaeda, it's the other way about: Sharia laws comes into practice before the holy war overthrows the taghut (tyrannical) regime.

ISIS further claims that al-Zarqawi had a five-phase process for establishing the caliphate, and that he had accomplished three of them by the time al-Baghdadi arrived on the scene: the immigration of foreign fighters to the land of jihad (*hijrah*), their enlistment in the ranks of a militancy (*jama'ah*), and their undermining of the idolators (pretty much everyone but the Zarqawists and their allies).

JIHADI RECRIMINATIONS

One of the more curious epiphenomena of this breakup is seeing Jolanist loyalists accuse Baghdadis of working for the other side. Many al-Nusra supporters have pointed to how the Syrian Air Force had largely refrained for the better part of a year (2013–2014) from bombing rather conspicuous ISIS installations in Raqqa. Al-Nusra has a point.

A recent study conducted by the Carter Center found that, prior to ISIS's military advances across Syria and Iraq in July and August 2014, the regime had "largely abstained from engaging [ISIS] unless directly threatened. . . .Prior to this [ISIS] offensive, the Syrian government had directed over 90% of all air raids against opposition positions."

By Damascus's own admission, it spent the better part of 2013 and 2014 mostly leaving ISIS alone in order to focus its aerial campaign against FSA and other rebel groups—for the simple reason that letting black-clad terrorists run around a provincial capital, crucifying and beheading people, made for great propaganda. One adviser to the regime told the *New York Times* that ignoring ISIS targets helped with the "tarring [of] all insurgents" as extremists.

We have also seen how the regime chooses to deal with terrorism by infiltration. An early defector from ISIS told CNN's Arwa Damon in February 2012 he witnessed would-be suicide bombers being told by their battlefield emirs that they were going off to attack regime installations. In reality, they were sent on suicide missions against other rebels. "There were a lot of regime locations we could have taken without sustaining losses of our fighters," the defector Abu Ammara said, "and we would receive orders to retreat."

Some of this may owe to ISIS's financial dependence on selling Syria's oil back to the regime. As a Western intelligence source told the *Daily Telegraph* in January 2014, just a month before al-Qaeda formally severed its ties with ISIS, "The regime is paying al-Nusra to protect oil and gas pipelines under al-Nusra's control in the north and east of the country, and is also allowing the transport of oil to regime-held areas. We are also now starting to see evidence of oil and gas facilities under ISIS control."

"Whatever Bashar al-Assad and Abu Bakr Al-Baghdadi may think of one another personally," Frederic Hof, the former State Department adviser on Syria, wrote, "their top tactical priority in Syria is identical: destroy the Syrian nationalist opposition to the Assad regime."

Alkhouri said that this charge of ISIS's collusion or conspiracy with the regime is widespread in al-Qaeda circles. "Five or six weeks ago, I came across a document—the person who released it said it came from air force intelligence—which said that Syrian intelligence has about 250 informants in the ranks of ISIS. I was not shocked in the least. I like to do reverse-engineering. How can I prove this by eliminating the noise? This is what you see: for many months, ISIS was very much capable of attacking regime soldiers but chose not to, preferring instead to transfer literally hundreds of its fighters to other areas in Syria that had been liberated by the FSA, Nusra, and other Islamist brigades. Why is ISIS doing this? Nusra says it's for the expansion of its power: 'Let other fighters repel or expel the regime, we'll move in and rule the land after all the heavy lifting is done.'"

On Twitter, a popular account known as Baghdadi Leaks has been dishing what it says is inside intelligence on ISIS—and about the backstory of its emir. No one knows who runs the account, but the likelihood is high that it's either an al-Qaeda operative or affiliate or perhaps a defector from ISIS looking to embarrass his erstwhile confederates by airing their dirty laundry. The portrait made of al-Baghdadi on this account is that of a mid-level member of ISI from 2006 to 2010 who rose through the ranks after having used his house as a drop site for secret communications between fighters and their commanders. "His job was apparently that of a go-between," said Alkhouri. "If this is true, then he was definitely privy to secret communications—dates of operations, claims of responsibilities, the top structure of ISI's Shura Council, who was powerful and who was not. And *that* means he was also privy to how Syria's military intelligence was running rat lines into Iraq. This is how Nusra wants to scandalize him. 'Baghdadi called Zawahiri a quisling, an upholder of Sykes-Picot? Yeah, well, look who's talking.'"

13

SHAKEDOWN OF THE

SHEIKHS

ISIS CO-OPTS THE TRIBES

"Terrain is fate in ground combat operations," according to Jim Hickey, the US army colonel who helped capture Saddam in 2003. "Iraq is a tribal society, and families in the tribes are tied to specific pieces of ground. That's going to shape this fight dramatically. It shaped the fight when the British were there in the First and Second World Wars. It shaped the fight when we were there."

Much the same can be said of the Jazira, which has in the last two years served as ISIS's strategic heartland, and the reason for its inextricability from Syria. It was here, after all, that Abu Ghadiyah had his safe house and countless other rat-line runners and "border emirs" kept their forward operating bases for AQI.

The Baathist regimes in Syria and Iraq viewed tribes and dealt with them differently. Prewar Iraqi state television channels prominently featured tribal traditions and folklore and Saddam personally mingled with both Sunni and Shia sheikhs, dispensing various incentives—such as smuggling and gray-market rights—for their continued fealty. It was this established patronage system that AQI self-defeatingly tried to disrupt in the mid-2000s, precipitating Sahwa in Iraq.

In Syria, by contrast, the Assad regimes were generally ambivalent about the tribes and strategically inept in co-opting them. True, the regime opportunistically exploited the tribes to create social rifts on demand, such as when it Arab-ized Kurdish-dominated areas in northern Syrian, the better to contain restive Kurdish nationalism. However, the al-Assads never deemed the ancient filial confederations in their desert hinterland as significant or important as Saddam had his own.

Since its advent in the 1960s, the Syrian branch of the Baath Party saw in tribalism a twofold threat: first, tribal bonds between clans in eastern Syria and northwestern Iraq were seen as a potential advantage for the rival Iraqi branch. Second, particularly in the early years of its ascent to power, the Baath Party regarded "retrograde" tribalism as antithetical to the party's "progressive" ideology.

Damascus's clumsy engagement with the tribes came back to haunt it when the Syrian uprising began. Many of the early demonstrations in Deraa, for example, were driven by tribal linkages and expressed in tribal rhetoric. Protestors called for "*fazaat houran*," the collective help of the people of the Houran valley, where Deraa is located. When the Syrian security forces used violence to suppress these demonstrations, Deraawis called on their "cousins" in the Gulf to come to their assistance.

Tribal networks played an even more pronounced role after the rebellion became militarized in early 2012. Fund organizers helped arm rebel groups in various parts of the country by appealing to their kin abroad, especially in Saudi Arabia, Kuwait, and Bahrain.

Members of the Ugaidat tribe in Homs, for example, would reach out to their fellow Ugaidat members from eastern Syria who were living in the Gulf and had readier access to fund-raising. Some pan-Syrian rebel coalitions were also formed partly because of tribal links. The Ahfad al-Rasoul brigade was led by Maher al-Nuaimi from Homs and Saddam al-Jamal from Deir Ezzor; both hailed from the same tribe. "People from al-Wa'ar al Qadeem and al-Dar al Kabeera in Homs, and others from the countrysides of Hama and Damascus connected with us," an FSA financier relayed to us. "We knew each other through tribal connections."

What started as an asset for the revolution soon became one for its jihadist deformity. Several factors explain al-Qaeda's and ISIS's purchase in Syria's tribal regions.

The first has to do with the relationship between population density and geography. Tribes have their highest concentrations in Deir Ezzor, Hasaka, Raqqa, and Deraa; they constitute a full 90 percent of the population in each of those four provinces. They also number around two million in Aleppo's rural districts. Overall, tribes account for 30 percent of Syria's overall population, and yet they inhabit about 60 percent of its territory. In other words, tribes are bound to the countryside, where insurgents have found it far easier to navigate and bivouac. As in Iraq, this is where Zarqawists tend to coalesce whenever they've been booted out of urban terrain or are plotting a massive offensive against rival groups.

AL-RAFDAN'S REVENGE

In 2012 Syrian tribalism was most effectively harnessed by Jabhat al-Nusra, then still a part of ISI. One of the first al-Nusra cells in Syria, in fact, was in a small town in Deir Ezzor known as al-Ghariba, where nearly every resident belonged to the same family. Because Deir Ezzor connects Syria to Iraq, many of al-Ghariba's inhabitants found it easy to join the Iraqi insurgency in 2003 and 2004 and imbibe Zarqawist propaganda.

The al-Assad regime uncovered the al-Nusra cell in al-Ghariba in January 2012 and almost completely eliminated it, killing dozens of its members. Al-Nusra then relocated to a nearby town, al-Shuhail, which had long been a hub for arms smuggling between Iraq and Syria. The town was named for the tribe that inhabits it, and most of the resident families had deep-rooted connections to Salafism. Members of the Hajr family, for instance, joined the Fighting Vanguard, a group that fought the regime in Hama as part of the Muslim Brotherhood's uprising in the 1970s and 1980s. After the US invasion of Iraq, many Hajr kin joined the Sunni insurgency. And after the Syrian uprising, when al-Nusra moved in, dozens of Hajr men joined the embryonic AQI franchise. Sometime in the summer of 2012, the town was effectively run by al-Nusra, earning it the nickname Shuhailistan.

"If you spoke about Jabhat al-Nusra in a negative way, you were effectively insulting the Shuhail," said Amir Al-Dandal, a member of a prominent tribe in Deir Ezzor, and an organizer for the FSA. Even the internecine war between al-Nusra and ISIS took on a tribal inflection. In April 2013, al-Nusra and Jaish Muta, another rebel group in Shuhail, fought against members of the al-Bu Assaf clan, part of the Albu Saraya tribe, which is the third-largest in Deir Ezzor. Members of the al-Bu Assaf later backed ISIS in the dispute.

Similarly, when Aamer al-Rafdan, a senior al-Nusra member, defected to ISIS after the rupture, he did so less out of ideological preference and more out of patrilineal allegiance. Al-Rafdan was from al-Bekayyir, a tribe based in Jedid Ugaidat, which for decades had been at odds with the Shuhail. Al-Rafdan's ship-jump allowed ISIS to seize control of the Conoco gas plant in Mayadeen, Deir Ezzor, delivering up a valuable resource prize to the Baghdadists and exacerbating what had been a long-running territorial dispute between the al-Bekayyir and the Shuhail. "The fighting had everything to do with the tribes, not with jihadi politics, and it was resolved on a tribal basis," said al-Dandal. "The tension was finally ended because the al-Bekayyir and the Shuhail both realized that any conflict would lead to greater problems in the future. The issue was resolved absent ISIS or al-Nusra's intervention." The truce was short-lived, however. The Shuhail expelled al-Rafdan and ISIS from Jedid Ugaidat. Then, in July 2014, ISIS conquered the Shuhail tribe, an event that had wide reverberations across Deir Ezzor.

A series of towns and villages swiftly succumbed to the jihadist blitz. Fayyadh al-Tayih, a former al-Nusra member who joined ISIS in December 2013, told us: "From the beginning, we believed that al-Shuhail was the real problem. If we were to take them, everyone else would surrender."

Triumphant, al-Rafdan began to exact revenge. He imposed harsh conditions on the Shuhail, exiling some members for a period of three months. (Even this was a tribally orientated form of punishment.) The fall of the town and tribe marked a decisive end to the al-Nusra's purchase in eastern Syria, granting ISIS more or less total control over the province of Deir Ezzor.

The sacking of Deir Ezzor was remarkable, given that Jedid Ugaidat was the only place where ISIS had ever carved out a real presence for itself; and even there, it had so alienated the local population that it had been temporarily expelled.

MONEY TALKS

Al-Nusra's routing in Deir Ezzor also derived from matériel exigencies, namely its struggle to control the province's energy resources. The Albu Ezzedine tribe asked another clan, the al-Dhaher, which was loyal to al-Nusra, to share in the revenue of smuggled oil from the al-Omar oil field, located in a desert region near Shuhail. When al-Nusra refused and claimed the revenue for itself, members of Albu Ezzedine joined ISIS.

Predictably, Sahwa took root in places where ISIS had little to no organic support from the populace. ISIS's wholesale take-over of Raqqa owed heavily to the fact that this province, more than any other, was essentially occupied by non-native fighters who fought and repelled minimal regime forces in 2013. There was no local rebel infrastructure in place beforehand, and the only military challenge that ISIS faced in Raqqa came from Ahrar al-Sham and al-Nusra, both of which were significantly spent forces after suffer-ing mass defections to ISIS following the al-Qaeda divorce.

By contrast, rebel forces in Idlib, Aleppo, the Damascus countryside, and Deir Ezzor had fought the regime's forces and more or less governed their liberated areas for about a year before ISIS was formed and could simply move in to conquer the con-querors.

In Iraq ISIS's reign has been characterized by much the same native-foreigner dichotomy. In Mosul residents were alienated by jihadists moving in from Tal Afar, the border town where AQI resisted US forces in 2005 and dispatched child suicide bombers. Mosulawis look down on Tal Afarians, considering the mostly Turkomen population to be poor, uneducated, and unruly.

Similar complaints are often heard in other ISIS-controlled ter-ritories where raids carried out by members from one city or town on shops or residents in another are often ascribed to preexisting socioeconomic tensions.

ISIS'S DIVIDE-AND-RULE STRATEGY

ISIS is the first and only jihadist franchise in history to successfully pit members of the same tribe against one another. This was on grim display in August 2014 when members of the Shaitat in Deir Ezzor participated in the killing of hundreds of their fellow tribes-men, at the behest of ISIS. The same coerced fratricide happened again in the Iraqi town of Hit, where members of the Albu Nimr took part in the execution of dozens of their kinsman in October 2014. Such divide-and-rule tactics ensure that any tribal uprising against ISIS will necessarily be a fratricidal one.

In Qa'im, the other border town where the first rumblings of Sahwa were felt in 2005, a preexisting division between two tribes, the Karbala and the Mihlawiyeen, manifested in the position either eventually took on AQI. Members of the Karbala joined the Zarqawists, and the tribe lost dozens of its members in an American air raid against Rawa, where seventy insurgents were killed. Al-Mihlawiyeen, however, was opposed to AQI and later joined the Awakening councils.

Unsurprisingly, bribery has played its part in tearing tribes apart. In April 2013, after the rupture with al-Nusra, ISIS secretly sought to co-opt young tribal leaders by offering to share oil and smuggling revenues and promising them positions of authority currently held by their elders. Younger tribesmen were seen as more credible and popular, owing to their participation in the anti-Assad rebellion, whereas their seniors mainly sided with the regime or stayed neutral. One tribal figure from Albu Kamal explained how ISIS deftly used this generational-political divide in one prominent family months before it had even established any presence in the area. "They [ISIS] are giving him a portion of an oil well in the area," the figure told us in December 2013. "They know that if they are to be eradicated in our area, who would be able to rally up people around him? Most of the other tribes in our area have no leadership; we have leadership and influence. They give him money, they protect him and consult with him on everything. The other option is, they would assassinate him."

Such strategic forward-planning is what helped ISIS take otherwise impervious towns in Deir Ezzor in the summer of 2014, such as al-Muhassan, Shaitat, and Albu Kamal. In Mo Hassan, the seizure came as a shock to most local rebels, as the town was known to be hostile to ISIS. Its population is famously secular and has produced many professional soldiers and officers in the Syrian Arab Army. But ideology played no role whatsoever. ISIS simply bought its way in before it fought its way in, relying on the enormous stocks of American- and Saudi-made weapons it had seized from the Iraqi Security Forces in Mosul in June 2014.

ISIS AS MEDIATOR

ISIS has also shown itself to be remarkably adept at arbitrating disputes in tribal areas. It mediated a historic reconciliation in November 2014 between two warring tribes in the Syrian border town of Albu Kamal, ending what had amounted to a War of the Roses–style thirty-year argument between al-Hassoun and al-Rehabiyeen, whose members would occasionally fight each other. "We learned they had tensions so we brought both of them together and got them to reconcile," an ISIS member who was involved in the reconciliation told us. "They agreed and were happy."

As part of its administration of ruled territory, ISIS has appointed an emir in charge of "tribal affairs," a Saudi national known as Dhaigham Abu Abdullah, based in Qa'im. He receives envoys to discuss local grievances or complaints—in many cases, residents from newly captured towns in eastern Syria cross the nonexistent border to meet with Abu Abdullah as they would a federal court judge. "People are racing to win the trust of the State," said an ISIS member from Deir Ezzor, who accompanied one of those convoys of arbitration-seekers to Anbar. "[ISIS] is a new authority in our area and people rush to present themselves as leaders to push for their personal interests, and tribalism is above everything for these people. Our leaders know this, we're not stupid."

In areas where killings were carried out by fellow tribesmen or a tribe from a neighboring town, ISIS uses foreign jihadists or

leaders from other regions to keep the peace. Here the importa-
tion of non-natives appears to be well considered. Saddam al-Jamal,
who was responsible for the killing of seventy locals in his hometown of Albu Kamal, was not given a leadership role when ISIS
returned to the area. Instead, he was tasked with the management
of a refugee camp near Iraq. Al-Rafdan, the vengeance-taker from
Shuhail, was reassigned to Raqqa.

Unlike al-Assad, but rather like Saddam, then, ISIS has made
tribal outreach an integral part of its governing strategy, the better to
keep the impossibility of another Awakening an integral part of its
war strategy. Where it hasn't scared or tempted tribesmen into submission with propaganda about "repentance" and the consequences
of not seeking it, it has inserted itself as a buffer between feuding
clans, relying, no doubt, on the experience and hard-won knowledge
of its former Baathist leadership. Not for nothing did al-Baghdadi,
in announcing the formation of ISIS in April 2013, explicitly refer
to two categories of people: Muslims and the tribes of Syria.

ISIS's success in playing tribes, or members of the same tribe,
against one another is a product of policies it has followed since its
battlefield resurgence in 2011. It has followed a divide-and-rule
policy to ensure that social and tribal rivalry and hostility are more
pronounced than any unified enmity to ISIS. That will undoubtedly
complicate the issue of working with tribes to defeat ISIS militarily,
because even if some members of one tribe decide to become sahwats, chances are they'll be fighting their own kinsmen.

It is a fear often voiced by sheikhs in both Iraq and Syria.
As Frederic Wehrey of the Carnegie Endowment for International Peace wrote, ISIS "has proven to be a more adaptable and
entrenched opponent today than its predecessor was in the mid-
2000s, deploying a potent mix of extreme violence and soft power
to both coerce and co-opt the tribes. Underpinning all of this are
truisms that often elude tribal enthusiasts: tribal authority is fickle,

hyper-localized, often artificially constructed, and therefore hard to fully harness."

The volte-face situation in Iraqi Sunni areas was just as much a product of the policies of Nouri al-Maliki—and more directly the military campaign in Anbar in early 2014. The antigovernment protests in that province following the US withdrawal saw the rise of mainstream Sunni religious and tribal figures, politically in the protests camps and militarily in the Anbar desert—even though ISI was present in the background. Instead of taking these figures' concerns seriously, al-Maliki portrayed his military campaign in Anbar in unequivocally sectarian terms. In a speech he delivered on Christmas 2013, he characterized it as an ancient war between the partisans of the Prophet's grandson Hussain and the son of the first Ummayad ruler, Yazid, in the seventh century.

This disastrous miscalculation arguably cost al-Maliki his premiership. It certainly helped open the door for ISIS's return in Anbar. "Once things settle down, the tribes will realize how the [al-Assad and al-Maliki] regimes marginalized them and get back to their senses," the ISIS mediation official told us. "They are our people, but they need to know that they cannot get it their way. They have to understand we are the only ones who can help them and protect them."

ISIS's tribal strategy does have its limitations; the biggest being that it is still regarded as a temporary governing force, an ally that was made out of convenience or brute necessity. The tribes accept the temporary situation as the best of all worlds, and because they don't want their areas turned into combat zones. But they don't endorse ISIS ideologically or join it en masse because they calculate that its reign won't last forever. Smaller tribes are joining ISIS, many of them driven by power politics rather than any sympathy for takfirism or the caliphate.

14

AL-DAWLA

THE ISLAMIC "STATE" SLEEPER CELLS

Abu Adnan came early to the meeting with us in a five-star hotel in Sanliurfa, also known as Urfa, in southern Turkey, near the Syrian border. Abu Adnan was in his late thirties and had been referred by a contact as someone who had inside knowledge about ISIS. He introduced himself as a doctor who worked in makeshift hospitals in ISIS-controlled territories. He initially seemed curious to know what we thought of the "state," for which he provided medical services, and our appraisal of attitudes toward it in the Middle East and internationally. He listened attentively, as did a younger companion who sat next to him.

Then Abu Adnan came clean, revealing that he wasn't just a doctor but also an *amni*, a security official for ISIS. He declined to answer specific questions about his job and dodged others, but he proudly explained that there are dozens of men like him working with ISIS outside of Syria, many in neighboring countries. "A believer does not get stung from the same hole twice," Abu Adnan said, referring to a saying attributed to the Prophet Muhammad, which is more or less the Islamic equivalent of "Fool me once . . ."

"We cannot afford to wait for others to spy on us," he said. "Information is the foundation and the pillar for everything. We need to know if there are activities outside the borders that might affect us in the future. We need to have a presence outside our territories. We need to do all that without compromising the state, so it is important to have reliable, efficient, and trusted people doing that."

Amniyat, or security units, are one of the vital organs of ISIS intelligence and counterintelligence, developed thanks to the former Iraqi Mukhabarat officers in its ranks. Amniyat, in fact, is headed by Abu Ali al-Anbari, the former intelligence officer in Saddam's regime. In ISIS territories these units are known to carry out raids to arrest wanted individuals and to probe security-related cases. However, little else is publicly known about the work of Amniyat. Even within a local ISIS structure, they have to operate separately from other sectors, such as the clerical authority, the military, and *khidmat al-muslimeen* ("Muslim Services").

Another ISIS member, Abu Moawiya al-Sharii, who serves the organization as a *sharii*, or cleric, confirmed that walls of separation exist between and among local ISIS affiliates. "Each one has a speciality," Abu Moawiya said. "I don't know what the military commanders do or know, and they don't know what an amni knows."

Such separation of powers helps with ISIS's pretense of statehood, reminiscent of the walled-off bureaucracies and departments in any government. But it also guards against infiltration and espionage—a particular obsession among ISIS's upper cadres and no doubt also a holdover from their Baathist origins. Even though ISIS tends to be more flexible in its recruitment and membership requirements than Nusra, it has established an elaborate and layered internal security apparatus to insulate its core leadership from provincial officers, and vice versa. "Our enemies are clever and determined," Abu Adnan said. "What we can do is to make sure the body of the state is strong, so that it can heal no matter how far they weaken it. So even if they destroy us in one area, you can be sure we're still there. We don't have to be exposed and visible."

At the hotel in Sanliurfa, Abu Adnan gave no outward sign of belonging to a takfiri organization known for its bearded and black-clad militants just miles to the south. He was clean-shaven and dressed in modern attire—more Mohamed Atta than Abu Bakr al-Baghdadi. Yet in the course of the interview he thumbed through his mobile phone photos to show himself mingling and posing with ISIS leaders in Raqqa, northern Hasaka, and Aleppo. He said that security officers, depending on the seniority of their position, have to learn a range of skills, from military training to political orientation to communication skills to clandestine activity. Abu Adnan claimed to have network of smugglers on the Syrian-Turkish border who would help potential fighters enter Syria to join ISIS. They operated in plain sight of the Turkish authorities and, like Abu Adnan, wouldn't be conspicuously out of place in any Western city.

"ISIS moves with incredible speed," Chris Harmer, the analyst at the Institute for the Study of War said, trying to explain how the terror army not only mobilizes forces but springs up in places where they previously had no discernible presence. "They have embedded, nested sleeper cells that start picking people off. We saw this in Mosul in June. Clearly, they had a list of people they were going to kill in the first seventy-two hours in the seizure of the city."

Mayser Hussain, a paramedic from Sahl al-Ghab, Hama, explained how ISIS has outfoxed the FSA there. "We have a group of 580 fighters from Sahl al-Ghab and Mount Shahshabu; many of them have secretly pledged allegiance to ISIS, as a sleeper cell. They're ready to fight. They haven't made it public because the FSA group in the region, Suqour al-Ghab Brigades, is dominant. Suqour al-Ghab has around four thousand fighters, so they can't fight it."

Hussain said that the group that pledged allegiance to ISIS used to be known as al-Farouq; now it's called Jabhat Sham. "I used to work with them when they were al-Farouq. Lately they offered me to join them as a paramedic. They told me that because I've been defending them in public and online, because I grew a beard and trimmed my mustache . . .'We are ready, and we are preparing ourselves to take the whole region.'"

ISIS, Hussain said, has experience recruiting from FSA cadres and offers incentives for mainstream rebels to defect to its ranks. A current policy is that anyone who has fought with the FSA, Ahrar al-Sham, or al-Nusra against ISIS and leaves to join al-Baghdadi's army is more likely to be promoted within its ranks. Abu Bilal, the FSA financier whose house was burned down by ISIS, told us the story of Obeida al-Hindawi, a former FSA fighter, who had worked for ISIS in secret for three to six months before declaring his affiliation. During that time, al-Hindawi received funding through local channels, all linked to external FSA donors. He was in regular communication with a Tunisian emir in al-Muhassan, where his mother's family hails from and where, as we examined in a previous chapter, ISIS has recruited tribesmen.

"During his secret allegiance, Obeida objected to our plan to join the fight against ISIS and he said that we should distance ourselves from it. He single-handedly recruited FSA members and convinced his former colleagues to join. Two of his brothers who led the brigade in the town were killed. He then became the commander of the brigade. Suddenly, he stopped fighting and said he no longer had any money or that his cars stopped working. It was all a ruse; he'd been with ISIS for a while at that point."

The one group that knew al-Hindawi's true affiliation was al-Nusra, which Abu Bilal said had better intelligence than anyone else in the area. "Nusra stormed Obeida's house in April or May. Everyone was asking why. Nusra said he was an ISIS member who paid money to people to join. He'd fled and went to Raqqa. He announced his allegiance when he returned from Raqqa to al-

Muhassan, as ISIS took Busaira, a town in Deir Ezzor, in June, and two days before they advanced into Nusra's stronghold in the town of Shuhail. He raised the ISIS flag and built a checkpoint and activated all the sleeper cells." Al-Hindawi was later involved in the execution of Shaitat tribesmen in nearby villages.

Zakaria Zakaria, a journalist from Hasaka, said that ISIS's infiltration of al-Nusra was equally impressive. When many al-Nusra jihadists in Hasaka wanted to defect to ISIS in early 2012, ISIS told them to stay put for the time being. "When ISIS made it public later on, already half of the members were with them, and the rest either fled to Turkey or joined."

OVERTAKING THE FSA

A mere twenty-six miles north of Aleppo, al-Bab had fallen to the FSA the previous summer and served as a fallback base for battalions laying siege to Aleppo, sections of which were being progressively peeled away from the regime.

One of the authors met Barry Abdul Lattif while reporting from al-Bab and the Bab al-Hadid quarter of Aleppo in late July 2012, in the midst of Ramadan. An early pro-revolution media activist, Lattif had earned a reputation among foreign correspondents for being a charismatic but unnerving adrenaline junkie. He loved to chase the regime's Sukhoi fighter jets and attack helicopters as much as he loved to take queasy Western journalists (such as us) into the most forbidding war zones in Syria. A day before our visit, he had sustained a small shrapnel injury, the result, we were told, of sniper bullets ricocheting off the ground in Salaheddine, which was then the fiercely contested Stalingrad of Aleppo, a city laid waste by aerial bombardment and round-the-clock shelling.

The al-Bab of Ramadan 2012 had offered one of the most encouraging signs of the anti-Assad revolution. The FSA presence guarding the town was mostly financed by local merchants, not foreign donors, and perhaps because it was salaried by the community it protected, it exhibited none of the taints of corruption or venality that would come to characterize the larger rebel camp later. Fighters stationed in the downtown barracks of the al-Khatib Brigade (one of the many units so named for Hamza al-Khatib, a thirteen-year-old boy who was killed by al-Assad's forces in 2011) would flash the peace sign or insist on posing for photographs.

But it was al-Bab's civil society that seemed so pregnant with promise. The Assad regime had all but destroyed al-Bab's city hospital and so, in order to tend to the wounded, local volunteers and professional doctors set up a makeshift field hospital in the basement of a mosque. They keep meticulous records of those they treated, which, they said, included civilians, FSA fighters, but also al-Assad's soldiers and even some shabiha. By nightfall, the streets of a pastoral Levantine hamlet were transformed into ecstatic scenes of protest and municipal action. Because all government services were stopped after al-Bab fell to the opposition, the people of the town had to take care of themselves. So FSA fighters put down their Kalashnikovs and picked up brooms and garbage bags, joined by white-gloved volunteers who rode around on motorbikes that looked like large hair dryers.

"Where are the terrorists here?" Lattif had asked that summer, mocking the regime's propaganda that everyone and anyone who stood up against it was al-Qaeda.

The terrorists arrived a year later.

Now living in Turkey and working for RMTeam, a Syrian research and humanitarian aid organization, Lattif recounted how ISIS moved into al-Bab and ultimately seized control of the entire town. "After they announced their 'state' and after they defected from al-Qaeda, they started to arrest activists around the liberated areas. For the first time, I saw it—it was August 2013, they came to al-Bab and they captured some bad FSA battalions."

What made the battalions "bad"? "They were thieves. They kidnapped some civilians and asked for money to set them free," Lattif said. "So Daesh arrested the battalions. In the early days, the civilians liked Daesh; they didn't know that it had its own project and its own plans for al-Bab."

The regime had never stopped bombarding al-Bab. According to Lattif, it had hit a school next to the hospital, which had by then been partially restored to working order. Twelve medics, Lattif said, were killed in that attack. Believing that the presence of takfiris would only invite further collective punishment on the town, the people began protesting against ISIS. "It lasted for three or four days. After that, some FSA brigades negotiated with Daesh for Daesh to leave the city. So they withdrew to the farmland around al-Bab. But they stayed there, just above the city, hovering, very close. And every day they captured new people, more FSA fighters from the bad battalions. They didn't yet capture any activists, they just issued threats against them—for me, especially. Almost everybody in the city asked me every day on Facebook if I was still free. They warned me that I was in danger, that Daesh was coming for me."

It was after ISIS seized near-total control of Raqqa, Lattif said, that it returned to al-Bab in force, creating a "siege" around the city. It began clashing with the FSA battalions as well as Ahrar al-Sham and al-Nusra fighters. "There were not too many men from those two groups in al-Bab at this point," Lattif said. The FSA was still the predominant insurgency, with around 1,500 fighters in al-Bab (many of them imported from neighboring areas, such as Minbij and Aleppo), followed distantly by Ahrar al-Sham, and then al-Nusra.

To force al-Bab into surrender, ISIS resorted to a favored tactic of the regime: starvation. It kept stealing the wheat from silos just outside the city, and the FSA was enlisted to stop the plunder lest the residents, already suffering, run out of bread. ISIS raided the main al-Bab headquarters for Liwa al-Tawhid, the largest brigade in Aleppo, killing around twenty-one men, Lattif said. Then the "regime bombarded the city with helicopters. It targeted only civilians in the center of the city. So Daesh took the advantage of that attack and came inside. It saw the opportunity created by the regime."

Al-Assad, Lattif insisted, was very crafty. "He wanted to give the impression to the civilians that Daesh and the regime are one. His goal was to start a civil war with the FSA."

By January 2014—the month that Syria's minor *sahwa* began— ISIS had brought snipers to strategic locations throughout al-Bab. They began picking off civilians and rebels. "They shot everyone," Lattif said. "I was in the al-Bab media office when Daesh took about a quarter of the city, in the southern district. Suddenly, everything went silent. There was no sound at all. All the fighting had stopped.

"We closed our office and went back to our homes. At about 11:00 at night, I went to take a look around the city to see what was happening. I saw Liwa al-Tawhid leave. There were no armed fighters left in al-Bab. I don't know where they went."

Ahrar al-Sham, he said, maintained a presence around the city but not inside it. "I stayed with them until morning. It was Friday night. I saw many Ahrar al-Sham fighters with cars with machine guns enter the city at around 4:00 a.m. Then, about an hour and a half later, three trucks, all filled with ammunition and rockets and all belonging to Ahrar al-Sham, drove out of al-Bab. There was an emir of Ahrar al-Sham who came over to us and asked the fighters I was with to leave our checkpoint because we were the last checkpoint in the city. Everyone had left for Aleppo, he told us."

ISIS took sole control of al-Bab that morning.

The safe house where one of the authors had stayed belonged to a rebel fighter named Abu Ali, a personal friend of Lattif. "He left his wife and children with my family. ISIS took control of his house. Abu Ali's family stayed for four, maybe five months. Now they're with him in Aleppo." Lattif's family, however, are still in al-Bab.

WHEN ISIS RULES

At first, Lattif said, ISIS treated civilians "gently," even assuming some of the civil administrative duties that had been handled by volunteers and the FSA. They fixed damaged roads, planted flowers in the street, cultivated gardens, and cleaned the local schools. But not long thereafter, Lattif said, ISIS instituted Sharia law, forcing women to wear what he called "the Daesh clothes"—the *niqab* or full head-and-face covering. "They banned hairdressing. Beard shaving is also forbidden. No woman can leave her house without a male escort now. There's no smoking, no *shisha* [hookah], no playing cards. They've made everything bad for civilians now. They force the people to go [to] the mosque for prayers, to close their businesses. No one can walk in the street during prayers. They kidnapped almost everybody working in the relief centers. About a month ago [November 2014], they closed the school. If you want to study now, you have to go to the Daesh school in the mosque."

Torture is common, too. ISIS has taken to arresting members of the FSA, whom they accuse of being agents of foreign intelligence services. Also sentences for various ISIS-designated crimes are carried out publicly in al-Bab's town square. These range from dismemberments to beheadings, depending on the offense. "They cut off heads and hands in the square. Do you remember the hookah place?" Lattif was referring to a popular cafe in central al-Bab where, in 2012, he had outlined for his vision of a free and democratic Syria. "The beheadings are taking place now in front of there. They shut down the hookah place, of course."

In the first months after ISIS seized control of al-Bab, the regime refrained from bombing the city. Then, in November 2014, the Syrian Air Force started up again, dropping barrel bombs—"flying IEDs," which have proved some of the deadliest ordnance used by the regime in the war— that killed sixty-two civilians in one air strike. According to Lattif, the Air Force dropped a barrel bomb in the main street of al-Bab, nowhere near any ISIS location.

This followed ISIS's eastern offensive against a series of regime military installations, such as the Tabqa air base in Deir Ezzor, the Division 17 base in Raqqa, and the Regiment 121 base in Hasaka—a noticeable uptick in the group's anti-regime sorties that followed directly after its blitz into central and northern Iraq. "The regime wants al-Bab to stay under the control of Daesh," Lattif said. "Assad has soldiers about fifteen kilometers west of al-Bab, but they never try to take the city back. Now, every time the regime sends its forces against the north areas of Aleppo, ISIS also attacks some places in the north. Both [the] regime and ISIS are attacking the FSA at the same time, but separately. The regime sees many benefits of ISIS's control of al-Bab and Raqqa—without them, allied forces won't strike Syria. The regime lost its authority in the beginning of the revolution. To get it back, it needs terrorists in Syria. Now there are many voices in the West saying that al-Assad is the only force against terrorists in the Middle East. Now the main players in Syria are the terrorists, Daesh, Jabhat al-Nusra, and the regime."

ISIS VS. ASSAD

Lattif's story conforms not just to what the Syrian opposition has been saying for years—that al-Assad and ISIS are, at the very least, tacit allies in a common war against the FSA and Islamist rebels—but to what regime loyalists have begun to say lately as well. To sack Tabqa, Division 17, and Regiment 121, ISIS relied on weapons looted from fallen Iraqi Security Forces bases in Ninewah and Anbar. As we've seen, prior to June 2014, when Mosul fell to ISIS, al-Assad's forces had largely refrained from fighting the takfiris in Syria while insisting in their propaganda that those were all they ever fought. After the fall of Mosul, however, the regime sensed a

renewed opportunity to partner with the West as an agent of counterterrorism. So Syrian warplanes began bombing dozens of ISIS
targets in Raqqa, or so they made a show of doing. "They did not
bomb the [ISIS] headquarters until June, and even then only after
it had been evacuated," Masrour Barzani, the Iraqi Kurdish intelligence head told the *Guardian* in late August 2014. "We are all
paying the price now."

After the takeover of Division 17, ISIS executed upward of
fifty Syrian soldiers, beheading some and then photographing the
lopped-off heads in Raqqa, according to Rami Abdel Rahman of
the London-based Syrian Observatory for Human Rights, who
told Agence France-Presse: "There is a clear shift in the ISIS strategy. It has moved from consolidating its total control in areas under
its grip. It is now spreading. For ISIS, fighting the regime is not
about bringing down Assad. It is about expanding its control."

This was all too much for many Assad loyalists. By the summer
of 2014, after seeing how little resistance ISIS faced in its eastern
offensive, many pro-regime activists began denouncing their own
side. In a video posted online, they accused the regime of nothing
short of treason at Tabqa air base, justifying their criticism by citing
a statement once made by Hafez al-Assad: "I don't want anyone to
be silent about a mistake." The video shows Syrian officers speaking
confidently about their fight against ISIS, but the narrator explains
that they were duped into believing that helicopters full of fifty tons
of ammunition and supplies were on the way. In the event, the only
helicopters that arrived carried no cargo to Tabqa but plenty of it
away: namely, the head of the air base, Adel Issa, along with of three
of his generals. This was eighteen hours before the base was stormed
by ISIS militants. The video also accuses Syria's information minister,
Omran al-Zoubi, of covering up this treachery and then lying about
its grisly aftermath. Assad's own cousin, Douraid al-Assad, is quoted
as saying: "I call for the expulsion of the defense minister, the chief

of staff, the air force chief, the information minister, and everyone involved in the fall of the Tabqa military base and its consequences." Finally, the video ends with statements such as: "Our bullets—nine of them are directed to the traitors and one to the enemy."

Elia Samaan, a Syrian official with the Ministry of Reconciliation, had openly inquired as to the absence of the Syrian Air Force in the war against ISIS in June 2014, after al-Baghdadi's men tore back into Syria from Iraq with renewed vigor and much stolen matériel. Though he discounted the allegation that the regime in any way colluded or cooperated with ISIS, Samaan admitted to the *New York Times*'s Anne Barnard that fighting the terrorist group was not a "first priority" for Damascus. Instead, al-Assad had been all too "happy to see ISIS killing" the FSA and Islamic Front instead of his own troops. When the Syrian Air Force finally escalated its air campaign against ISIS, it ended up killing, as per Lattif's account, more innocents than militants. Khaled, an ISIS fighter, told Barnard, "Most of the air strikes have targeted civilians and not ISIS headquarters. Thank God."

MINBIJ

Where ISIS may have thrived in part from the Assad regime's malign neglect, it also benefited from savvy politicking against what Lattif called the "bad FSA battalions."

Ayman al-Zawahiri had counseled al-Zarqawi, in the early years of AQI, not just about the folly of slaughtering Iraq's Shia, but about the need for effective Islamic governance in the areas ruled by al-Qaeda in Iraq. "[I]t's imperative that, in addition to force, there be an appeasement of Muslims and a sharing with them in governance," al-Zawahiri wrote his field commander in 2005. What he had advocated was something akin to the steady application of jihadist soft power. While clearly shirking al-Zawahiri's injunction about Shia, ISIS has more or less heeded his advice on creating popular incentives for Islamic governance. Minbij is a case in point.

A city of approximately two hundred thousand situated strategically between Aleppo, Raqqa, and the Turkish border, Minbij was abandoned by Syrian regime forces in November 2012, after which residents set up a municipal administration for self-rule. Soon, the city became an important but temporary symbol for the Syrian revolution that a post-Assad state needn't be a Hobbesian nightmare at all. That idyll lasted for about a year.

Accusations that nationalistic or secular rebel groups were behaving like brigands or gangsters were rife throughout Syria, often making more hard-line Islamist factions, including al-Nusra, seem models of discipline and fairness by comparison. Fortified with nearly all of al-Nusra's former foreign fighter contingent, ISIS established a base in the city in April 2013, operating side by side with several other armed factions, and continued to serve as a small but feared gendarmerie of about fifty men.

ISIS used its base to quietly reach out to the local population, inviting people to its *madhafa* (meeting place) to socialize and also to learn about al-Baghdadi's broad Islamic project for the region. ISIS mediated disputes and responded to complaints from locals, acting as de facto mukhtars in a city devoid of any state authority. However, ISIS's presence in Minbij grew steadily and quietly; rented houses were used as secret weapon and ammunition stockpiles, making the true extent of the jihadist presence publicly calculable. Also, its policy of arbitration grew less transparent and more severe. ISIS arrested FSA fighters without resorting to the Sharia commissions established by the rebels; it intimidated secular activists and controlled whatever resources it could lay its hands on to try and buy off the rest of the population through the dispensation of social services. It kept its fighters away from the front lines and instead struck tactical deals with FSA and other Islamist groups: in exchange for suicide bombers, who could be used to detonate

VBIEDs at regime checkpoints or to blow up military installations with surplus matériel, the rebels who were fighting al-Assad's forces would share their war booty with ISIS. By September 2013 ISIS's heavy-handedness and its play for monopolistic control of the city's services boiled over into outright confrontation with rival groups.

It declared war against Kurds in Minbij, vowing to "cleanse" the region of the Kurdistan Workers' Party (PKK), whose Syrian branch, the Democratic Union Party (PYD) of Kurdistan was the most powerful armed faction among Syria's Kurdish minority.

In October rebel forces in Minbij seized the flour mills from ISIS and told the jihadists to refrain from bypassing military and Sharia councils in the city in the settlement of public disputes. When the rebels in Aleppo and Idlib declared war against ISIS in January 2014, local forces in Minbij overran the ISIS base and killed or captured all of its fighters.

However, according to several residents from Minbij who spoke to the authors, locals *sympathized* with ISIS and lamented its expulsion. "People did not see anything but good things from ISIS, even though they did not like its religious ideas," said resident Shadi al-Hassan. "They also know that those who fought it were the worst people in the area." ISIS's retreat from Idlib and northern Aleppo helped it return to Minbij with a vengeance. It took control of the city after it sent reinforcements from Raqqa and northeastern Aleppo. Soon it established a full-fledged system of governance, impressing city denizens and displaced refugees alike. Hard as it may be to believe, given the luridness of ISIS's atrocities, Syrians actually flocked in large number to join the jihadist group or work with it at the local level. ISIS members had different roles: some were dedicated to fighting, while others acted as security, administered medical services, operated bakeries, ran Sharia courts, and so on. For the local community, the difference was quickly felt: ISIS provided safety and security; its methods of justice were swift, and nobody was exempt from punishment, including its own fighters who deviated from the strict moral code it had laid down. Consequently, kidnappings, robberies, and acts of extortion all but disappeared.

Ayman al-Mit'ib, a Minbij resident who since November 2013 had been internally displaced in Minbij, said, "There is no absolute support for its acts but no absolute opposition to its acts either. The reason why people support the Islamic State is its honesty and practices compared to the corruption of most of the FSA groups. Some FSA groups joined it, too."

The story of how ISIS grew in Minbij rings true in other areas under its control, particularly where FSA factions failed to rein in corruption or human rights abuses. A defector from the Syrian army, for instance, told the *Guardian* in November 2013 how ISIS operated like a virus in Syria by taking over other battalions and the territories they controlled. "What they do is attack the weaker units on the pretext that their commander is a bandit or a looter—they only fight one force at a time," he said, adding that once ISIS was ensconced in a city, it spread outward, seizing towns and villages surrounding that urban hub.

Indeed, one of the first rebel leaders to be publicly executed by ISIS was Hassan Jazra of Ghuraba al-Sham. Jazra had been a watermelon merchant before the revolution, then a peaceful protestor against al-Assad, and finally a rebel who stole to finance his military activity. In an obituary for Jazra, journalist Orwa Moqdad wrote, "Aleppo knew Hassan Jazra as a thief. Yet he did not leave his post at the front for a year and a half in the face of regular army attacks. He was a son of the protest movement who was driven by deteriorating circumstances to become a military leader . . .that became increasingly typical over the course of the war." ISIS executed him, along with six of his fighters, in November 2013. The execution was used by ISIS to prove a point: those who sought self-gain from the war, or who strayed from a pure revolutionary path, were as bad as the regime. Although in death Jazra's reputation depended on whom you asked, for ISIS his execution was a necessary form of justice. Its popularity went up accordingly. After that, it began to assert itself even more in rebel-held areas.

Governance has been a winning strategy for ISIS. Its model of governance has driven many to join its ranks, work with it, or at least not to oppose its existence in their areas. Since this aspect is key to its existence and survivability, it is important to understand how the group set out to winning hearts and minds despite its pathological brutality.

When the Syrian rebels started to control areas across the country, lawlessness was somewhat tolerated by the local communities as a necessary price before the removal of the regime. Also, as it came to be exposed later, some FSA-affiliated groups engaged in theft and robbery and claimed the Assad forces were behind it. As time went by, however, lawlessness became more pronounced and a major source of grievance for the local communities. Some FSA factions opted to leave the front lines and busy themselves with moneymaking activities in their areas. Factionalism, profit-making, and incompetence started to alienate people.

Toward the end of 2012, independent Islamist factions started to gain a foothold as they proved to be more effective, in terms of governance and fighting, than the ragtag militias of the FSA. Across the country, Islamists began to hold sway in rebel-held areas. They established Sharia committees, regulated resources, and ran government facilitates. In some areas, al-Nusra worked with Islamists to strengthen the enforcement mechanism of the Sharia courts. But the model did not prove sustainable for several reasons.

Since most of Islamist insurgents received financial backing from a variety of donors who demanded a say in how the money would be spent, division was inevitable. Ideological differences also contributed to the inability to establish strong courts and security forces. Islamists were also more attuned to the local communities and could enforce Sharia law only through mediation and public consent, especially when the matter involved another armed group or a powerful family. Even al-Nusra, which was far more powerful and disciplined than other forces up until the rise of ISIS, had to retract some of its decisions to avoid clashes with local families. Al-Nusra, as well as Islamists, also shied away from enforcing their rules to avoid alienating the population.

ISIS's model was high-risk. It was consistent and determined about enforcing its rules, often at the cost of turning more powerful local forces against it. Even at times when it seemed clear that ISIS had little future in Syria—around February 2014, for instance—it insisted on its ways. It would not tolerate any rivalry or recognize any Sharia commissions other than its own. It demanded uniformity at any cost. "If you're an FSA commander and you have a civilian relative, [FSA and other rebels] would accept mediation," said Hassan al-Salloum, a former rebel commander from Idlib residing in Antakya, Turkey, referring to the time when ISIS was still a marginal player in Syria. "But with ISIS, if I complain about an FSA member, they would go and bring him to interrogate him. They would not accept mediation. People started to go to complain to them. People made them intervene. A person comes to them and asks for help. FSA would not do it. ISIS gets you what you want, and then you start talking about it. If I hit one of my soldiers, he goes to ISIS. They give him weapons, salary, pocket money."

Once ISIS controls an area, it establishes a semblance of order and shows zero tolerance for any rivalry or public display of weapons. It immediately disarms the local communities, primarily of heavy weapons. For Syrians who lived under the control of FSA militias, the change was welcome. "You can drive from Aleppo to Raqqa to Deir Ezzor and into Iraq, and nobody will bother you," a resident of Deir Ezzor said. "Before, you'd have to be stopped at ad hoc checkpoints and you [would] have to bribe this and tolerate that."

Lawlessness is even more irksome for those who work in transportation or trade or live in areas that have oil fields. Whole armed groups were formed to control oil fields, impose road taxes, escort oil traders, perpetrate smuggling, or to accumulate wealth in any way possible. Constant shooting, random killing, kidnapping, and extortion were common in most places. It was often the case that when a person with heavily armed relatives killed another person, the family of the victim despaired of justice, unless they had allies in a militia that could ask for justice through a Sharia commission. The situation changed 180 degrees when ISIS came. People seemed pleasantly surprised at first, sometimes to the extent that they would overplay their sense of relief. "We never felt this safe for twenty years," said one old resident of Deir Ezzor. "We no longer hear shooting. We no longer hear so-and-so killed so-and-so. We can travel with no problems." Later, the same people expressed satisfaction with the current situation but were less keen to praise ISIS's rule.

One of the most cited praises for ISIS in its territories is that it gets the job done. Unlike the FSA and Islamist groups, ISIS will send a patrol to fetch someone if another person files a complaint about him. Even if the complaint in question dates back to the years before the uprising, said one resident who was involved in such a case, ISIS will settle the situation if the person has the appropriate documents. Rifaat al-Hassan, from Albu Kamal, told the story of an uncle who lost hundreds of thousands of Syrian pounds years before the uprising, in a fraud scheme by a local businessman. When ISIS controlled the city of Albu Kamal, the fraudulent man was arrested and forced by ISIS to return all money taken unlawfully.

More important, laws apply to ISIS members and commanders too; ISIS has executed scores of members and commanders for unlawfully profiteering or abusing power. In November 2014, ISIS executed one of its leaders in Deir Ezzor after it accused him of embezzlement and robbery. According to the group, the commander robbed residents after claiming they were apostates. Similar stories are commonly told by members of communities under ISIS control. Imad al-Rawi, from the Iraqi border town of Qa'im, who pledged allegiance to ISIS in August 2014, spoke of ten ISIS members who were executed because they sold tobacco they seized from smugglers. "When they raid shops that sell tobacco, they don't burn the tobacco," al-Rawi said. "When they raid a house, they also steal from it. The state executed them when it discovered them. None of those members smoked, they just sold the tobacco."

With such tactics, ISIS established itself as a viable law enforcer and won credit from two important societal segments: those who were disillusioned with the Syrian revolution and started to reminisce about safety and security under the regime, and those who were alienated by the FSA and Islamist factions. For those categories, among others, ISIS served an acceptable temporary role. "The regime made mistakes and repeated them," said Ghassan al-Juma, from Hasaka. "The FSA, too, made mistakes, and nobody could stop them. But when ISIS makes mistakes, it does not repeat them. You go and complain. If nobody responds to your complaint, you go to the perpetrator's leader, and you always get what you want if you are right."

In Iraq ISIS also sought to avoid the mistakes it had made in the years prior to the Awakening councils. Part of its strategy in the areas it controlled was to win hearts and minds and reach out to the local community leaders. After the takeover of Mosul, ISIS members avoided being heavily present in the streets. Residents of Mosul said that in the first weeks after the Iraqi Security Forces left the city, most of the fighters roaming the streets were from the neighborhoods.

In Mosul and elsewhere, ISIS allowed local forces to govern their own state of affairs, especially in areas where it felt relatively secure or lacked manpower. The reduced visibility of ISIS helped establish confidence in the new order, especially in the Iraqi cities. In Syrian areas, before it established control, ISIS had less leeway to do so given the dominance of hostile rebel groups. Instead, it benefited from sleeper cells and loyalists from within those communities to incrementally establish a foothold. The group's notorious brutality helped it create a sense of calm in the first days before it started reaching out to people.

"People were terrified of ISIS because its reputation preceded it," said al-Rawi from Qa'im. "At first, people avoided them, but once they started meeting people in mosques and engaging them, people became too comfortable with them. They liked their dedication and slowly started working with them even if they were still not with them. [ISIS] interfered when they had to. Local people were more present."

That is still particularly the case in areas where ISIS is in need of manpower. After the takeover of Mosul, ISIS came up with a new system of membership for existing local forces that it still does not trust. It called them *munasir* ("supporter")—to be distinguished from *ansar*, a term jihadists use to refer to local members of a group as opposed to *muhajirin*, or foreign fighters. A munasir has to pledge allegiance to ISIS without having access to its structure. These second-tier members receive salaries and mostly work to fill low-level municipality and police roles in their areas, tasks ISIS often refers to as khidmat al-muslimeen. This strategy helps ISIS be less visible and thus more capable of dodging responsibility, and increases rivalry within the local community over governance. ISIS can call on such forces to serve as reinforcement to its troops on the front lines, such as in Kobane, according to residents in Raqqa. Despite the leeway it allows for local forces, ISIS still has an overarching military, religious, and political control.

The combination of brute force and effective governance means that the local population has little motivation and a huge deterrent to rise up against ISIS, particularly in the absence of a viable and acceptable alternative. Such policies also make it much harder for any force from outside to retake these areas from ISIS, owing to the difficulty of filling the void and forming new alliances with the local communities.

EVERYWHERE AND NOWHERE

While it tends to be minimally visible as a military force, ISIS also refrains from micromanaging a town as much as possible. Local forces and their relatives often run day-to-day administrative affairs. Typically when ISIS takes over a new town, the first facility it establishes is a so-called Hudud Square, to carry out Sharia punishments, such as crucifixions, beheadings, lashings, and hand-loppings. (This is the area in al-Bab that Barry Abdul Lattif referred to as the town square, just opposite the shuttered hookah cafe.) It then establishes a Sharia court, police force, and security operation station. The work of Sharia police, known as *hisbah*, is not restricted to the implementation of sharia, but also to the regulation of the marketplace, and these police forces are more active in urban centers. ISIS divides regions into wilayat (provinces, of which there are roughly sixteen in Iraq and Syria) and smaller *qawati'* (townships). One military commander, one or more security commanders, and a general emir are appointed for each township. They all answer to a *wali* (governor).

Top leaders don't live in the same province they rule. For example, the governors of Minbij, al-Bab, and the parts of Deir Ezzor ISIS designated as Wilayat al-Khair (from the city of Deir Ezzor to the borders of Albu Kamal) tend to live in Raqqa or in Shaddadi, in Hasaka. The governor of Wilayat al-Furat (Albu Kamal and Qa'im) lives in Iraq and rarely travels to Syria. The same applies to the governors of Iraqi provinces.

Raqqa and Mosul serve as ISIS's de facto capitals, and envoys from its territories often meet in palaces occupied by the group. ISIS members are instructed to display very few of their weapons in public; as in Minbij, they hide arms in confiscated homes.

Checkpoints are also manned by a small number of fighters, in some cases by those who have recently joined ISIS and are still undergoing basic training.

When ISIS security units carry out an operation, foreign and local fighters from the town and nearby towns gather as reinforcements. The exaggerated show of force in cases of security operations is a hallmark of ISIS's deterrent strategy. This everywhere-but-nowhere strategy serves at least two purposes for ISIS. First, it deters local forces from rebelling against it, because it allows flexibility for locals to run their own affairs, within limits. Second, it enlists ISIS as the paramount conflict resolver. It is very common for residents to voice their anger about one another rather than about ISIS as an organization, with some going so far as to claim that foreign fighters are more disciplined and better behaved than natural-born residents.

ISIS allows fighters from other groups to keep their arms after it overruns an area, so long as these fighters continue to fight exclusively on the front lines. Anyone who receives weapons, ammunition, and food from ISIS must report to an ISIS emir and serve a set number of hours per week. Leave of absences from the battlefield require the relinquishing of weapons. Members of other groups have to follow a similar pattern if they wish to govern in their areas. In Fallujah and newly captured areas in Syria, ISIS offers a stark choice: pledge allegiance or leave. "At first, ISIS sets harsh conditions to pressure them," an FSA fighter from Deir Ezzor said of the jihadists' administration of the province in the summer of 2013. "It tells them that if you don't turn up at the [Deir Ezzor] airport regularly, you have to hand over your arms."

Disarming the local communities is also key to residents accepting ISIS. During FSA rule, buying and carrying weapons became necessary protection for moving from place to place in the face of rampant lawlessness and theft. As one resident from Hasaka put it, "Everybody carried weapons, from children on up. If you didn't have a gun, you'd walk into the market and be scared. If you got into a small fight, you were doomed." ISIS thus caters to popular fears about the absence of law and order by offering itself as the only alternative to societal collapse. Like any government, it seeks to retain a monopoly on violence.

TAKFIRINOMICS

ISIS has married its authoritarian governance with a remarkably successful war economy. FSA and Islamist groups that controlled oil fields in eastern Syria, for example, did dedicate some of the revenue to run schools and supply electricity, telecommunications, water, food, and other services. Some villages and towns saw a decline in such services because ISIS distributed oil revenue to other towns under its control in Syria and Iraq, establishing its own pan-territorial patronage system. As a result, in oil-rich areas, warlordism—a side effect of strictly localized rebel governance—dropped steadily.

ISIS also forced municipality personnel to work, unlike previous groups that had allowed Syrian state employees to continue to receive their salaries (mostly from the regime) while they sat at home and did nothing, no doubt with attendant kickbacks. "The streets are cleaner now; 70 percent of the employees were not working, even though they received salaries," said a former media activist with the FSA from Deir Ezzor. "They cancelled the customary day off on Saturday; they're supposed to make Thursday the day off instead."

Regulations and price control are another area in which ISIS's governance proved successful. It banned fishermen from using dynamite and electricity to catch fish. It also prohibited residents in the Jazira from using the chaos of war to stake new land claims, principally in the Syrian desert, where they had tried to build new homes or establish businesses, much to the chagrin of their neighbors. ISIS also limited the profit margins on oil by-products, ice, flour, and other essential commodities. Before ISIS controlled eastern Syria, an oil well produced around thirty thousand barrels per day, and each barrel sold for two thousand Syrian pounds—eleven dollars at the current exchange rate. Local families that worked in refineries would make two hundred liras (a little more than one dollar) on each barrel they refined primitively. After ISIS took over, a barrel of oil became cheaper because it fixed the price of a liter of oil at fifty pounds (thirty cents).

ISIS also banned families from setting up refineries close to residences under the threat of confiscation, a policy that led some families to quit the oil business altogether. Collectively, price control and regulations balanced the decline in resources and services.

Subsidies from Gulf countries, where many of those who live in ISIS-controlled areas work, also helped some families afford electricity-generating engines and oil by-products. "Those in the Gulf who used to send once a month now send twice a month because they understand the situation," said the former FSA media activist. "Also, there is no big difference in value. In 2010 a kilo of chicken was 190 pounds [$1] and is now 470 [$2.60]."

Oil was a major revenue generator for ISIS until the coalition air strikes began. Before that, ISIS was thought to have earned millions of dollars a month from oil in Syria and Iraq—$1 to 2 million a day. The revenue dropped significantly after the air strikes. But oil smuggling to neighboring countries such as Turkey and Jordan, and to other areas in Syria and Iraq, still makes significant revenue for ISIS. The sharp decline in oil production affected civilians more than it affected ISIS, which could still generate wealth from other sources, but it hampered ISIS's ability to provide for the local communities, especially much-coveted materials such as gas cylinders. "I estimate that the impact of air strikes was 5 percent," said the media activist, who still lives in Deir Ezzor. "They affected oil primarily. Food is plenty, and most of it comes from Turkey or Iraq. Borders are open; if you don't like prices here, you go to Anbar. I see the situation as normal."

ISIS's oil market savvy has impressed and shocked many observers, although Derek Harvey isn't one of them. "I know for a
fact that the Saddamists who were smuggling the oil in the '90s, to
evade UN sanctions, are now doing so for ISIS," he said. "People
are saying that they're selling it for thirty-five dollars a barrel. What
we bombed recently is some of the local refineries. If you're selling
it at that price, it's fifty to fifty-five dollars off the current market
price. But here's what happens: these middlemen are selling it, and
there's a kickback coming back in to ISIS's senior leaders. They're
getting another twenty, twenty-five dollars a barrel in kickbacks,
but that's not on the books or being factored in by everybody. It's
going back into the kitty of financiers at the top of the pyramid. The
ISIS fighters in Deir Ezzor would not be aware of that."

Locals in eastern Syria had learned to survive on remittances
from the Gulf and local economies even before the uprising. High
oil prices led many to rely less on agricultural products since the
energy had to be spent pumping water from the Euphrates or
Tigress rivers to their farmlands many miles away. After the war
started, cheaper oil revived the Syrian agribusiness—smuggling and
livestock trade markets began booming again. When ISIS seized
control of the Jazira, people were already buying their own oil for ir-
rigation and electricity and didn't need to rely on subsidized services.

Germany's foreign intelligence agency, the Bundesnachrichten-
dienst (BND), has cautioned against "overblown" speculation about
ISIS's high oil revenue because there is a tendency to discount the
massive overhead and spending inside its territories. But, as per
Harvey, ISIS pockets most of this revenue, as it sometimes taxes
residents for services supplied by the regime, such as electricity
and telecommunication. Unlike Islamist groups that operated re-
gime-established facilities for the local communities gratis, ISIS
has developed a surcharge economy to replenish its own coffers.

ISIS also makes millions from *zakat* (different forms of Islamic alms payable to the state). Zakat is extracted from annual savings or capital assets (2.5 percent), gold (on values exceeding $4,500), livestock (two heads out of 100 heads owned by a farmer), dates, crops (10 percent if irrigated by rain or a nearby stream or river, and 5 percent if irrigation costs money), and profits (2.5 percent).

ISIS also imposes annual taxes on non-Muslims living in its territories, especially Christians (1.25 grams of gold for the rich and half of that for moderate-income individuals). It makes money by stealing dressed up as civil penalties: it confiscates the properties of displaced or wanted individuals or as punishment for fighting ISIS. This includes, of course, enormous stocks of weapons and ammunition as part of its community disarmament policies.

While donations from foreign sponsors constitute a meager percentage of its treasury, deep-pocked individuals, whether foreign donors or members who have joined the group, still contribute to the group.

More significantly, *ghanima* (war spoils, which in ISIS's definition encompasses robbery and theft) is one of the group's largest and most valuable sources of income. ISIS seized millions of dollars worth of American and foreign military equipment after it forced three Iraqi divisions to flee in June 2014, and it has also seized large stockpiles of weapons as well as equipment, facilities, and cash from Syria's regime and rebel groups. Artifacts are also lucrative for ISIS—one man interviewed in Turkey said trade in artifacts grew during ISIS rule, with one of his cousins smuggling into Turkey golden statues and coins found in Mari ancient ruins, eleven kilometers away from Albu Kamal.

EPILOGUE

Days before the video showing James Foley's beheading was aired around the world, Iraq's authoritarian prime minister, Nouri al-Maliki, resigned under US and Iranian pressure, ostensibly addressing the political impasse for which the rise of ISIS has been blamed. His successor was a fellow member of the Dawa Party, the sixty-two-year-old Haider al-Abadi, who had spent years of exile in London. Many Iraqi Sunnis we talked to at the time praised al-Abadi as an improvement on al-Maliki, but none thought he could or would make a substantive difference in the way Iraq was governed. This, they all said, owed to the endemic sectarian dimensions of the nation's politics and Tehran's overweening influence on Baghdad.

It didn't bode well for the new premier's tenure that in one of his first press conferences he advocated a strategic partnership between the United States and Iran in combating ISIS—a partnership that many Sunnis believed started in 2003. "The American approach us to leave Iraq to the Iraqis," Sami al-Askari, a former Iraqi MP and senior advisor to al-Maliki, told Reuters. "The Iranians don't say leave Iraq to the Iraqis. They say leave Iraq to us."

One of the world's leading state sponsors of terrorism now presents itself as the last line of defense against terrorism. Quds Force commander Qassem Suleimani has overseen the creation of a multipronged shadow army consisting of the very same Special Groups not only responsible for killing American soldiers and countless Sunni civilians in Iraq, but now equally committed to propping up the murderous regime in Damascus. According to Phillip Smyth, there are now more than fifty "highly ideological, anti-American, and rabidly sectarian" Shia militias operating and recruiting in Iraq. The conditions have been recreated, in other words, for exactly the same sectarian holy war envisioned by al-Zarqawi in 2004—only this time, it will be played out in two countries at the same time. As a former Iraqi official put it, "I'm not very hopeful. This is almost like a last chance for Iraq to remain as a unified state."

Despite al-Abadi's calls for national unity, the sectarian bloodletting continues. According to Human Rights Watch, ISF and Shia militias have executed 255 prisoners in six villages and towns since June 9, 2014, a day before the fall of Mosul. Eight of the victims were boys younger than eighteen. On August 22, 2014, the Musab Bin Omair mosque in Diyala—where ISIS has anticipated its fiercest battles—was raided by ISF personnel and Asaib Ahl al-Haq militants dressed in plainclothes. They massacred dozens.

Al-Abadi's Interior Minister, Mohammed al-Ghabban, is also a senior official in the Badr Organization, which means that a notorious death squad has once again been given purview over Iraq's police force. The Badr has lately been accused of "kidnapping and summarily executing peopl[and] expelling Sunnis from their homes, then looting and burning them, in some cases razing entire villages," according to Human Rights Watch's Iraq researcher Erin Evers. "The [United States] is basically paving the way for these guys to take over the country even more than they already have."

Nearly every major Iraqi offensive against ISIS has borne Suleimani's fingerprints. In late October, when ISIS was driven from Jurf al-Sakher, a town about thirty miles southwest of Baghdad along the Euphrates River Valley, agents of the Quds Force and Lebanese Hezbollah were embedded with some seven thousand Iraqi Security Forces soldiers and militiamen, providing training and distributing arms. The entire operation was planned by Suleimani.

Indirectly supported by US warplanes, Asaib Ahl al-Haq and Kata'ib Hezbollah, a US-designated terrorist entity, played a lead combat role in ending ISIS's months-long siege of Amerli, a Shia Turkomen town of about fifteen thousand, in November 2014. Suleimani was photographed smiling in Amerli shortly after it was retaken.

US Abrams tanks have been photographed in the possession of Kata'ib Hezbollah, making ISIS not the only terrorist organization to have requisitioned American materiel intended for the ISF.

What has the last seven months of US-led air strikes in Syria and Iraq accomplished? The Pentagon announced that sixteen out of the twenty oil refineries ISIS had been using to fund its activities were rendered inoperable. According to Dr. Hisham al-Hashimi, by the end of 2014, ISIS had lost 90 percent of its oil-driven revenue, nine out of eleven weapons warehouses in Iraq, and three out of ten warehouses in Syria. Adding to this seemingly impressive list of damage was the elimination of thirty ISIS leaders in air strikes. These included a dozen high-ranking officials such as Abu Muslim al-Turkmani, al-Baghdadi's deputy, Ridwan Taleb al-Hamdouni, the "governor" of Mosul, and the military commanders of Ramadi, Salah ad-Din, Fallujah and Ninewah. Al-Abadi has claimed that al-Baghdadi himself was injured in a sortie on al-Qaim. Washington says that ISIS has lost around seven hundred square kilometers of terrain.

While it is certainly true that the momentum of ISIS's blitzkrieg in Iraq has been stalled considerably—it no longer threatens to take Erbil, much less Baghdad—its defeats so far have been tactical. "Purely from a military perspective, the single factor that stands out the most to me is that ISIS has always had the strategic initiative," said Chris Harmer. "There are times when they've been more active in one place than another. But they've never been on the strategic defensive. Tactically, they've been on the defensive: they took Mosul Dam, then lost it. They took Bayji Oil Refinery, then lost it. But is ISIS 'losing'? No."

ISIS has suffered mainly within enemy lines rather than in its geostrategic heartlands across Syria and Iraq. Sinjar and Bayji, for example, are crucial to the Kurds. Baqubah and Dhuluiya provide entryways into Baghdad and thus matter greatly to the ISF and Shia militias, which have ethnically cleansed them, according to Ayad Allawi, now the vice president for reconciliation. Despite some 1,700 air strikes, ISIS has still managed to advance in places where it has either a natural constituency or can dominate a Sunni population too fearful or indifferent to rise up against it. Two months into Operation Inherent Resolve, the jihadists sacked Hit, the town where Adam Such glimpsed an early and localized Sahwa in 2005. Other villages and hamlets in Anbar have fallen since.

As Derek Harvey demonstrated a decade ago, just because jihadists have been expelled from ethnically mixed terrain, such as Baghdad, doesn't mean they've been defeated or are less capable of conducting operations. ISIS continues to rule more or less uncontested in al-Bab, Minbij, Jarablous, Raqqa, southern Hasaka, Tal Afar, Qa'im, and outside the city center of Ramadi. Rebellion from within in these areas is extremely unlikely in the short term. In Haditha and Amiriya Fallujah, Sunni tribes are divided over what do about ISIS—and the consequence is tribal infighting, which only forecloses on the possibility of another Awakening.

According to al-Hashimi, ISIS has compensated for its 10 percent territorial losses in Iraq by *gaining* 4 percent in Syria, though you wouldn't know it to listen to US officials. "The strategy with respect to Syria has not changed," Alistair Baskey, a spokesman for the National Security Council, told reported in November 2014.

"While the immediate focus remains to drive [ISIS] out of Iraq, we and coalition partners will continue to strike at [ISIS] in Syria to deny them safe haven and to disrupt their ability to project power."

Except that ISIS has more than a "safe haven" in Syria, and it continues to project even more power since Operation Inherent Resolve began. Today it controls roughly a third of the geography of the country. Even in the most fiercely contested battle for Kobane, it continues to hang on to parts of the Syrian-Turkish border town, which even the White House sees as more "symbolic" than strategically essential—and this is three months into the most intense US aerial sorties waged in all of Syria.

Those who have understood the long-term challenges posed by ISIS have not been rewarded. In October 2014 Defense Secretary Chuck Hagel sent a two-page memo to the National Security Council outlining his concerns about America's strategy in Syria. He was fired as defense secretary at the end of the following month, in part because he cautioned that the continued failure to confront the al-Assad regime—which members of the Obama administration have rightly called a "magnet" for terrorism—would only redound to al-Baghdadi's benefit. It has also redounded to al-Assad's.

"What's amazing is how we keep making the same mistakes over and over again, in Iraq but also in the broader Middle East," Ali Khedery told us. "I've seen senior American officials waste time tweeting about the number of air strikes. Who cares about these tactical developments? Sunnis are being radicalized at record proportions. A counterterrorism approach isn't going to work with ISIS. We saw that in Iraq, and we'll see it in Syria."

The law of unintended consequences reigns supreme. Just as US warplanes began striking ISIS locations in Syria, mainstream rebels who have received American weapons took to criticizing the operation for its one-sidedness. "The sole beneficiary of this foreign interference in Syria is the Assad regime, especially in the absence of any real strategy to topple him," Harakat Hazm (the Movement of Steadfastness) posted to its Twitter account in late September 2014. "Last Friday, for the first time I can recall, opponents of the government of President Bashar al-Assad burned an American flag," wrote Robert Ford, the former US ambassador to Syria who resigned in protest over the Obama administration's Syria policy, in the *New York Times*. That was in early October 2014.

Of course, the US isn't *only* targeting ISIS in Syria—it's also targeting Jabhat al-Nusra. In one strike, in the town of Kafr Daryan, Idlib, an ad hoc refuge for internally displaced Syrians was reportedly hit in an attempt to bomb installations belonging to al-Nusra, specifically a subunit of it known as the Khorasan Group, which the White House says was plotting attacks on Western targets. This has only aggravated Syrian grievances against America; as one rebel media activist put it, if "the raids had targeted the regime and a large number people had been killed by mistake, we would have said they were a sacrifice for our salvation." It has also strengthened al-Nusra, which has been joined by ISIS in waged localized, opportunistic campaigns against US-backed rebel groups, now branded as little more than mujahidin-hunting hirelings of the Pentagon. The White House's stated plan of training five hundred rebels a year for the sole purpose of fighting ISIS isn't set to start until the spring of 2015, but already it has had profound negative consequences on the battlefield.

True, the contingency that al-Nusra will ever formally reconcile with ISIS is remote. However, it doesn't have to in order for a jihadist civil war—or even a jihadist cold war—to affect the Western designs in the region, and at home. ISIS has pledged rhetorical solidarity with al-Nusra against a common "crusader" enemy in Syria. It has also offered its warm congratulations to Al-Qaeda in the Arabian Peninsula's recent handiwork in the West.

On January 7, 2015, Said and Chérif Kouachi, two French

brothers, slaughtered a dozen journalists and cartoonists at the offices of satirical magazine *Charlie Hebdo* in Paris. Two days later, one of the brothers' accomplices, Ahmed Coulibaly, seized the Hyper Cacher kosher market in the same city, killing four customers before the French police shot him.

The Kouachi brothers were part of a French cell responsible for sending men to join AQI in the early days of the insurgency. Like al-Zarqawi, both had been radicalized first in a mosque, and then in a prison. They read al-Maqdisi. Chérif was arrested before he could join the Sheikh of the Slaughterers.

Coulibaly has claimed inspiration and pledged allegiance to al-Zarqawi's successor, al-Baghdadi.

Many are now asking if the streets of Europe, and eventually the United States, are to serve as the blood-soaked arenas for a game of one-upmanship between a jihadist parent company and its former subsidiary. It's a good question.

More than eleven years after the United States invaded Iraq, a deadly insurgency adept at multiple forms of warfare has proved resilient, adaptable, and resolved to carry on fighting. A legacy of both Saddam and al-Zarqawi, ISIS has excelled at couching its struggle in world-historical terms. It has promised both death and a return to the ancient glories of Islam. Thousands have lined up to join it, and even more have already fallen victim to it.

The army of terror will be with us indefinitely.

NOTES

INTRODUCTION

x   Islamic State of Iraq and al-Sham: Technically "ISIS" no longer exists. The official name for the organization is now the Islamic State. We have stuck with "ISIS" purely for the sake of convenience, realizing that there's an intense debate on nomenclature. *Daesh,* which many of our interviewees use, is the Arabic acronym for "Dawla al-Islamiya fil Eraq wa Sham," or the Islamic State in Iraq and al-Sham. Although the acronym doesn't have a specific meaning, it is considered pejorative because of the hard sound of its pronunciation. The combination of letters in Arabic connotes thuggishness, harshness, and obtuseness.

CHAPTER 1

2   Zarqa was the biblical staging ground: Loretta Napoleoni, *Insurgent Iraq: Al-Zarqawi and the New Generation* (New York: Seven Stories Press, 2005) 29–30.

2   Zarqawi was an unpromising student: Napoleoni, *Insurgent Iraq,* 260.

2   He drank and bootlegged alcohol: Mary Anne Weaver, "The Short, Violent Life of Abu Musab al-Zarqawi," *The Atlantic,* July 1, 2006, www.theatlantic.com/magazine/archive/2006/07/the-short-violent-life-of-abu-musab-al-zarqawi/4983.

2   His first stint in prison: Loretta Napoleoni, "Profile of a Killer," *Foreign Policy,* October 20, 2009, foreignpolicy.com/2009/10/20/profile-of-a-killer.

2   Worried that her son was descending: Weaver, 2006.

3   It was a city of perpetual waiting: Jean-Charles Brisard, *Zarqawi: The New Face of Al-Qaeda* (New York: Other Press, 2005) 16.

4   If Azzam was the Marx: Fawaz A. Gerges, *The Far Enemy: Why Jihad Went Global* (New York: Cambridge University Press, 2005) 135.

4   Untold millions of dollars passed through: Lawrence Wright, *The Looming Tower* (New York: Vintage, 2007); Gerges, *The Far Enemy,* 134.

4   Some of the world's most notorious: Gerges, *The Far Enemy,* 76.

5   By the end of the decade: Peter L. Bergen, *The Osama bin Laden I Know: An Oral History of al Qaeda's Leader* (New York: Free Press, 2006), 64–65.

5   He had been the emir: Bergen, *The Osama bin Laden I Know,* 63, 66–67.

5   In late November 1989: Napoleoni, *Insurgent Iraq,* 52–53.

5   Theories as to the likely culprits: Bergen, *The Osama bin Laden I Know,* 93.

5   One of the arrivals: Weaver, 2006.

5   In the spring of 1989: Brisard, *Zarqawi,* 17.

6   Rather than return to Jordan: Ibid.

6   Among those were the brother of Khalid Sheikh Mohammed: Brisard, *Zarqawi,* 21.

6   Despite his remedial Arabic: Ibid.

6   He also met his future brother-in-law: Brisard, *Zarqawi,* 21; Bergen, *The Osama bin Laden I Know,* 32.

6   Al-Hami had lost a leg to a land mine: Weaver, 2006.

6   She traveled to Peshawar for the wedding: "هذا بيان للناس - أبو مصعب الزرقاوي," YouTube video, 34:05, posted by al ansaralshari3a, March 25, 2012, www.youtube.com/watch?v=EUrLMFautCI.

6   According to al-Hami: Brisard, Zarqawi, 22.
6   Al-Hami returned to Jordan: Brisard, *Zarqawi*, 23–24.
6   He cast his lot with the Pashtun warlord: Brisard, *Zarqawi*, 24.
7   It graduated the masterminds: "KSM trains at Sada camp," GlobalSecurity.org, last modified January 11, 2006, www.globalsecurity.org/security/profiles/ksm_trains_at_sada_camp.htm; "Hambali trains at Sada camp," GlobalSecurity.org, last modified January 11, 2006, www.globalsecurity.org/security/profiles/hambali_trains_at_sada_camp.htm.
7   As recounted by Loretta Napoleoni: Napoleoni, *Insurgent Iraq*, 55.
7   The first was "the days of experimentation,": Ibid.
7   The second was the "military preparation period,": Ibid.
7   Clausewitz for terrorists: Ibid.
7   Al-Zarqawi returned to Jordan in 1992: Brisard, *Zarqawi*, 28.
7   Their fears were proven out in 1993: Brisard, *Zarqawi*, 29.
8   Together, in a Levantine shadow play: Brisard, *Zarqawi*, 36.
8   Al-Maqdisi was a pedantic scholar: Brisard, *Zarqawi*, 37.
8   "He never struck me as intelligent": Jeffrey Gettleman, "Zarqawi's Journey: From Dropout to Prisoner to Insurgent Leader," *New York Times*, July 13, 2004, www.nytimes.com/2004/07/13/international/middleeast/13zarq.html
8   Al-Maqdisi first gave al-Zarqawi: Brisard, *Zarqawi*, 226–27.
8   Aware that the GID was tracking: Brisard, *Zarqawi*, 39.
8   He was charged and convicted: Weaver, 2006.
9   Amin was further instructed: Napoleoni, *Insurgent Iraq*, 64–65.
9   Both were sentenced in 1994: Brisard, *Zarqawi*, 43.
9   Time in prison made al-Zarqawi more focused: Weaver, 2006.
9   He got his underlings: Brisard, *Zarqawi*, 48.
9   "He could order his followers": Gettleman, 2004.
9   By means of coercion or persuasion: Brisard, *Zarqawi*, 48.
9   He beat up those he didn't like: Ibid.
10 "The note was full of bad Arabic, like a child wrote it": Gettleman, 2004.
10 Unable to develop arguments: Ibid.
10 At one point, he was thrown into: Napoleoni, *Insurgent Iraq*, 70.
10 It was in prison that al-Zarqawi: Napoleoni, *Insurgent Iraq*, 75–76.
10 The mentor-scholar helped: Weaver, 2006.
10 A few of these even caught the attention of bin Laden: Bruce Riedel, *The Search for Al Qaeda: Its Leadership, Ideology, and Future* (Washington, D.C.: Brookings Institution Press, 2010) 93–94.
10 According to "Richard," a former top-ranking counterterrorism official: Interview with former top-ranking counterterrorism official, December 2014.
11 Many Islamists who hadn't actually committed terrorism: Brisard, *Zarqawi*, 57.
11 Al-Zarqawi left Jordan in the summer of 1999: Brisard, *Zarqawi*, 59.
11 Al-Zarqawi was arrested briefly in Peshawar: Napoleoni, *Insurgent Iraq*, 97.
11 Told that he would only receive his passport back: Brisard, *Zarqawi*, 67.
11 Al-Zawahiri was present at the meeting: Bryan Price, Dan Milton, Muhammad al-Ubaydi, and Nelly Lahoud, "The Group That Calls Itself a State: Understanding the Evolution and Challenges of the Islamic State," Combating Terrorism Center at West Point, December 16, 2014, www.ctc.usma.edu/posts/the-group-that-calls-itself-a-state-understanding-the-evolution-and-challenges-of-the-islamic-state.
12 In the early 1990s al-Qaeda had targeted: Bergen, *The Osama bin Laden I Know*, 197.
12 One of these contacts was Abu Muhammad al-Adnani: Price et al., 2014.
13 The camp was built with al-Qaeda start-up money: Brisard, *Zarqawi*, 71–72.
13 According to former CIA analyst Nada Bakos: "Tracking Al Qaeda in Iraq's Zarqawi Interview With Ex-CIA Analyst Nada Bakos," Musings on Iraq blog, June 30, 2014, musingsoniraq.blogspot.com/2014/06/tracking-al-qaeda-in-iraqs-zarqawi.html.

NOTES

13 The physical activity at Heart: Interview with former top-ranking counterterrorism official, December 2014.
13 Al-Zarqawi fielded mainly Palestinian and Jordanian recruits: Brisard, *Zarqawi*, 72.
13 As the name implied, the Soldiers of the Levant were: Weaver, 2006.
13 Some of the camp's graduates: Napoleoni, *Insurgent Iraq*, 125–26; Brisard, *Zarqawi*, 88.
13 The Jordanian authorities claimed: Napoleoni, *Insurgent Iraq*, 125–26; Weaver, 2006.
13 Jund al-Sham grew exponentially: Weaver, 2006.
14 Repeatedly between 2000 and 2001: Ibid.
14 Repeatedly al-Zarqawi refused: Napoleoni, *Insurgent Iraq*, 98–99; Weaver, 2006.
14 "I never heard him praise anyone apart from the Prophet": Napoleoni, *Insurgent Iraq*, 98–99.
14 Whether owing to his arrogance: Weaver, 2006.
14 One of al-Zarqawi's lieutenants at Heart: Brisard, *Zarqawi*, 77.
14 After the September 11 attacks: Brisard, *Zarqawi*, 115.
14 The targets of this conglomerate were two: Napoleoni, *Insurgent Iraq*, 106–07; Brisard, *Zarqawi*, 115–16, 122.
14 On February 3, 2003: Napoleoni, *Insurgent Iraq*, 116–17.
15 "We first knew of Zarqawi . . .Interview with one of the authors, December 2014.
15 "Jihadists gain more from friendships . . .": Interview with one of the authors, December 2014.
16 Al-Zarqawi and his convoy: Napoleoni, *Insurgent Iraq*, 109.
16 According to a member of al-Zarqawi's entourage: Ibid.
16 Saif al-Adel, the al-Qaeda security chief: Price et al., 2014.
17 He visited a Palestinian refugee camp: Brisard, *Zarqawi*, 96, 99–100.
17 Shadi Abdalla, bin Laden's former bodyguard: Brisard, *Zarqawi*, 95.
17 Al-Zarqawi also went to Syria: Brisard, *Zarqawi*, 96.
17 A high-level GID source told: Weaver, 2006.
18 It was in deference to al-Zawahiri: Bill Roggio, Threat Matrix: A Blog of the Long War Journal, May 12, 2014, www.longwarjournal.org/threat-matrix/archives/2014/05/iran_owes_al_qaeda_invaluably.php
19 As early as October 2002: Riedel, *The Search for Al Qaeda*, 87–88; Gerges, *The Far Enemy*, 252.
19 A year later, bin Laden wrote a letter: Riedel, *The Search for Al Qaeda*, 88.
19 In opposition bin Laden advocated: Ibid.
19 He put out a global casting call: Riedel, *The Search for Al Qaeda*, 10–11, 87–89, 132.
19 To hurt the "far enemy,": Riedel, *The Search for Al Qaeda*, 88.

CHAPTER 2

20 Bin Laden's injunction was fully realized: Kevin Woods, James Lacy, and Williamson Murray, "Saddam's Delusions," *Foreign Affairs*, May/June 2006, www.foreignaffairs.com/articles/61701/kevin-woods-james-lacey-and-williamson-murray/saddams-delusions.
21 But he had very much prepared: Michael R. Gordon and Bernard E. Trainor, *The Endgame: The Inside Story of the Struggle for Iraq, from George W. Bush to Barack Obama* (New York: Vintage Books, 2013) 20–21.
21 He beefed up one of his praetorian divisions: Ibid.
21 In their magisterial history of the Second Gulf War: Ibid.
21 The man who anatomized this strategy: Gordon & Trainor, *The Endgame*, 18–20.
22 Added to their ranks were more disaffected Iraqis: Gordon & Trainor, *The Endgame*, 14; "Coalition Provisional Authority Order Number 1: De-Ba'athification of Iraqi Society," The Coalition Provisional Authority, May 16, 2003, www.iraqcoalition.org/regulations/20030516_CPAORD_1_De-Ba_athification_of_Iraqi_Society_.pdf; Sharon Otterman, "IRAQ: Debaathification," Council on Foreign Relations, April 7, 2005, www.cfr.org/iraq/iraq-debaathification/p7853#p9.

NOTES

23 To distinguish the latter from disfigured veterans: Brian Owsley, "Iraq's Brutal Decrees Amputation, Branding and the Death Penalty," Human Rights Watch/Middle East, June 1995, www.hrw.org/reports/1995/IRAQ955.htm.

23 The regime thus introduced a proscription: Napoleoni, *Insurgent Iraq*, 146.

23 Some of Iraq's new-minted faithful: Joel Rayburn, *Iraq After America: Strongmen, Sectarians, Resistance* (Stanford, California: Hoover Institution Press, 2014) 101.

23 Most of the officers who were sent to the mosques: Rayburn, *Iraq After America*, 102.

24 Many graduates of the program, Rayburn notes: Ibid.

24 One such person was Khalaf al-Olayan: Rayburn, *Iraq After America*, 113.

24 Mahmoud al-Mashhadani showed the folly: Rayburn, *Iraq After America*, 114.

25 "If you talk to the Shiites, they understand . . .": Interview with one of the authors, October 2014.

25 It was for this reason that George H. W. Bush: Gordon & Trainor, *The Endgame*, 5.

26 The elder Bush had hoped: Ibid.

26 The violent implementation of democracy: Rayburn, *Iraq After America*, 105.

26 It was carried out by a twenty-six-year-old Moroccan man: Carolina Larriera, "Remembering Sergio Vieira de Mello Ten Years After the Attack on the UN in Baghdad," *The Huffington Post*, October 19, 2013, www.huffingtonpost.com/carolina-larriera/remembering-sergio-vieira_b_3779106.html.

27 This "embellishment" evidently included the diplomat's role: Christopher Hitchens, "Why Ask Why?: Terrorists Attacks Aren't Caused by Any Policy Except That of the Bombers Themselves," *Slate*, October 3, 2005, www.slate.com/articles/news_and_politics/fighting_words/2005/10/why_ask_why.html.

27 "According to Harvey, it provided Zarqawi's men the cars SSO provided the vehicles . . .": Gordon & Trainor, *The Endgame*, 22; "Iraq's Security Services: Regime Strategic Intent—Annex C," Central Intelligence Agency, April 23, 2007, www.cia.gov/library/reports/general-reports-1/iraq_wmd_2004/chap1_annxC.html; "Special Security Organisation—SSO: Al Amn al-Khas," GlobalSecurity.org, last modified July 28, 2011, www.globalsecurity.org/intell/world/iraq/khas.htm.

27 The idea was, if you understood who the terrorists were: Derek Harvey interview with one of the authors, October 2014.

28 According to a study conducted by the Jamestown Foundation: Murad Batal al-Shishani, "Al-Zarqawi's Rise to Power: Analyzing Tactics and Targets," *Terrorism Monitor* Vol. 3 No. 22, The Jamestown Foundation, November 18, 2005, www.jamestown.org/single/?tx_ttnews%5Btt_news%5D=610&no_cache=1#.VIk1cDHF8ei.

28 The same month Tawhid wal-Jihad bombed the Jordanian embassy: Riedel, *The Search for Al Qaeda*, 100, 105; Lawrence Joffe, "Ayatollah Mohammad Baqir al-Hakim," obituary, *The Guardian*, August 29, 2003, www.theguardian.com/news/2003/aug/30/guardianobituaries.iraq.

28 In fact, it was al-Zarqawi's father-in-law, Yassin Jarrad: Napoleoni, *Insurgent Iraq*, 108, 160–161; "Imam Ali Mosque," GlobalSecurity.org, last modified July 9, 2011, www.globalsecurity.org/military/world/iraq/an-najaf-imam-ali.htm; Bassem Mroue, "Alleged Al Qaeda Militant Is Hanged," *The New York Sun* via The Associated Press, July 6, 2007, www.nysun.com/foreign/alleged-al-qaeda-militant-is-hanged/57989; Ben Wedemean, "FBI to Join Mosque Bombing Probe," CNN.com, September 1, 2003, www.cnn.com/2003/WORLD/meast/08/31/sprj.irq.main.

29 It went on to state, "The unhurried observer . . .": Musab Al-Zarqawi, "Letter from Abu Musab al-Zarqawi to Osama bin Laden," Council on Foreign Relations, February 1, 2004, www.cfr.org/iraq/letter-abu-musab-al-zarqawi-osama-bin-laden/p9863. nemeses was the Badr Corps: For the sake of consistency, we have chosen to use Badr Corps throughout, however, it was eventually renamed the Badr Organization.

29 "[T]he Badr Brigade . . . has shed its Shi'a garb . . .": Ibid.

29 If we succeed in dragging them into the arena of sectarian war: Ibid.

NOTES

30 That figure may have been exaggerated: "Iraq: Islamic State Executions in Tikrit," Human Rights Watch, September 2, 2014, www.hrw.org/news/2014/09/02/iraq-islamic-state-executions-tikrit.

30 Members of the first two categories were then carted away elsewhere: "Iraq: ISIS Executed Hundreds of Prison Inmates," Human Rights Watch, October 30, 2014, www.hrw.org/news/2014/10/30/iraq-isis-executed-hundreds-prison-inmates.

30 Al-Zarqawi proved a dire pioneer: Brisard, *Zarqawi*, 142–43.

30 An imprecation was then recited by his captors: Brisard, *Zarqawi*, 131.

31 Though Al-Zarqawi retained an audiovisual squad: Brisard, *Zarqawi*, 143.

31 Writing to his former protégé: Riedel, *The Search for Al Qaeda*, 103.

31 However, as former CIA analyst Bruce Riedel has observed: Riedel, *The Search for Al Qaeda*, 102–03.

32 As scholar Michael W. S. Ryan has noted: Michael W. S. Ryan, "Dabiq: What Islamic State's New Maga www.jamestown.org/programs/tm/single/?tx_ttnews[tt_news]=42702&cHash=0efbd71af77fb92c064b9403dc8ea838#.VLGK7caJnzL

32 Before Blackwater attained international notoriety: "Four Blackwater Agents Hung in Fallujah Iraq March 31, 2004," YouTube video of ABC broadcast, 2:41, posted by WARLORDSMEDIUM, December 11, 2011, www.youtube.com/watch?v=bln0q8E5onE.

32 The failure of foresight seems staggering: Gordon & Trainor, *The Endgame*, 23, 56–57.

33 According to Wael Essam, a Palestinian journalist: Interview with the authors, November 2014.

33 The beheading of Nicholas Berg: Gordon & Trainor, *The Endgame*, 113.

33 The main American weapon against Zarqawists: Gordon & Trainor, *The Endgame*, 114.

33 McChrystal assessed that the threat posed: Ibid.

34 By then adept at the uses of psychological warfare: Bergen, *The Osama bin Laden I Know*, 364.

34 It would be the Saudi billionaire's enterprise: Riedel, *The Search for Al Qaeda*, 105.

34 It was also accompanied by F/A-18 Hornet jets: Gordon & Trainor, *The Endgame*, 117–18.

34 In total, three "torture houses" were uncovered in the city: Gordon & Trainor, *The Endgame*, 119.

35 Roughly a quarter of all insurgents killed: Lt. Colonel Kenneth Estes, *US Marine Corps Operations in Iraq, 2003-2006* (Marine Corps History Division), 66; CQ Researcher, *Global Issues: Selections from CQ Researcher* (CQ Press, 2014), ebook.

35 America was waging a "total war against Islam,": Napoleoni, *Insurgent Iraq*, 183.

36 In December 2004 bin Laden answered al-Zarqawi's bayat: Ibid.

36 The title was somewhat deceptive: Riedel, *The Search for Al Qaeda*, 105.

36 As Bruce Riedel recounts, some al-Qaeda ideologues: Riedel, *The Search for Al Qaeda*, 12–13.

36 Here the thirteenth-century Islamic theologian: Riedel, *The Search for Al Qaeda*, 100.

36 Al-Zarqawi was thus seen as upholding: Riedel, *The Search for Al Qaeda*, 105; Napoleoni, *Insurgent Iraq*, 150–53.

36 As Riedel puts it: Riedel, *The Search for Al Qaeda*, 106.

36 He had the United States and its European allies: Riedel, *The Search for Al Qaeda*, 106., "Mapping the Global Muslim Population," PewResearch, October 7, 2009, www.pewforum.org/2009/10/07/mapping-the-global-muslim-population.

37 He had, according to his Saudi admirer: Riedel, *The Search for Al Qaeda*, 105.

37 One insurgent stronghold was Haifa Street: Gordon & Trainor, *The Endgame*, 123; "Haifa St, Baghdad, Iraq," Google Maps, accessed January 17, 2015, www.google.com/maps/place/Haifa+St,+Baghdad,+Iraq/@33.3263295,44.3705687,12z/data=!4m2!3m1!1s0x15577f4a7ecb0a21:0x808bf83e3e9c97e9.

37 Haifa Street in particular was a totem: Gordon & Trainor, *The Endgame*, 123.

38 In Dora [yet another district of Baghdad infiltrated by insurgents]: Ibid.

39 The ease with which Mosul collapsed: Gordon & Trainor, *The Endgame*, 124.

NOTES

39 They were especially brutal to any Iraqi soldier: Gordon & Trainor, *The Endgame*, 126.

CHAPTER 3

40 Al-Zarqawi's sinister strategy hewed closely: Translation of *The Management of Savagery* by William McCants. Abu Bakr Najri, *The Management of Savagery: The Most Critical Stage Through Which the Umma Will Pass*, May 23, 2006, azelin.files.wordpress.com/2010/08/abu-bakr-naji-the-management-of-savagery-the-most-critical-stage-through-which-the-umma-will-pass.pdf.

42 Less than 1 percent of Sunnis cast ballots: Rayburn, *Iraq After America*, 110.

42 On February 28, 2005, a suicide bomb killed: Warzer Jaff and Robert E. Worth, "Deadliest Single Attack Since Fall of Hussein Kills More Than 120," *New York Times*, February 28, 2005, www.nytimes.com/2005/02/28/international/middleeast/28cnd-iraq.html.

42 In one horrifying instance: "Interview Col. H.R. McMaster," Frontline End Game, June 19, 2007, www.pbs.org/wgbh/pages/frontline/endgame/interviews/mcmaster.html.

43 "If they perceive failure, they may take other actions . . .": Gordon & Trainor, *The Endgame*, 36.

43 "[Al-]Zarqawi, or the Iraqis he had working for him . . .": Interview with one of the authors, December 2014.

44 It also contains the largest phosphate mines in the Middle East: Napoleoni, *Insurgent Iraq*, 190.

44 Building on Adam Such's experience in Hit: "Anbar Before and After The Awakening Pt. IX: Sheik Sabah Aziz of the Albu Mahal," Musings on Iraq blog, January 23, 2014, musingsoniraq.blogspot.com/2014/01/anbar-before-and-after-awakening-pt-ix.html.

45 In the Albu Mahal's Hamza Battalion: Hannah Allam and Mohammed al Dulaimy, "Marine-led Campaign Kill Friends and Foes, Iraqi Leaders Say," McClatchy DC via Knight Ridder Newspapers, May 16, 2005, www.mcclatchydc.com/2005/05/16/11656_marine-led-campaign-killed-friends.html.

45 The graduates of the Qa'im program: Gordon & Trainor, *The Endgame*, 172; Rayburn, *Iraq After America*, 110–11.

45 A third of the Desert Protectors' members quit: Ibid.

45 Appalled by how the Sunni boycott: Col. Gary W. Montgomery and Timothy S. McWilliams, eds., *Al-Anbar Awakening: From Insurgency to Counterinsurgency in Iraq, 2004–2009*, Vol. 2, Marine Corps University Press, 2009, www.marines.mil/Portals/59/Publications/Al-Anbar%20Awakening%20Vol%20II_Iraqi%20Perspectives%20%20PCN%2010600001200_1.pdf.

46 Its first initiative was to encourage Sunnis: Monte Morin, "Officer Killed by Suicide Bomb Had High Hopes for Ramadi," *Stars and Stripes*, January 9, 2006, www.stripes.com/news/officer-killed-by-suicide-bomb-had-high-hopes-for-ramadi-1.43384.

46 On the fourth day of the glass factory drive: Monte Morin, "Suicide Bomb Kills Dozens of Iraqi Police Recruits, Two Americans," Stars and Stripes, January 6, 2006, www.stripes.com/news/suicide-bomb-kills-dozens-of-iraqi-police-recruits-two-americans-1.43269.

46 Still too vulnerable to al-Zarqawi's strong-arm tactics: Stephen Biddle, Jeffrey A. Friedman, and Jacob N. Shapiro, "Testing the Surge: Why Did Violence Decline in Iraq in 2007?" *International Security*, Vol. 37, No. 1, Summer 2012, 20.

CHAPTER 4

48 Sunni voter turnout was around 80 percent: Rayburn, *Iraq After America*, 119.

49 Additionally, less moderate non-AQI insurgents: Gordon & Trainor, *The Endgame*, 191–92.

49 Kanan Makiya, a scholar of Baathist Iraq: Kanan Makiya, *Cruelty and Silence: War, Tyranny, Uprising, and the Arab World* (New York: Jonathan Cape, 1993).

50 He founded his own paramilitary organization: Nada Bakri, "In Lebanon, New Cabinet Is Influenced by Hezbollah," *New York Times*, June 13, 2011, www.nytimes.com/2011/06/14/world/middleeast/14lebanon.html.

NOTES

50 The Battle of Najaf in August 2004: Gordon & Trainor, *The Endgame*, 101.

51 Ansari worked for the Quds Force's Department 1000: Ibid.

51 The Supreme Council for Islamic Revolution in Iraq (SCIRI): Rayburn, *Iraq After America*, 15–17.

51 SCIRI's armed wing: "Iraqi Miniser's Son Misses Flight, Forces Plane Back: Airline," Reuters, March 6, 2014, www.reuters.com/article/2014/03/06/us-lebanon-iraq-plane-idUSBREA2519B20140306; Rayburn, *Iraq After America*, 73–75.

51 "The mullahs ran a very subversive campaign": Interview with one of the authors, June 2014.

51 A former CIA officer not long ago described Suleimani: Dexter Filkins, "The Shadow Commander," *The New Yorker*, September 30, 2013, www.newyorker.com/magazine/2013/09/30/the-shadow-commander.

52 For Petraeus, Iran had: Gordon & Trainor, *The Endgame*, 423.

52 Not only had the Quds Force officer: Gordon & Trainor, *The Endgame*, 313, 351–52.

52 Al-Muhandis was selected to oversee: Gordon & Trainor, *The Endgame*, 151, 159; Filkins, 2013.

52 When detonated, the heat from the EFP: David Axe, "Real E.F.P.: Pocket-Sized Tank Killer," Defense Tech, February 14, 2007, defensetech.org/2007/02/14/real-e-f-p-pocket-sized-tank-killer.

53 Another JSOC raid in Erbil: Gordon & Trainor, *The Endgame*, 324–25.

53 "By exposing Iran's secret deal": "Treasury Targets Key Al-Qa'ida Fuding and Support Network Using Iran as a Critical Transit Point," US Department of the Treasury, July 28, 2011, www.treasury.gov/press-center/press-releases/Pages/tg1261.aspx.

54 "They were there, under Iranian protection, planning operations,": Filkins, 2013.

54 After December 2005 SCIRI was placed: Gordon & Trainor, *The Endgame*, 140.

55 "We either stop them or give Iraq to Iran": Gordon & Trainor, *The Endgame*, 141.

55 But, by way of trying to limit the damage: Ibid.

55 The counterpart brigade in charge of West Baghdad: Gordon & Trainor, *The Endgame*, 146.

55 According to a State Department cable: "Islamic Human Rights Organization Alleges Iraqi Forces Detainee Abuse in Ninewa," Wikileaks, June 16, 2005, wikileaks.org/plusd/cables/05BAGHDAD2547_a.html.

55 Other Iraqi government institutions: Gordon & Trainor, *The Endgame*, 222.

56 Hospitals, meanwhile, were refashioned: Gordon & Trainor, *The Endgame*, 221–222.

56 It also had ready access: Ibid.

56 When US soldiers finally opened the door: Gordon & Trainor, *The Endgame*, 185–86.

57 Only the "most criminal terrorists" were detained: Ibid.

57 Testifying to the grim cooperation: Edward Wong and John F. Burns, "Iraqi Rift Grows After Discover of Prison, *New York Times*, November 17, 2005, www.nytimes.com/2005/11/17/international/middleeast/17iraq.html.

57 In 2006 the US government found: "Testimony of Dr. Matthew Levitt, Fromer-Wexler fellow and director of the Stein Program on Counterterrorism and Intelligence at The Washington Institute for Near East Policy," US House Financial Services Committee, November 13, 2014, financialservices.house.gov/uploadedfiles/hhrg-113-ba00-wstate-mlevitt-20141113.pdf.

57 According to Laith Alkhouri: Interview with one of the authors, November 2014.

58 From 2005 to 2010 subsidies from Gulf Arab donors: US House Financial Services Committee, 2014.

58 Oil smuggling from the Bayji Oil Refinery: Gordon & Trainor, *The Endgame*, 231; Benjamin Bahney, Howard J. Shatz, Carroll Ganier, Renny McPherson, and Barbara Sude, *An Economic Analysis of the Financial Records of al-Qa'ida in Iraq* (National Defense Research Institute, 2010) e-book.

58 A Defense Intelligence Agency assessment: Gordon & Trainor, *The Endgame*, 231.

58 AQI's resources had by then eclipsed: US House Financial Services Committee, 2014.

58 In July 2005 al-Zawahiri sent him a letter: "Zawahiri's Letter to Zarqawi (English

Translation)," Combating Terrorism Center at West Point, October 2013, www.ctc.usma. edu/posts/zawahiris-letter-to-zarqawi-english-translation-2.

58   Al-Zawahiri counseled al-Zarqawi to avoid the "mistakes of the Taliban,": Riedel, *The Search for Al Qaeda*, 104.

58   There was one enemy: Combating Terrorism Center at West Point, 2013.

59   Fearing that the Islamic Republic's response: Riedel, *The Search for Al Qaeda*, 104.

59   The CIA leaked the critical missive: Riedel, *The Search for Al Qaeda*, 103.

59   The day of the bombing: Ellen Knickmeyer and K.I. Ibrahim, "Bombing Shatters Mosque in Iraq," *Washington Post*, February 23, 2006, www.washingtonpost.com/wp-dyn/content/article/2006/02/22/AR2006022200454.html.

59   Grand Ayatollah Ali al-Sistani called for peaceful protests: Ibid.

59   One of Iraq's NGOs found: Gordon & Trainor, *The Endgame*, 194.

59   The al-Askari Mosque bombing accomplished: Ellen Knickmeyer and Muhanned Saif Aldin, "Tense Calm Prevails as Iraqi Forces Seal Off River Town," *Washington Post*, October 18, 2006, www.washingtonpost.com/wp-dyn/content/article/2006/10/17/AR2006101700254.html; Rayburn, *Iraq After America*, 120.

60   Bodies were dumped in the Tigris River: Joshua Partlow and Saad al-Izzi, "Scores of Sunnis Killed in Baghdad," *Washington Post*, July 10, 2006, www.washingtonpost.com/wp-dyn/content/article/2006/07/09/AR2006070900139.html; Gordon & Trainor, *The Endgame*, 214.

60   The Mahdi Army also set up checkpoints: Jon Lee Anderson, "Inside the Surge," *The New Yorker*, November 19, 2007, www.newyorker.com/magazine/2007/11/19/inside-the-surge; "Ghazaliya, Baghdad, Iraq," Google Maps, accessed January 17, 2015, www.google.com/maps/place/Ghazaliyah,+Baghdad,+Iraq/@34.0092759,43.8541015,9z/data=!4m2!3m1!1s0x15577d6b25af61b3:0x1c37973c4265e31e; Gordon & Trainor, *The Endgame*, 213–14.

60   Uniformed Iraqi policemen were enlisted: Gordon & Trainor, *The Endgame*, 213–14.

60   Sunni insurgents paid the Shia back: Rayburn, *Iraq After America*, 87–88.

60   AQI and other Islamist insurgent groups: Gordon & Trainor, *The Endgame*, 213–14.

60   This was the issue put forth in a classified memo: "Text of U.S. Security Adviser's Iraq Memo," *New York Times*, November 29, 2006, www.nytimes.com/2006/11/29/world/middleeast/29mtext.html.

60   "Reports of nondelivery of services to Sunni areas": Ibid.

61   He may even have once escaped: Riedel, *The Search for Al Qaeda*, 106.

61   To find al-Zarqawi through his underlings: Gordon & Trainor, *The Endgame*, 206.

61   US forces discovered that their target: Ibid.

› 61   Iraqi soldiers found al-Zarqawi first: Gordon & Trainor, *The Endgame*, 207.

61   Jordanian intelligence, which had claimed: Dexter Filkins, Mark Mazzetti and Richard A. Oppel Jr., "How Surveillance and Betrayal Led to a Hunt's End," *New York Times*, June 9, 2006, www.nytimes.com/2006/06/09/world/middleeast/09raid.html.

61   All foregoing words of caution to the contrary: Riedel, *The Search for Al Qaeda*, 106.

62   The Mujahidin Advisory Council he installed: Eben Kaplan, "Abu Hamza al-Muhajir, Zarqawi's Mysterious Successor (aka Abu Ayub al-Masri)," Council on Foreign Relations, June 13, 2006, www.cfr.org/iraq/abu-hamza-al-muhajir-zarqawis-mysterious-successor-aka-abu-ayub-al-masri/p10894.

62   Al-Masri had belonged to: Gordon & Trainor, *The Endgame*, 230.

62   For one thing, he took the Iraqization program further: Rayburn, *Iraq After America*, 121; Ahmed S. Hashim, "The Islamic State: From al-Qaeda Affiliate to Caliphate," Middle East Policy Council, Vol. 21, No. 4, Winter 2014, www.mepc.org/journal/middle-east-policy-archives/islamic-state-al-qaeda-affiliate-caliphate.

62   Its demesne was Ninewah, Anbar, and Salah ad Din provinces: Rayburn, *Iraq After America*, 121, 136.

62   ISI's appointed leader, Abu Omar al-Baghdadi: Gordon & Trainor, *The Endgame*, 230;

Rayburn, *Iraq After America*, 128.

63   After his succession became public, US forces captured: Gordon & Trainor, *The Endgame*, 230.

63   Al-Zarqawi, he said, saw himself in messianic terms: Ibid.

63   "He came from outside . . .": Interview with one of the authors, October 2014.

63   Both men wanted to establish: Gordon & Trainor, *The Endgame*, 230; Hashim, 2014.

63   Most of the Sunni groups that joined ISI protested: Hashim, 2014.

63   Ultimately, they resorted to killing jihadists: Interview with one of the authors, November 2014.

64   In May 2014 he issued a statement: Price et al., 2014.

65   Digital intelligence on ISI: Bill Roggio, "Iraqi Troops Kill Senior al Qaeda in Iraq Leader," The Long War Journal, November 7, 2008 www.longwarjournal.org/archives/2008/11/iraqi_troops_kill_se.php.

65   The *Wall Street Journal* reported: Greg Jaffe, "At Lonely Iraq Outpost, GIs Stay as Hope Fades," *Wall Street Journal*, May 3, 2007, www.wsj.com/articles/SB117813340417889827.

66   Abu Ghazwan's overview: Gordon & Trainor, *The Endgame*, 233.

66   He had once been a detainee of the coalition: Gordon & Trainor, *The Endgame*, 233; "Fire Marshal Ronald P. Bucca," Officer Down Memorial Page, accessed January 17, 2015, www.odmp.org/officer/16195-fire-marshal-ronald-p-bucca.

66   In Bucca, al-Rahman not only learned: Gordon & Trainor, *The Endgame*, 32–33, 233–34.

66   As Michael Gordon and Bernard Trainor recount: Gordon & Trainor, *The Endgame*, 234.

CHAPTER 5

68   "The history of the Anbar Awakening is very bitter . . ."a former high-ranking official: Interview with the authors, August 2014.

69   Barrels of purloined crude were imported: Gordon & Trainor, *The Endgame*, 244.

69   Two sheikhs from the Albu Aetha and Albu Dhiyab tribes: Myriam Benraad, "Iraq's Tribal 'Sahwa': Its Rise and Fall," Middle East Policy Council, Vol. 18, No. 1, Spring 2011, www.mepc.org/journal/middle-east-policy-archives/iraqs-tribal-sahwa-its-rise-and-fall.

69   Nighttime vigilantism gained: Gordon & Trainor, *The Endgame*, 244.

70   What made Ramadi different: Kirk Semple, "Uneasy Alliance Is Taming One Insurgent Bastion," *New York Times*, April 29, 2007, www.nytimes.com/2007/04/29/world/middleeast/29ramadi.html.

70   al-Rishawi was ready to cut a new deal: Gordon & Trainor, *The Endgame*, 250.

70   "People with ties to the insurgents . . ."a US lieutenant had told the journalist George Packer: George Packer, "The Lesson of Tal Afar," *The New Yorker*, April 10, 2006, www.newyorker.com/magazine/2006/04/10/the-lesson-of-tal-afar.

70   The council quickly expanded: Gordon & Trainor, *The Endgame*, 252.

71   Just before New Year 2007: Gordon & Trainor, *The Endgame*, 253.

71   Abdul al-Rishawi's general success: Ibid.

71   "I swear to God . . ." the sheikh told the *New York Times*: Edward Wong, "An Iraqi Tribal Chief Opposes the Jihadists, and Prays," *New York Times*, March 3, 2007, www.nytimes.com/2007/03/03/world/middleeast/03sheik.html

71   He was assassinated by the jihadists: Alissa J. Rubin and Graham Bowley, "Bomb Kills Sunni Sheik Working With US in Iraq," *New York Times*, September 13, 2007, www.nytimes.com/2007/09/13/world/middleeast/13cnd-iraq.html

72   The emir told him that while foreign occupiers: Gordon & Trainor, *The Endgame*, 263.

72   The new strategy demanded confronting: Jason Burke, *The 9/11 Wars* (New York: Penguin, 2012), 267.

72   Petraeus and Marine Lieutenant General James Mattis: Burke, *The 9/11 Wars*, 265.

73   A mixture of soldiering and policing: Joint Chiefs of Staff Joint Publication 3-24, *The Patraeus Doctrine: The Field Manual on Counterinsurgency Operations*, US Army, 2009.

73   In 2007 the US Government Accountability Office: Glenn Kessler, "Weapons Given to

Iraq Are Missing," *Washington Post*, August 6, 2007, www.washingtonpost.com/wp-dyn/content/article/2007/08/05/AR2007080501299.html.

73   The US military's solution was a partition: Burke, *The 9/11 Wars*, 271.

74   A military intelligence analysis: Gordon & Trainor, *The Endgame*, 209.

74   Furthermore, the overwhelming cluster of attacks: Ibid.

75   If a detonated IED turned out to be a dud: Gordon & Trainor, *The Endgame*, 210.

75   As they had done the prior year in Ramadi: Gordon & Trainor, *The Endgame*, 370.

75   The group's fallback base was in nearby Buhriz: Ibid.

75   Sergeant 1st Class Benjamin Hanner told the *Washington Post*: Joshua Partlow, "Troops in Diyala Face A Skilled, Flexible Foe," *Washington Post*, April 22, 2007, www.washingtonpost.com/wp-dyn/content/article/2007/04/21/AR2007042101467_pf.html.

76   Shawn McGuire, a staff sergeant recalled to Gordon and Trainor: Gordon & Trainor, *The Endgame*, 375.

77   In an interview with the *Washington Post*: Jackie Spinner, "Marines Widen Their Net South of Baghdad," *Washington Post*, November 28, 2004, www.washingtonpost.com/wp-dyn/articles/A16794-2004Nov27.html.

77   After being handed a list of the top-ten AQI operatives: Gordon & Trainor, *The Endgame*, 381.

77   In Ameriya, a neighborhood: Gordon & Trainor, *The Endgame*, 384.

78   No doubt leery of seeing a replay: Ibid.

78   In a June 2010 Pentagon news briefing: Gen. Raymond Odierno, "DOD News Briefing with Gen. Odierno from the Pentagon," US Department of Defense, June 4, 2010, www.defense.gov/transcripts/transcript.aspx?transcriptid=4632.

79   In *Iraq After America*, Joel Rayburn recounts: Rayburn, *Iraq After America*, 124.

80   Several months before his death, he had conducted a Skype call: Interview with one of Jibouri's interlocutors, November 2014.

81   Dr. Jaber al-Jabberi . . . told us: Interview with one of the author, August 2014.

CHAPTER 6

83   Not only had the internationally publicized and condemned torture: Alissa J. Rubin, "US Military Reforms Its Prisons in Iraq," *New York Times*, June 1, 2008, www.nytimes.com/2008/06/01/world/africa/01iht-detain.4.13375130.html.

83   According to one US military estimate: Interview with Joel Rayburn, October 2014.

83   Owing to the spike in military operations: Craig Whiteside, "Catch And Release in the Land of Two Rivers," War on the Rocks, December 18, 2014, warontherocks.com/2014/12/catch-and-release-in-the-land-of-two-rivers.

84   In a PowerPoint presentation he prepared for CENTCOM: Major General D.M Stone, "Detainee Operations," United States Marine Corps, PowerPoint presentation, November 2014.

86   A former ISIS member interviewed by the *Guardian*: Martin Chulov, "Isis: The Inside Story," *The Guardian*, December 11, 2014, www.theguardian.com/world/2014/dec/11/-sp-isis-the-inside-story.

86   Abu Ahmed recounted: Ibid.

87   Craig Whiteside, a professor at the Naval War College: Whiteside, 2014.

88   Anthony Shadid, then a foreign correspondent for the *Washington Post*: Anthony Shadid, "In Iraq, Chaos Feared as US Closes Prison," *Washington Post*, March 22, 2009, www.washingtonpost.com/wp-dyn/content/article/2009/03/21/AR2009032102255_pf.html.

89   "It was easy to capture al-Qaeda people," Rayburn told us.: Interview with one of the authors, October 2014.

90   No longer useful to al-Maliki: Burke, *The 9/11 Wars*, 430.

90   Conditions were especially grim in Diyala: Gordon & Trainor, *The Endgame*, 591.

90   Such prejudicial justice didn't apply to Shia prisoners: Gordon & Trainor, *The Endgame*, 592.

90 Shadid interviewed Colonel Saad Abbas Mahmoud: Shadid, 2009.
91 The original plan for the Awakening: Gordon & Trainor, *The Endgame*, 591.
91 The Iraqi agency tasked: Gordon & Trainor, *The Endgame*, 593.
91 Moreover, al-Maliki showed little interest: Ibid.
91 Mullah Nadim Jibouri . . . claimed: Interview with one of the authors, November 2014.
91 The US assessment of his dictatorial tendencies: Gordon & Trainor, *The Endgame*, 614.
92 Odierno, with good reason, saw: Gordon & Trainor, *The Endgame*, 609.
92 He would need to form a government: Gordon & Trainor, *The Endgame*, 617.
93 The following day, Iraq's president: Rayburn, *Iraq After America*, 213–14.
93 Al-Maliki formed a government in 2010: Gordon & Trainor, *The Endgame*, 620.
93 Odierno, for one, saw how flagrant manipulation: Gordon & Trainor, *The Endgame*, 619
93 Vice President Joseph Biden . . . is recorded: Gordon & Trainor, *The Endgame*, 615.
93 "I know one guy . . ." Khedery told us.: Interview with one of the authors, November 2014; Ali Khedery, "Why We Stuck With Maliki—and Lost Iraq," *Washington Post*, July 3, 2004, www.washingtonpost.com/opinions/why-we-stuck-with-maliki--and-lost-iraq/2014/07/03/0dd6a8a4-f7ec-11e3-a606-946fd632f9f1_story.html.
94 As much of the consequences of the surge: "Blowback Against Glenn Greenwald #1," Anonymous Mugwump blog, May 25, 2013, anonymousmugwump.blogspot.co.uk/2013/05/blowback-against-glenn-greenwald-1.html
94 There was actually little debate: "Five Myths About ISIS," Anonymous Mugwump blog, October 5, 2014, anonymousmugwump.blogspot.co.uk/2014/10/five-myths-about-isis.html.
94 But al-Maliki didn't: Gordon & Trainor, *The Endgame*, 673–674.
96 Al-Hashimi was allowed to fly off: Adrian Blomfield and Damien McElroy, "Iraq In Fresh Turmoil as Prime Minister Nuri al-Maliki Orders Arrest of Vice President," *The Telegraph*, December 19, 2011, www.telegraph.co.uk/news/worldnews/middleeast/iraq/8966587/Iraq-in-fresh-turmoil-as-Prime-Minister-Nuri-al-Maliki-orders-arrest-of-vice-president.html.
96 He remained in exile He later fled to Turkey: Associated Press in Baghdad, "Iraq Vice President Sentenced to Death Amid Deadly Wave of Insurgent Attacks," *The Guardian*, September 9, 2012, www.theguardian.com/world/2012/sep/09/iraq-vice-president-hashemi-death-sentence.
96 They claimed to be searching for the killer: Joel Rayburn, "Iraq Is Back on the Brink of Civil War," *New Republic*, May 8, 2013, www.newrepublic.com/article/113148/iraqs-civil-war-breaking-out-again.
98 According to the Obama administration: Jessica D. Lewis, "Al-Qaeda in Iraq Resurgent," *Middle East Security Report 14*, Institute for the Study of War, September 2013, www.understandingwar.org/sites/default/files/AQI-Resurgent-10Sept_0.pdf.
98 ISIS then sacked Fallujah: Sinan Adnan and Aaron Reese, "Beyond the Islamic State: Iraq's Sunni Insurgency," *Middle East Security Report 24*, Institute for the Study of War, October 2014, www.understandingwar.org/sites/default/files/Sunni%20Insurgency%20in%20Iraq.pdf

CHAPTER 7

99 Abed al-Sattar, the Anbar Awakening leader: Edward Wong, "An Iraqi Tribal Chief Opposes the Jihadists, and Prays," *New York Times*, March 3, 2007, www.nytimes.com/2007/03/03/world/middleeast/03sheik.html.
100 As scholar Eyal Zisser has noted: Eyal Zisser, "Hafiz al-Asad Discovers Islam," *Middle East Quarterly*, March 1999, www.meforum.org/465/hafiz-al-asad-discovers-islam.
100 Up until recently, for example, despite a national Syrian law: Fares Akram, "Hamas Leader Abandons Longtime Base in Damascus," *New York Times*, January 27, 2012. www.nytimes.com/2012/01/28/world/middleeast/khaled-meshal-the-leader-of-hamas-vacates-damascus.html.
100 Today, the regime relies overwhelming on the paramilitary assets: David Axe, "Iran Transformed Syria's Army into a Militia that Will Help Assad Survive Another

Year," Reuters, December 17, 2014, blogs.reuters.com/great-debate/2014/12/16/iran-transformed-syrias-army-into-a-militia-that-will-help-assad-survive-another-year; Amos Harel, "Iran, Hezbollah Significantly Increases Aid to Syria's Assad," *Haaretz*, April 6, 2012, www.haaretz.com/news/middle-east/iran-hezbollah-significantly-increase-aid-to-syria-s-assad-1.422954.

101   In 2007 CENTCOM announced: "Three Major Terror Busts in Iraq—Iran, Syria Connections Exposed, Say US Officials," ABC News, March 22, 2007, abcnews.go.com/blogs/headlines/2007/03/three_major_ter; Burke, *The 9/11 Wars*, 171.

101   According to Major General Kevin Bergner: Bill Roggio, "Al Qaeda in Iraq Operative Killed Near Syrian Border Sheds Light on Foreign Influence," The Long War Journal, October 3, 2007, www.longwarjournal.org/archives/2007/10/al_qaeda_in_iraq_ope.php.

101   A study published in 2008: Peter Bergen, Joseph Felter, Vahid Brown, and Jacob Shapiro, *Bombers, Bank Accounts, & Bleedout: Al-Qa'ida's Road In and out of Iraq*, Combating Terrorism Center at West Point, July 2008, https://www.ctc.usma.edu/wp-content/uploads/2011/12/Sinjar_2_FINAL.pdf.

102   "In border villages and cities," the CTC study stated: Ibid.

102   Al-Assad, of course, has always denied: Ibid.

102   as Jason Burke's *The 9/11 Wars* shows: Burke, *The 9/11 Wars*, 171.

103   Bassam Barabandi, a former diplomat: Interview with one of the authors, December 2014.

103   The former diplomat described for us: Interview with one of the authors, December 2014.

103   Tony Badran, an expert on Syria: Interview with one of the authors, December 2014.

104   Badran mentioned . . . the curious case: "Death of a Cleric," *NOW Lebanon*, October 5, 2007, now.mmedia.me/lb/en/commentaryanalysis/death_of_a_cleric.

104   As recounted by journalist Nicholas Blanford: Ibid.

104   Blanford argued that al-Qaqa: Ibid.

105   Habash told us that he first met al-Qaqa in 2006: Interview with one of the authors, December 2014.

106   "According to reports in the Arabic press": Interview with one of the authors, December 2014.

106   Fatah al-Islam later posted: Graham Bowley and Souad Makhennet, "Fugitive Sunni Leader Thought to Have Been Captured or Killed in Syria," *New York Times*, November 10, 2008, www.nytimes.com/2008/12/10/world/africa/10iht-syria.4.18569673.html.

107   Most of the insurgents Syria funneled: Gordon & Trainor, *The Endgame*, 231.

107   "crisis management cell": Ian Black and Martin Chulov, "Leading Syrian Regime Figures Killed in Damascus Bomb Attack," *The Guardian*, July 18, 2012, www.theguardian.com/world/2012/jul/18/syrian-regime-figures-bomb-attack; Michael Weiss, "What the Assault on the Assad Regime Means," *The Telegraph*, July 20, 2012, blogs.telegraph.co.uk/news/michaelweiss/100171767/what-the-assault-on-the-assad-regime-means.

107   Abu Ghadiyah, the Treasury Department alleged: Bill Roggio, "US Strike in Syria 'Decapitated' al Qaeda's Facilitation Network," The Long War Journal, October 27, 2008, www.longwarjournal.org/archives/2008/10/us_strike_in_syria_d.php.

107   According to a State Department cable: "Gen. Patraeus's Meeting with P.M. Maliki," Wikileaks, January 7, 2009, www.wikileaks.org/plusd/cables/09BAGHDAD31_a.html.

108   He was an al-Qaeda financier: "Treasury Designates Members of Abu Ghadiyah's Network Facilitates Flow of Terrorists, Weapons, and Money from Syra to al Qaida in Iraq," US Department of the Treasury, February 28, 2008, www.treasury.gov/press-center/press-releases/Pages/hp845.aspx.

108   Abu Ghadiyah's predecessor: James Joyner, "Zarqawi Financial Network Independent," Outside the Beltway, January 25, 2005, www.outsidethebeltway.com/zarqawi_financial_network_independent.

108   Petraeus had even sought permission: Gordon & Trainor, *The Endgame*, 461.

108   Stanley's McChrystal's JSOC: Roggio, October 2008.

109   He asked al-Assad to end: Gordon & Trainor, *The Endgame*, 577.

109   Maura Connelly, the charge d'affaires: "UK Foreign Secretary Miliband's

Nov. 17 18 Trip to Damascus,"Wikileaks, November 19, 2008, www.wikileaks.org/plusd/cables/08DAMASCUS821_a.html.

109 Perhaps it was with the foregoing episode: "Cable 09DAMASCUS384, Re-engaging Syria: Dealing with Sarg Diplomacy,"Wikileaks, June3, 2009, wikileaks.org/cable/2009/06/09DAMASCUS384.html.

110 In December 2014 Martin Chulov: Chulov, December 2014.

110 More than one hundred people: Ibid.

111 In November 2009 his government aired: Steven Lee Myers, "Iraq Military Broadcasts Confession on Bombing," *New York Times*, August 23, 2009, www.nytimes.com/2009/08/24/world/middleeast/24iraq.html.

111 But it recalled its ambassador from Damascus: "Iraq and Syria Recall Envoys," *Al Jazeera*, August 25, 2009, www.aljazeera.com/news/middleeast/2009/08/20098251602328210.html.

111 One of the men he refused to turn over: Khaled Yacoub Oweis, "US Security Team to Visit Syria, Focus on Iraq," Reuters, August 11, 2009, www.reuters.com/article/2009/08/11/us-syria-usa-sb-idUSTRE57A5Y120090811.

111 For a short time, al-Assad had tried: Gordon & Trainor, *The Endgame*, 610; Hugh Naylor, "Syria is Said to Be Strengthening Ties to Opponents," *New York Times*, October 7, 2007. www.nytimes.com/2007/10/07/world/middleeast/07syria.html.

111 Iraqi Foreign Minister Hoshyar Zebari told: Tony Badran, "The 'Lebonization' of Iraq," *NOW Lebanon*, December 22, 2009, now.mmedia.me/lb/en/commentaryanalysis/the_lebanonization_of_iraq.

112 The Iraqi general struggled: Chulov, December 2014.

112 As relayed in a State Department cable: "Syrian Intelligence Chief Attends CT Dialogue With S/CT Benjamin,"Wikileaks, February 24, 2010, wikileaks.org/plusd/cables/10DAMASCUS159_a.html.

113 He explained his own peculiar method: Ibid.

113 The answer to that question lay in Mamlouk's follow-up: Ibid.

CHAPTER 8

114 ISIS's history, according to *Dabiq*'s reconstruction: "The Return of Khilafah," *Dabiq*, Issue 1, July, 2014, media.clarionproject.org/files/09-2014/isis-isil-islamic-state-magazine-Issue-1-the-return-of-khilafah.pdf.

115 The first was the killing of Abu Khalaf: Bill Roggio, "US Kills Senior Syrian-based al Qaeda Facilitator in Mosul,"The Long War Journal, January 28, 2010, www.longwarjournal.org/archives/2010/01/us_kills_senior_syri.php.

115 A US official later said: Ibid.

115 Al-Rawi named two couriers: Gordon & Trainor, *The Endgame*, 623.

116 Laith Alkhouri, the counterterrorism expert, said.: Interview with one of the authors, November 2014.

117 "No one thought he wanted competition . . .": Ibid.

117 He's said to have lived in modest quarters: Ruth Sherlock, "How a Talented Footballer Became World's Most Wanted Man, Abu Bakr al-Baghdadi," *The Telegraph*, November 11, 2014, www.telegraph.co.uk/news/worldnews/middleeast/iraq/10948846/How-a-talented-footballer-became-worlds-most-wanted-man-Abu-Bakr-al-Baghdadi.html.

117 Al-Baghdadi wore glasses: Ibid.

117 Dr. Hisham al-Hashimi, an expert on ISIS: Interview with one of the authors, December 2014.

117 According to one of his neighbors: Sherlock, November 2014.

118 by late 2003 he had founded his own Islamist faction: Hashim, 2014.

118 a year after that, he was enrolled: Chulov, December 2014.

119 Abu Ahmed, the former high-ranking ISIS member: Ibid.

119 according to Abu Ahmed, he started causing problems: Ibid.

119   When al-Baghdadi was released: Ibid.

119   In 2007 he joined the Mujahideen Shura Council: Hashim, 2014.

123   "The brutality, the tradecraft . . .": Interview with one of the authors, October 2014.

124   Harvey's insight is all the more compelling: Ben Hubbard and Eric Schmitt, "Military Skill and Terrorist Technique Fuel Success of ISIS," *New York Times*, August 27, 2014, mobile. nytimes.com/2014/08/28/world/middleeast/army-know-how-seen-as-factor-in-isis-successes.html.

124   The first is Abu Abdul-Rahman al-Bilawi: Ruth Sherlock, "Inside the Leadership of Islamic State: How the New 'Caliphate' Is Run," *The Telegraph*, July 9, 2014, www.telegraph. co.uk/news/worldnews/middleeast/iraq/10956280/Inside-the-leadership-of-Islamic-State-how-the-new-caliphate-is-run.html.

124   Originally from al-Khalidiya in Anbar: Hisham al-Hashimi,"Revealed: The Islamic State 'Cabinet,' From Finance Minister to Suicide Bomb Deployer," *The Telegraph*, July 9, 2014, www.telegraph.co.uk/news/worldnews/middleeast/iraq/10956193/Revealed-the-Islamic-State-cabinet-from-finance-minister-to-suicide-bomb-deployer.html.

124   The second influencer, according to al-Hashimi: Ibid.

124   Somewhere in between, according to the *Wall Street Journal*: Siobhan Gorman, Nour Malas, and Matt Bradley, "Brutal Efficiency: The Secret to Islamic State's Success," *Wall Street Journal*, September 3, 2014, www.wsj.com/articles/the-secret-to-the-success-of-islamic-state-1409709762.

124   Iraqi and Syrian militants think al-Anbari: Siobahn Gorman, Nour Malas, and Matt Bradley, "Disciplined Cadre Runs Islamic State," *Wall Street Journal*, September 3, 2014, www.wsj.com/articles/SB20001424052970204545604580127823357609374.

125   according to a cache of internal documents: "Exclusive: Top ISIS Leaders Revealed," *Al Arabiya News*, February 13, 2014, english.alarabiya.net/en/News/2014/02/13/Exclusive-Top-ISIS-leaders-revealed.html.

125   Another former US detainee: Hubbard & Schmitt, 2014.

125   Another graduate of both Bucca: "3 Senior ISIS Leaders Killed in US Airstrikes," CBS News, December 18, 2014, www.cbsnews.com/news/3-senior-isis-leaders-killed-in-u-s-airstrikes.

125   A former lieutenant colonel: Sherlock, July 2014.

125   Baghdad is said to have "handpicked": Hubbard & Schmitt, 2014.

125   The *New York Times* reported: Ibid.

126   Michael Pregent, a former US military: Interview with one of the authors, October 2014.

126   Known internationally as the "red-bearded jihadist": "Red-Bearded Chechen Fighter Is Face of ISIS," Sky News, July 3, 2014, news.sky.com/story/1293797/red-bearded-chechen-fighter-is-face-of-isis.

126   Abu Omar al-Shishani, or Tarkhan Batirashvili: Gorman et al. "Disciplined Cadre," 2014.

126   He fought in the 2008 Russo-Georgian War: Nina Akhmeteli, "The Georgian Roots of Isis Commander Omar al-Shishani," BBC News, July 8, 2014, www.bbc.com/news/world-europe-28217590.

126   Al-Shishani even hung up the phone: Ibid.

126   Released in 2010: Bassem Mroue, "Chechen in Syria a Rising Star in Extremist Group," Associated Press, July 2, 2014, bigstory.ap.org/article/chechen-syria-rising-star-extremist-group.

126   Teimuraz told the BBC: Akhmeteli, 2014.

127   The Chechen first emerged in Syria: Mroue, 2014.

127   In November 2014 Kadyrov announced: Joanna Paraszczuk, "The Chechen Leader With a Grudge and the IS Commander with Nine Lives," Radio Free Europe Radio Liberty, November 14, 2014, www.rferl.org/content/islamic-state-why-kadyrov-claims-shishani-killed/26692100.html.

128   Some of them even made impressive incursions: Mroue, 2014.

128   Menagh finally fell: Nour Malas and Rima Abushakra, "Islamists Seize Airbase Near Aleppo," *Wall Street Journal*, August 6, 2013, www.wsj.com/articles/SB1000142412788732

342060457865225087294205 8.

128 Largely a morale boost: Anne Barnard and Hwaida Saad, "Rebels Gain Control of Government Air Base in Syria," *New York Times*, August 5, 2013, www.nytimes. com/2013/08/06/world/middleeast/rebels-gain-control-of-government-air-base-in-syria. html; Michael Weiss, "Col. Oqaidi on al-Qaeda, UN Inspectors, and Kurdish Militias," *NOW Lebanon*, August 18, 2013, now.mmedia.me/lb/en/interviews/col-oqaidi-on-al-qaeda-un-inspectors-and-kurdish-militias.

128 Khalid wrote in a statement: Joanna Paraszczuk, "Military Prowess of IS Commander Umar Shishani Called Into Question," Radio Free Europe Radio Liberty, November 6, 2014, www.rferl.org/content/umar-shishani-military-prowess-islamic-state/26677545. html.

129 Stories about pretty, middle-class teenage: Allan Hall, "One of the Teenage Austrian 'Poster Girls' Who Ran Away to Join ISIS Has Been Killed in the Conflict, UN Says," *Daily Mail*, December 18, 2014, www.dailymail.co.uk/news/article-2879272/One-teenage-Austrian-poster-girls-ran-away-join-ISIS-killed-conflict-says.html.

129 copycats who are stopped: "Austria Detains Teenage Girls Who Wanted to Marry ISIS Fighters," NBC News, January 11, 2015, www.nbcnews.com/storyline/isis-terror/austria-detains-teenage-girls-who-wanted-marry-isis-fighters-n284096.

130 In 1940 George Orwell wrote an essay: "George Orwell Reviews *Mein Kampf* (1940)," Open Culture, August 19, 2014, www.openculture.com/2014/08/george-orwell-reviews-mein-kampf-1940.html.

CHAPTER 9

131 Bashar al-Assad gave an interview: "Interview With Syrian President Bashar al-Assad," *Wall Street Journal*, January 31, 2011, www.wsj.com/articles/SB10001424052748703833204 576114712441122894.

131 Just three days before his interview: "Syria: Gang Attacks Peaceful Demonstrators; Police Look On," Human Rights Watch, February 3, 2011, www.hrw.org/news/2011/02/03/ syria-gang-attacks-peaceful-demonstrators-police-look; Lauren Williams, "Syria Clamps Down on Dissent with Beatings and Arrests," *The Guardian*, February 24, 2011, www. theguardian.com/world/2011/feb/24/syria-crackdown-protest-arrests-beatings.

131 on February 17, a spontaneous protest erupted: Molly Hennessy-Fiske, "Syria: Activists Protest Police Beating, Call for Investigation," *Los Angeles Times*, February 17, 2014, latimesblogs.latimes.com/babylonbeyond/2011/02/syria-activists-protest-police-beating-call-for-investigation.html.

131 Although the protest was carefully directed: Ibid.

131 That demonstration came to an end: Rania Abouzeid, "The Syrian Style of Repression: Thugs and Lectures," *TIME*, February 27, 2011, content.time.com/time/world/ article/0,8599,2055713,00.html.

132 Similar protests soon broke out in Damascus: Dane Vallejo and Michael Weiss, "Syria Media Briefing: A Chronology of Protest and Repression," The Henry Jackston Society, May 2011, henryjacksonsociety.org/cms/harriercollectionitems/Syria+Media+Briefing.pdf.

132 One woman held at the Palestine Branch: Fergal Keane, "Syria Ex-Detainees Allege Ordeals of Rape and Sex Abuse," BBC News, September 25, 2012, www.bbc.com/news/ world-middle-east-19718075.

133 Caesar testified before US Congress: Josh Rogin, "Syrian Defector: Assad Poised to Torture and Murder 150,000 More," *The Daily Beast*, July 31, 2014, www.thedailybeast.com/ articles/2014/07/31/syrian-defector-assad-poised-to-torture-and-murder-150-000-more.html.

133 Stephen Rapp, the State Department's ambassador-at-large: Josh Rogin, "US: Assad's 'Machinery of Death' Worst Since the Nazis," *The Daily Beast*, July 7, 2014, www.thedailybeast. com/articles/2014/07/07/u-s-assad-s-machinery-of-death-worst-since-the-nazis.html.

134 one of the favored slogans: "The Syrian regime says, 'Al Assad or we'll burn the country down,'" YouTube video, 7:24, posted by Tehelka TV, October 30, 2013, www.youtube.com/

watch?v=wnBGHaTkgW8.

135 What Zakarya meant: James Reynolds, "Syria Torture Accounts Reinforce Human Rights Concerns," BBC News, July 3, 2012, www.bbc.com/news/world-middle-east-18687422.

135 said Shiraz Maher, an expert on radicalization: Interview with one of the authors, November 2014.

135 In 2010 Nibras Kazimi published: Nibras Kazimi, *Syria Through Jihadist Eyes: A Perfect Enemy* (Stanford, CA: Hoover Press, 2010), 63.

136 "The sectarianism was carefully manufactured . . .": Interview with one of the authors, November 2014.

136 According to one who was detained: Ruth Sherlock, "Confessions of an Assad 'Shabiha' Loyalist: How I Raped and Killed for £300 a Month," *The Telegraph*, July 14, 2012, www.telegraph.co.uk/news/worldnews/middleeast/syria/9400570/Confessions-of-an-Assad-Shabiha-loyalist-how-I-raped-and-killed-for-300-a-month.html.

137 Most of them were women and children: Stephanie Nebehay, "Most Houla Victims Killed n Summary Executions: UN," Reuters, May 29, 2012, www.reuters.com/article/2012/05/29/us-syria-un-idUSBRE84S10020120529.

137 The shabiha were readily identifiable: Harriet Alexander and Ruth Sherlock, "The Shabiha: Inside Assad's Death Squads," *The Telegraph*, June 2, 2012, www.telegraph.co.uk/news/worldnews/middleeast/syria/9307411/The-Shabiha-Inside-Assads-death-squads.html.

137 an investigation by the United Nations: "Report of the Independent International Commission of Inquiry on the Syrian Arab Republic," Human Rights Council, 21st Session, August 15, 2012, www.ohchr.org/Documents/HRBodies/HRCouncil/RegularSession/Session21/A-HRC-21-50.doc.

137 Victoria Nuland accused Iran: Chris McGreal, "Houla Massacre: US Accuses Iran of 'Bragging' about Its Military Aid to Syria," *The Guardian*, May 29, 2012, www.theguardian.com/world/2012/may/29/houla-massacre-us-accuses-iran.

137 With as many as one hundred thousand recruits: Sam Dagher, "Syria's Alawite Force Turned Tide for Assad," *Wall Street Journal*, August 26, 2013, www.wsj.com/articles/SB10001424127887323997004578639903412487708.

138 IRGC operative Sayyed Hassan Entezari said: Axe, 2014.

138 Each brigade of the National Defense Force: Ibid.

138 Reuters conducted interviews: "Insight: Syrian Government Guerrilla Fighters Being Sent to Iran for Training," Reuters, April 4, 2013, www.reuters.com/article/2013/04/04/us-syria-iran-training-insight-idUSBRE9330DW20130404.

138 The camp at which Samer: Farnaz Fassihi, Jay Solomon, and Sam Dagher, "Iranians Dial Up Presence in Syria," *Wall Street Journal*, September 16, 2013, www.wsj.com/articles/SB10001424127887323864604579067382861808984.

138 According to an Iranian military officer: Ibid.

139 the National Defense Force has already: Michael Weiss, "Rise of the Militias," *NOW Lebanon*, May 21, 2013 now.mmedia.me/lb/en/commentaryanalysis/rise-of-the-militias.

139 Christian witnesses who spoke to the NGO: "No One's Left," Human Rights Watch, September 13, 2013, www.hrw.org/reports/2013/09/13/no-one-s-left-0.

139 This has resulted in high-profile Iranian fatalities: Filkins, 2013.

139 Tehran has relied only on operatives: Farnaz Fassihi and Jay Solomon, "Top Iranian Official Acknowledges Syria Role," *Wall Street Journal*, September 16, 2012, online.wsj.com/news/articles/SB10000872396390443720204578000482831419570.

139 Several members of IRGC Ground Forces: Will Fulton, Joseph Holliday, and Sam Wyer, *Iranian Strategy in Syria*, AEI's Critical Threats Project & Institute for the Study of War, May 2013, www.understandingwar.org/sites/default/files/IranianStrategyinSyria-1MAY.pdf.

140 A report published by the Institute for the Study of War: Ibid.

140 former Syrian prime minister Riyad Hijab declared: Karim Sadjadpour, "Iran: Syria's Lone Regional Ally," Carnegie Endowment for International Peace, June 9, 2014 carnegieendowment.org/2014/06/09/syria-s-lone-regional-ally-iran.

NOTES

140   As early as May 2011: "Administration Takes Additional Steps to Hold the Government of Syria Accountable for Violent Repression Against the Syrian People," US Department of the Treasury, May 18, 2011, www.treasury.gov/press-center/press-releases/Pages/tg1181. aspx.

140   Such support, as later came to light, included: Michael R. Gordon, "US Presses Iraq on Iranian Planes Thought to Carry Arms to Syria," *New York Times*, September 5, 2012, www. nytimes.com/2012/09/06/world/middleeast/us-presses-iraq-on-iranian-planes-thought-to-carry-arms-to-syria.html.

140   In 2012, when the Iraqis stopped denying: Ibid.

140   According to US intelligence: Arash Karami, "Iran News Site Profiles Head of Iraq's Badr Organization," *Al-Monitor*, November 13, 2014, www.al-monitor.com/pulse/ originals/2014/11/iran-news-site-profiles-badr-org.html.

141   In January 2014 the Meir Amit Intelligence: William Booth, "Israeli Study of Foreign Fighters in Syria Suggests Shiites May Outnumber Sunnis," *Washington Post*, January 2, 2014, www.washingtonpost.com/blogs/worldviews/wp/2014/01/02/israeli-study-of-foreign-fighters-in-syria-suggests-shiites-may-outnumber-sunnis.

141   Kata'ib Hezbollah has also lost: Phillip Smyth, "From Karbala to Sayyida Zaynab: Iraqi Fighters in Syria's Shi'a Militias," Combating Terrorism Center at West Point, August 27, 2013, www.ctc.usma.edu/posts/from-karbala-to-sayyida-zaynab-iraqi-fighters-in-syrias-shia-militias.

141   Ditto Muqtada al-Sadr's Mahdi Army: Suadad al-Salhy, "Iraqi Shi'ite Militants Fight for Syria's Assad," Reuters, October 16, 2012, www.reuters.com/article/2012/10/16/us-syria-crisis-iraq-militias-idUSBRE89F0PX20121016.

141   Phillip Smyth, an expert on the Special Groups: Phillip Smyth, "Breaking Badr, The New Season: Confirmation of the Badr Organization's Involvement in Syria," Jihadology blog, August 12, 2013, jihadology.net/2013/08/12/hizballah-cavalcade-breaking-badr-the-new-season-confirmation-of-the-badr-organizations-involvement-in-syria.

141   Iran has even sent "thousands": Farnaz Fassihi, "Iran Pays Afghans to Fight for Assad," *Wall Street Journal*, May 22, 2014, www.wsj.com/articles/SB10001424052702304908304579564161508613846.

141   Others are allegedly ex-Taliban fighters: Nick Paton Walsh, "'Afghan' in Syria: Iranians Pay Us to Fight for Assad," CNN, October 31, 2014, www.cnn.com/2014/10/31/world/meast/syria-afghan-fighter.

142   No IRGC-run subsidiary has been: Martin Chulov, "Syrian Town of Qusair Falls to Hezbollah in Breakthrough for Assad," *The Guardian*, June 5, 2013, www.theguardian.com/world/2013/jun/05/syria-army-seizes-qusair.

142   one Party of God paramilitary confessed: Mona Alami, "Hezbollah Fighter Details Opsin Qusayr," *NOW Lebanon*, June 4, 2013, now.mmedia.me/lb/en/interviews/hezbollah-fighter-details-ops-in-qusayr.

142   Abu Rami told the *Guardian* in July 2013: Martin Chulov and Mona Mahmood, "Syrian Sunnies Fear Assad Regime Wants to 'Ethnically Cleanse' Alawite Heartland," *The Guardian*, July 22, 2013, www.theguardian.com/world/2013/jul/22/syria-sunnis-fear-alawite-ethnic-cleansing.

142   al-Assad's first post-uprising interview: Andrew Gilligan, "Assad: Challenge Syria at Your Peril," *The Telegraph*, October 29, 2011, www.telegraph.co.uk/news/worldnews/middleeast/syria/8857898/Assad-challenge-Syria-at-your-peril.html.

143   But in February 2012: Wyatt Andrews, "Clinton: Arming Syrian Rebels Could Help al Qaeda," CBS News, February 27, 2012, www.cbsnews.com/news/clinton-arming-syrian-rebels-could-help-al-qaeda.

143   As the Violations Documentation Center: Glenn Kessler, "Are Syrian Opposition Fighters, 'Former Farmers or Teachers or Pharmacists'?" *Washington Post*, June 26, 2014, www. washingtonpost.com/blogs/fact-checker/wp/2014/06/26/are-syrian-opposition-fighters-former-farmers-or-teachers-or-pharmacists.

144 As Ambassador Frederic Hof: Frederic Hof, "Saving Syria is No 'Fantasy,'" *Politico*, August 11, 2014, www.politico.com/magazine/story/2014/08/mr-president-saving-syria-is-no-fantasy-109923.html.

145 he issued a general amnesty: "Assad Orders New Syrian Amnesty," *Al Jazeera*, June 21, 2011, www.aljazeera.com/news/middleeast/2011/06/2011621944198405.html.

145 Muhammad Habash, the former Syrian: Mohammed Habash, "Radicals Are Assad's Best Friends," *The National*, January 1, 2014, www.thenational.ae/thenationalconversation/comment/radicals-are-assads-best-friends.

145 There's a famous photograph: Joshua Landis, "Syria's Top Five Insurgent Leaders," Syria Comment blog, October 1, 2013 www.joshualandis.com/blog/biggest-powerful-militia-leaders-syria.

145 Future ISIS members were also amnestied: Ahmad al-Bahri, "ISIS Restructures Raqqa Under its New Ruling System," Syria Deeply, November 17, 2014, www.syriadeeply.org/articles/2014/11/6388/isis-restructures-raqqa-ruling-system.

145 according to the US State Department: "Designations of Foreign Terrorist Fighters," US Department of State, September 24, 2014, www.state.gov/r/pa/prs/ps/2014/09/232067.htm.

147 in January 2014, Major General Fayez Dwairi: Phil Sands, Justin Vela, and Suha Maayeh, "Assad Regime Set Free Extremists from Prison to Fire Up Trouble during Peaceful Uprising," *The National*, January 21, 2014, www.thenational.ae/world/syria/assad-regime-set-free-extremists-from-prison-to-fire-up-trouble-during-peaceful-uprising.

147 a twelve-year veteran of Syria's own Military: Ibid.

148 More intriguingly, Fares claimed: Ruth Sherlock, "Exclusive Interview: Why I Defected from Bashar al-Assad's Regime, by Former Diplomat Nawaf Fares," *The Telegraph*, July 14, 2012, www.telegraph.co.uk/news/worldnews/middleeast/syria/9400537/Exclusive-interview-why-I-defected-from-Bashar-al-Assads-regime-by-former-diplomat-Nawaf-Fares.html.

149 According to journalist Rania Abouzeid: Rania Abouzeid, "The Jihad Next Door," *Politico*, June 23, 2014. www.politico.com/magazine/story/2014/06/al-qaeda-iraq-syria-108214.html.

149 Among those making the journey: Ibid.

149 Major General Dwairi told the *National*: Sands et al., 2014.

149 Though his first point of contact in Hasaka: Abouzeid, 2014.

149 What has been established: Ibid.

149 Al-Jolani's cell allegedly waged: "Extremism Hits Home Stopping the Spread of Terrorism," *Per Concordian*, Vol. 5, No. 3, 2014, www.marshallcenter.org/mcpublicweb/MCDocs/files/College/F_Publications/perConcordiam/pC_V5N3_en.pdf.

150 Laith Alkhouri said.: Interview with one of the authors, November 2014.

151 Al-Jolani later explained to Al Jazeera: "Full Interview with Abu Mohammad al-Jolani," Internet Archive, posted by Abe Khabbaab (المهاجر خباب ابى), archive.org/details/golan2.

151 Al-Zawahiri issued two communiqués: Sheikh Ayman Al-Zawahiri, "Move Forward, O Lions of Sham," The Global Islamic Media Front, 2012, azelin.files.wordpress.com/2012/02/dr-ayman-al-e1ba93awc481hirc4ab-22onward-oh-lions-of-syria22-en.pdf.

151 Al-Zawahiri excoriated the al-Assad regime: Sheikh Ayman Al-Zawahiri, "Move Forward, O Lions of Sham," The Global Islamic Media Front, April 26, 2012, worldanalysis.net/modules/news/article.php?storyid=2125.

CHAPTER 10

157 The idea that a Kurd would join ISIS: Samantha Power, *A Problem from Hell: America and the Age of Genocide* (New York: HarperCollins, 2007), 244.

158 ISIS's spokesman, Abu Muhammad al-Adnani: "Abu Speech: Jihadist Kurds of Halabja Attack Lead 'Islamic State' Kobani," (كرد جهادي »أبو خطاب« »الدولة« »هجوم يقود حلبجة من ي على كوباني« (الاسلامية Al-Quds Al-Arabi, October 10, 2014, www.alquds.co.uk/?p=233274.

158 Charities that were started: "Kuwaiti Charity Designated for Bankrolling al Qaida

NOTES

Network," US Department of the Treasury, June 13, 2008, www.treasury.gov/press-center/press-releases/Pages/hp1023.aspx.

158   after decades of proselytization: Salem al-Haj, "Issue: Islamic Tide in Iraq's Kurdistan File Historical Reading," (ملف العدد: الـمد في الاسلامي فـي كردستان كـ عراق ال قراءة تاريخية) Al Hiwar. February 7, 2014, alhiwarmagazine.blogspot.ae/2014/02/blog-post_5030.html.

158   In Syria the Kurdish turn to ISIS: Jordi Tejel, *Syria's Kurds: History, Politics, and Society* (New York: Routledge, 2009), 90, 102.

159   Al-Baghdadi's deputy: "Abu Muslim al-Turkmani: From Iraqi Officer to Slain ISIS Deputy," Al Arabiya News, December 19, 2014, english.alarabiya.net/en/perspective/profiles/2014/12/19/Abu-Muslim-al-Turkmani-From-Iraqi-officer-to-slain-ISIS-deputy.html.

159   Abu al-Athir al-Absi: Radwan Mortada, "Al-Qaeda Leaks II: Baghdadi Loses His Shadow," *Al-Akhbar*, January 14, 2014, english.al-akhbar.com/node/18219.

159   Al-Absi formed a group: Suhaib Anjarini, "The War in Syria: ISIS's most Succesful Investment Yet," *Al-Akhbar*, June 11, 2014, english.al-akhbar.com/node/20133.

159   Al-Absi took a hard line: Mortada, 2014.

159   According to Wael Essam: Interview with one of the authors, November 2014.

160   Al-Absi was one of his staunchest defenders: Anjarini, 2014.

161   others fell out with their original insurgencies: Mitchell Prother, "ISIS's Victories May Win It Recruits from Rival Syrian Rebel Groups," McClatchy DC, June 23, 2014, www.mcclatchydc.com/2014/06/23/231236_isiss-victories-may-win-it-recruits.html.

161   issued a joint statement disavowing: "Syria Rebel Factions, Including al Qaeda-linked Nusra Front, Reject Authority of US-Backed Opposition SNC," CBS News, Septembe 25, 2013, www.cbsnews.com/news/syria-rebel-factions-including al qaeda linked nusra front reject-authority-of-us-backed-opposition-snc.

161   In October seven Islamist groups: "Charter of the Syrian Islamic Front," Carnegie Endowment for International Peace, January 21, 2013, carnegieendowment.org/syriaincrisis/?fa=50831.

161   Some Islamic Front commanders: Joanna Paraszczuk, "Syria: Truce Between ISIS's Abu Umar al-Shishani & Ahrar ash-Sham on Eastern Front in Aleppo Province," EA Worldview, January 8, 2014, eaworldview.com/2014/01/syria-claimed-truce-abu-umar-al-shishani-ahrar-ash-sham-eastern-front.

161   Liwa Dawud, once the most powerful: "1,000-strong Syrian Rebel Brigade Defects to Islamic State," RT, July 11, 2014, rt.com/news/171952-thousand-strong-defect-islamic-state.

162   fighters from the Islamic Front: Yusra Ahmed, "Nusra Front Suffers Defections to Join Rival ISIS," Zaman Al Wasl, October 24, 2014, www.zamanalwsl.net/en/news/7205.html.

162   ISIS benefits from the absence: Ahmed Abazid, "The Muslim Brotherhood and the Confused Position," Zaman Al Wasl, March 28, 2014, www.zamanalwsl.net/news/48054.html.

164   In areas fully controlled by ISIS: Liz Sly, "The Islamic State is Failing at Being a State," *Washington Post*, December 25, 2014, www.washingtonpost.com/world/middle_east/the-islamic-state-is-failing-at-being-a-state/2014/12/24/bfbf8962-8092-11e4-b936-f3afab0155a7_story.html.

165   had a reputation as a drug dealer: Ruth Sherlock, "Bodyguard of Syrian Rebel Who Defected to Isil Reveals Secrets of the Jihadist Leadership," *The Telegraph*, November 10, 2014, www.telegraph.co.uk/news/worldnews/islamic-state/11221995/Bodyguard-of-Syrian-rebel-who-defected-to-Isil-reveals-secrets-of-the-jihadist-leadership.html.

165   Aamer al-Rafdan joined ISIS: Anjarini, 2014.

166   In an article for the *New Statesman*: Shiraz Maher, "From Portsmouth to Kobane: The British Jihadis Fighting for Isis," *NewStatesman*, November 6, 2014, www.newstatesman.com/2014/10/portsmouth-kobane.

167   by September 2014 the CIA calculated: "CIA Says IS Numbers Underestimated," *Al*

NOTES

Jazeera, September 12, 2014, www.aljazeera.com/news/middleeast/2014/09/cia-triples-number-islamic-state-fighters-201491232912623733.html.

167 Missionary jihadists who were driven: interview with one of the authors, November 2014.

167 ISIS benefited from the Assadist massacres: Interviews with Syrian activists and rebels, 2013–2014.

168 Armed with knives and light weapons: Kyle Orton, "What to do About Syria: Sectarianism and the Minorities," The Syrian Intifada blog, December 24, 2014, kyleorton1991. wordpress.com/2014/12/24/what-to-do-about-syria-sectarianism-and-the-minorities.

168 Videos of torture also showed: Rafida and Nusayris are derogatory terms for Shia and Alawites respectively.

168 Saudi nationals often point to: "Kawalis al-Thawra Program, 7th episode with Mousa al-Ghannami," (الساعة الحلقة بعة ال ثورة كواليس-ال الحلقة-السا-تطبيق-تحدود بين حكمة حكمة الشرع وجهل وعش داع) YouTube video, 36:13, posted by موسى الغنامي, December 20, 2014, www.youtube.com/watch?v=sYtJ0XNMoKI.

CHAPTER 11

170 Slightly overstating the power of social media: "Head to Head—Will ISIL Put an End to Iraq?" YouTube video, 47:27, posted by Al Jazeera English, November 21, 2014, http://youtu.be/XkJl9UbG2lo.

170 Two weeks before the fall of the city: Nico Prucha, "Is This the Most Successful Release of a Jihadist Video Ever?" Jihadica blog, May 19, 2014, www.jihadica.com/is-this-the-most-successful-release-of-a-jihadist-video-ever. Video can be found at ihadology. net/2014/05/17/al-furqan-media-presents-a-new-video-message-from-the-islamic-state-of-iraq-and-al-sham-clanging-of-the-swords-part-4.

173 This not only maximized its viewership: J.M. Berger, "How ISIS Games Twitter," *The Atlantic*, June 16, 2014, www.theatlantic.com/international/archive/2014/06/isis-iraq-twitter-social-media-strategy/372856.

175 In the videos, this hadith is recited: "The Failed Crusade," *Dabiq*, Issue 4, October 2014, media.clarionproject.org/files/islamic-state/islamic-state-isis-magazine-Issue-4-the-failed-crusade.pdf.

175 Al-Baghdadi claimed to be a descendent: Hashim, 2014.

177 One of ISIS's governors, Hussam Naji Allami: "Mufti 'Daash' Legitimate: Hedma Shrines of Mosul, on the Basis of the 'Modern Prophetic,'" Al-Ghad, November 17, 2014, www. alghad.com/articles/836900.

177 the US State Department created a Twitter: Think AgainTurn Away, Twitter post, January 15, 2015, 11:04 a.m., twitter.com/ThinkAgain_DOS/status/555802610083852289.

177 Three days earlier, as the world was recovering: Dan Lamothe, "US Military Social Media Accounts Apparently Hacked by Islamic State Sympathizers," *Washington Post*, January 12, 2015, www.washingtonpost.com/news/checkpoint/wp/2015/01/12/centcom-twitter-account-apparently-hacked-by-islamic-state-sympathizer.

178 Though the White House downplayed: Eli Lake and Josh Rogin, "Islamic State's Psychological War on US Troops," *Bloomberg View*, January 15, 2015, www.bloombergview. com/articles/2015-01-15/islamic-states-psychological-war-on-us-troops; "ISIS Supporters Just Hacked the US Military's CENTCOM Twitter Account." Vox, posted by Zack Beauchamp, January 12, 2015, www.vox.com/2015/1/12/7532363/centcom-hack-isis.

CHAPTER 12

180 as the Associated Press reported: Bradley Klapper and Kimberly Dozier, "Al-Qaeda Building Well-Organized Network in Syria: US Intelligence Officials," *National Post*, August 10, 2015, news.nationalpost.com/2012/08/10/al-qaeda-building-well-organized-network-in-syria.

180 And al-Zawahiri's exhortation had paid off: Bradley Klapper and Kimberly Dozier, "US Officials: al-Qaeda Gaining Foothold in Syria," Yahoo! News, August 10, 2012, news.yahoo.com/us-officials-al-qaida-gaining-foothold-syria-201207990.html.

180   The rebels were also growing: Julian Borger, "Syria Crisis: West Loses Faith in SNC to Unite Opposition Groups," *The Guardian*, August 14, 2012, www.theguardian.com/world/2012/aug/13/syria-opposition-groups-national-council.

181   In a survey of the opposition: "Syrian Opposition Survey: June 1– July 2, 2012," The International Republican Institute and Pechter Polls, iri.org/sites/default/files/2012%20August%2017%20Survey%20of%20Syrian%20Opposition,%20June%201-July%202,%20 2012.pdf.

181   On December 11, 2012, the US Treasury Department: "Treasury Sanctions Al-Nusrah Front Leadership in Syria and Militias Supporting the Asad Regime," US Department of the Treasury, December 11, 2012, www.treasury.gov/press-center/press-releases/Pages/tg1797.aspx.

182   In December 2012, Syrians held: Ruth Sherlock, "Syrian Rebels Defy US and Pledge Allegiance to Jihadi Group," *The Telegraph*, December 10, 2012, www.telegraph.co.uk/news/worldnews/middleeast/syria/9735988/Syrian-rebels-defy-US-and-pledge-allegiance-to-jihadi-group.html.

182   the first al-Qaeda agent to confirm: Rania Abouzedi, "How Islamist Rebels in Syria Are Ruling a Fallen Provincial Capital," *TIME*, March 23, 2013, world.time.com/2013/03/23/how-islamist-rebels-in-syria-are-ruling-a-fallen-provincial-capital.

183   US Marines had famously helped: Paul Wood, "The Day Saddam's Statue Fell," BBC News, April 9, 2004, news.bbc.co.uk/2/hi/middle_east/3611869.stm.

183   Suddenly Islamists had just toppled: Rania Abouzeid, "A Black Flag in Raqqa," *New Yorker*, April 2, 2013, www.newyorker.com/news/news-desk/a-black-flag-in-raqqa.

183   Pamphlets were distributed: Abouzeid, March 2013.

183   In the *New Yorker*, Rania Abouzeid reconstructed: Abouzeid, April 2013.

184   Al-Baghdadi didn't just confine his message: Rita Katz and Adam Raisman, "Special Report on the Power Struggle Between al-Qaeda Branches and Leadership," INSITE on Terrorism blog, June 25, 2013, news.siteintelgroup.com/blog/index.php/about-us/21-jihad/3195-special-report-on-the-power-struggle-between-al-qaeda-branches-and-leadership-al-qaeda-in-iraq-vs-al-nusra-front-and-zawahiri.

184   al-Jolani left absolutely no doubt: Ibid.

184   What followed was a brief media intermission: Ibid.

185   Al-Zawahiri thereby "dissolved" ISIS: "Translation of al-Qaeda Chief Ayman al-Zawahiri's Letter to the Leaders of the Two Jihadi Groups," accessed January 18, 2015, s3.documentcloud.org/documents/710588/translation-of-ayman-al-zawahiris-letter.pdf.

185   Al-Suri, who was killed: Thomas Joscelyn, "Al Qaeda's Chief Representative in Syria Killed in Suicide Attack," The Long War Journal, February 23, 2014, www.longwarjournal.org/archives/2014/02/zawahiris_chief_repr.php.

185   was a veteran al-Qaeda agent: "Sources in Aleppo, Syrian Net: Syrian Regime Released from Abu Musab al-Suri and his Assistant Abu Khaled, Observers See a Threat to Washington," Aleppo Syrian Net, December 23, 2011, Accessed January 3, 2015, www.sooryoon.net/archives/41907.

185   He had helped found: Caleb Weiss, "Caucasus Emirate Eulogizes Slain Ahrar al Sham Leaders," The Long War Journal, September 15, 2014, www.longwarjournal.org/archives/2014/09/caucasus_emirate_eul.php.

186   The brainchild of Sir Mark Sykes: James Barr, A Line in the Sand: Britain, France and the Struggle That Shaped the Middle East (New York: Simon & Schuster, 2012), p. 12.

186   The agreement was, and still is, a synecdoche: Ian Black, "Isis Breach of Iraq-Syria Border Merges Two Wars into One 'Nightmarish Reality,'" *The Guardian*, June 18, 2014 www.theguardian.com/world/2014/jun/18/isis-iraq-syria-two-wars-one-nightmare.

186   Al-Baghdadi had earnestly taken up: Constanze Letsch, "Foreign Jihadis Change Face of Syrian Civil War," *The Guardian*, December 25, 2014, www.theguardian.com/world/2014/dec/25/foreign-jihadis-syrian-civil-war-assad.

190   On July 11 2013, Kamal Hamami: Paul Wood, "Key Free Syria Army Rebel 'Killed

by Islamist Group,'" BBC News, July 12, 2013, www.bbc.co.uk/news/world-middle-
east-23283079.
190 "We are going to wipe the floor with them,": "New Front Opens in Syria as Rebels Say al
Qaeda Attack Means War," Reuters UK, July 13, 2013, uk.reuters.com/article/2013/07/13/
uk-syria-crisis-idUKBRE96B08C20130713.
190 Similarly, when ISIS "accidentally" beheaded: Richard Spencer, "Al-Qaeda–Linked Rebels
Apologise After Cutting Off Head of Wrong Person," *The Telegraph*, November 14, 2013,
www.telegraph.co.uk/news/worldnews/middleeast/syria/10449815/Al-Qaeda-linked-
rebels-apologise-after-cutting-off-head-of-wrong-person.html.
191 It kidnapped revered opposition activists: "Rule of Terror: Living Under ISIS in Syria,"
Report of the Independent International Commission of Inquiry on the Syrian Arab
Republic, United Nations, November 14, 2014, www.ohchr.org/Documents/HRBodies/
HRCouncil/CoISyria/HRC_CRP_ISIS_14Nov2014.pdf.
191 it established monopolistic checkpoints: Tareq al-Abed, "The Impending Battle Between
FSA, Islamic State of Iraq and Syria," Al-Monitor, July 31, 2013, www.al-monitor.com/
pulse/security/2013/07/syria-possible-battle-fsa-islamic-state-iraq.html.
191 ISIS sent a car bomb to the base: Lauren Williams, "Islamist Militants Drive Free Syrian
Army Out of Raqqa," *The Daily Star Lebanon*, August 15, 2013 www.dailystar.com.lb/
News/Middle-East/2013/Aug-15/227444-islamist-militants-drive-free-syrian-army-out-
of-raqqa.ashx.
191 ISIS then expelled the brigade: Ibid.
191 In late December 2013: Michael Weiss, "Has Sahwa Hit the Fan in Syria?" *NOW Lebanon*,
January 8, 2014, now.mmedia.me/lb/en/commentaryanalysis/529244-has-sahwa-hit-the-
fan-in-syria.
191 Among the buildings targeted: Ibid.
192 Fares had taken to comparing: Ibid.
192 "The reason Kafranbel became . . .": Ibid.
192 On New Year's Day 2014: Ibid.
193 the brigade accused it of exceeding: Ibid.
193 the Islamic Front stated in a press release: Ibid.
193 This new mainstream front, Saoud told us: Interview with one of the authors, January 2015,
193 The last group to join this budding Sahwa: Ibid.
194 If these demands were not met: Ibid.
194 On January 5 the Islamic Front announced: Ibid.
195 A quaky truce brokered: Ibid.
195 Al-Jolani blamed ISIS for the week: Ibid.
195 ISIS had raised a defiant slogan: Richard Barrett, "The Islamic State," The Soufan Group,
November 2014, soufangroup.com/wp-content/uploads/2014/10/TSG-The-Islamic-State-
Nov14.pdf.
196 Abu Omar al-Shishani . . . signed: Yossef Bodansky, "The Sochi Olympics Terror Threat has
Links to Camps in Syria that are Supported by the US," *World Tribune*, January 24, 2014,
www.worldtribune.com/2014/01/24/the-sochi-olympics-terror-threat-has-links-to-camps-
in-syria-that-are-supported-by-the-u-s.
196 On February 2, 2014, global al-Qaeda: Liz Sly, "Al-Qaeda Disavows Any Ties with
Radical Islamist ISIS Group in Syria, Iraq," *Washington Post*, February 3, 2014, www.
washingtonpost.com/world/middle_east/al-qaeda-disavows-any-ties-with-radical-islamist-
isis-group-in-syria-iraq/2014/02/03/2c9afc3a-8cef-11e3-98ab-fe5228217bd1_story.html.
196 His real name is Maysara al-Juburi: Abu Bakr al Haj Ali, "Abu Maria: The Nusra
Leader Behind the Split with IS in Syria?," Middle East Eye, November 14, 2014, www.
middleeasteye.net/in-depth/features/changes-jabhat-al-nusra-indicate-changes-entire-
battlefield-1875666927.
197 ISIS further claims: Nibras Kazimi, "The Caliphate Attempted," Hudson Institute, July
1, 2008, www.hudson.org/research/9854-the-caliphate-attempted-zarqawi-s-ideological-

NOTES

heirs-their-choice-for-a-caliph-and-the-collapse-of-their-self-styled-islamic-state-of-iraq.

198 A recent study conducted by the Carter Center: "Syria: Countrywide Conflict Report #4," The Carter Center, September 11, 2014, www.cartercenter.org/resources/pdfs/peace/conflict_resolution/syria-conflict/NationwideUpdate-Sept-18-2014.pdf.

198 By Damascus's own admission: Kyle Orton, "The Assad Regime's Collusion with ISIS and al-Qaeda: Assessing the Evidence," The Syrian Intifada blog, March 24, 2014, kyleorton1991.wordpress.com/2014/03/24/assessing-the-evidence-of-collusion-between-the-assad-regime-and-the-wahhabi-jihadists-part-1.

198 One advisor to the regime told the *New York Times*: Michael Weiss, "Trust Iran Only as Far as You Can Throw It," *Foreign Policy*, June 23, 2014, foreignpolicy.com/2014/06/23/trust-iran-only-as-far-as-you-can-throw-it.

198 Some of this may owe to ISIS's financial: Ibid.

198 As a Western intelligence source told the *Daily Telegraph*: Ruth Sherlock. "Syria's Assad Accused of Boosting al-Qaeda with Secret Oil Deals," *The Telegraph*, January 20, 2014, www.telegraph.co.uk/news/worldnews/middleeast/syria/10585391/Syrias-Assad-accused-of-boosting-al-Qaeda-with-secret-oil-deals.html.

198 Frederic Hof . . . wrote: Frederic C. Hof, "Syria: Should the West Work with Assad?" Atlantic Council, July 10, 2014, www.atlanticcouncil.org/blogs/menasource/syria-should-the-west-work-with-assad.

CHAPTER 13

201 It was this established patronage system: William D. Wunderle, *A Manual for American Servicemen in the Arab Middle East: Using Cultural Understanding to Defeat Adversaries and Win the Peace* (New York: Skyhorse Publishing, 2013).

201 the Baath Party regarded: Carole A. O'Leary and Nicholas A. Heras, "Syrian Tribal Networks and their Implications for the Syrian Uprising," The Jamestown Foundation, June 1, 2012, www.jamestown.org/single/?no_cache=1&tx_ttnews%5Btt_news%5D=39452.

201 Protestors called for *"fazaat houran,"*: " ماش - فزعة حوران - اهداء للثورة نم بش " بلاسعودية"YouTube video, 7:28, posted by Shaam Network S.N.N., April 1, 2011, www.youtube.com/watch?v=Y4ww1xUrHMs.

202 Overall, tribes account for 30 percent: Nasser Al-Ayed, "Jihadists and Syrian Tribes," Global Arab Network, November 6, 2014, www.globalarabnetwork.com/studies/13181-2014-11-06-11-53-28.

202 Because Deir Ezzor connects Syria: Peter Neumann, "Suspects into Collaborators," *London Review of Books*, Vol. 36, No.7, April 3, 2014, www.lrb.co.uk/v36/n07/peter-neumann/suspects-into-collaborators.

203 Sometime in the summer of 2012: Karen Leigh, "In Deir Ezzor, ISIS Divides and Conquers Rebel Groups," Syria Deeply, August 11, 2014, www.syriadeeply.org/articles/2014/08/5930/deir-ezzor-isis-divides-conquers-rebel-groups.

206 Members of the Karbala joined: Interview with Wael Essam, November 2014.

CHAPTER 14

220 They did not bomb the [ISIS] headquarters until June: Martin Chulov, "Isis Fighters Surround Syrian Airbase in Rapid Drive to Recapture Lost Territory," *The Guardian*, August 22, 2014, www.theguardian.com/world/2014/aug/22/isis-syria-airbase-tabqa.

220 "There is a clear shift in the ISIS strategy . . .": "ISIS Take over Syria Army Base, Behead Soldiers: Activists," The Daily Star Lebanon, July 26, 2014, www.dailystar.com.lb/News/Middle-East/2014/Jul-26/265226-85-syria-troops-killed-in-jihadist-advance-activists.ashx.

220 Assad's own cousin, Douraid al-Assad, is quoted as saying: YouTube video, 7:29, posted by Syria.truth, September 15, 2014, www.youtube.com/watch?v=zsA7FQywurU#t=11.

221 When the Syrian Air Force finally escalated: Anne Barnard, "Blamed for Rise of ISIS, Syrian Leader is Pushed to Escalate Fight," *International New York Times*, August 22, 2014,

www.nytimes.com/2014/08/23/world/middleeast/assad-supporters-weigh-benefits-of-us-strikes-in-syria.html.

221 "[I]t's imperative that, in addition to force, there be an appeasement . . .": Price et al., 2014.

224 "What they do is attack the weaker units . . .": Ghaith Abdul-Ahad, "'Syria is Not a Revolution Any more—This is Civil War,'" *The Guardian*, November 18, 2013, www.theguardian.com/world/2013/nov/18/syria-revolution-civil-war-conflict-rivalry.

224 In an obituary for Jazra, journalist Orwa Moqdad wrote: Orwa Moqdad, "A Rebel Killed by Rebels," *NOW Lebanon*, December 19, 2013, now.mmedia.me/lb/en/reportsfeatures/526509-the-enemy-of-the-enemy.

230 One military commander: Hassan Abu Haniya, "Structural Construction of the 'Islamic State,'" Al Jazeera Center for Studies, November 23, 2014, studies.aljazeera.net/files/isil/20 14/11/2014112363816513973.htm

233 Before that, ISIS was thought to have earned millions: Scott Bronstein and Drew Griffin, "Self-Funded and Deep-Rooted: How ISIS Makes Its Millions," CNN, October 7, 2014, edition.cnn.com/2014/10/06/world/meast/isis-funding.

234 Germany's foreign intelligence agency: "German Spies Say Isis Oil Isn't Money Gusher," *The Local*, November 7, 2014, www.thelocal.de/20141107/spies-say-isis-oil-isnt-money-gusher.

235 Zakat is extracted from annual savings:"Zakat FAQs," Islamic Relief UK, accessed January 18, 2015, www.islamic-relief.org.uk/about-us/what-we-do/zakat/zakat-faqs/#trade.

235 ISIS also imposes taxes on non-Muslims: The Islamic State blog, the-islamic-state.blogspot.ae/2014/02/blog-post_26.html.

235 While donations from foreign sponsors: US House Financial Services Committee, 2014.

235 ISIS seized millions of dollars: Bronstein & Griffin, 2014.

235 It has also seized large stockpiles: "Dispatch from the Field: Islamic State Weapons in Iraq and Syria," Conflict Armament Research Ltd, September 2014, conflictarm.com/wp-content/uploads/2014/09/Dispatch_IS_Iraq_Syria_Weapons.pdf.

EPILOGUE

236 in one of his first press conferences: Jay Solomon, "Prime Minister Haider al-Abadi Pledges to Unify Iraq in Fight Against Islamic State," *Wall Street Journal*, September 25, 2014, www.wsj.com/articles/prime-minister-haider-al-abadi-pledges-to-unify-iraq-in-fight-against-islamic-state-1411688702.

236 "The Americans approach us to leave . . .": Phillip Smyth, "All the Ayatollah's Men," *Foreign Policy*, September 18, 2014, foreignpolicy.com/2014/09/18/all-the-ayatollahs-men.

237 According to Human Rights Watch: "Iraq Forces Executed 255 Prisoners in Revenge for Islamic State Killings—HRW," Reuters, July 12, 2014, news.yahoo.com/iraq-forces-executed-255-prisoners-revenge-islamic-state-133400715.html.

237 On August 22, 2014, the Musab Bin Omair mosque: "Iraq: Survivors Describe Mosque Massacre," Human Rights Watch, November 2, 2014, www.hrw.org/news/2014/11/01/iraq-survivors-describe-mosque-massacre.

237 The Badr has lately been accused of: Susannah George, "Breaking Badr," *Foreign Policy*, November 6, 2014, foreignpolicy.com/2014/11/06/breaking-badr.

237 "The [United States] is basically paving the way . . .": Ibid.

238 Indirectly supported by US warplanes: "US Military Conducts Air Strikes Against ISIL, Airdrops Humanitarian Aid Near Amirli," United States Central Command, August 30, 2014, www.centcom.mil/en/news/articles/us-military-conducts-airstrikes-against-isil-airdrops-humanitarian-aid-iraq.

238 US Abrams tanks have been photographed: Josh Rogin and Eli Lake, "Iran-Backed Militias Are Getting US Weapons," BloombergView, January 8, 2015, www.bloombergview.com/articles/2015-01-08/iranbacked-militias-are-getting-us-weapons-in-iraq.

238 The Pentagon announced: Maggie Ybarra, "Pentagon: Most of Islamic State's Oil

Refineries in Syria Have Been Destroyed," *Washington Times*, September 30, 2014, www. washingtontimes.com/news/2014/sep/30/pentagon-most-of-isis-oil-refineries-in-syria-have.

238   Al-Abadi has claimed: "Iraq: ISIS Leader Baghdadi Injured, Stays in Syria," Al Arabiya News, January 20, 2015, english.alarabiya.net/en/News/middle-east/2015/01/20/ISIS-leader-wounded-and-stays-mostly-in-Syria-says-Iraqi-PM.html.

240   Even in the most fiercely contested battle for Kobane: Dan Lamothe, "US Air Strikes in Syria Are Now Dwarfing Those in Iraq, Thanks to the Fight for One Town," *Washington Post*, October 16, 2014, www.washingtonpost.com/news/checkpoint/wp/2014/10/16/u-s-airstrikes-in-syria-are-now-dwarfing-those-in-iraq-thanks-to-the-fight-for-one-town.

240   In October 2014 Defense Secretary Chuck Hagel: Phil Stewart and Steve Holland, "Hagel, Under Pressure, Resigns as US Defense Secretary," Reuters, November 24, 2014, www. reuters.com/article/2014/11/24/us-usa-military-hagel-idUSKCN0J81AK20141124.

240   in part because he cautioned: Justin Sink, "Hagel Memo Criticized WH Syria Strategy," *The Hill*, October 30, 2014, thehill.com/policy/defense/222354-hagel-memo-criticized-wh-syria-strategy.

241   Harakat Hazm (the Movement of Steadfastness) posted: "US-Backed Rebel Group Criticizes Syria Strikes," AFP, September 23, 2014, news.yahoo.com/us-backed-rebel-group-criticises-syria-strikes-192612603.html.

241   wrote Robert Ford, the former US ambassador: Robert S. Ford, "Remember Our Syrian Allies," *New York Times*, October 3, 2014, www.nytimes.com/2014/10/04/opinion/remember-our-syrian-allies.html.

241   In one strike, in the town of Kafr Daryan, Idlib: Josh Levs, Paul Cruickshank, and Tim Lister, "Source: Al Qaeda Group In Syria Plotted Attack Against US with Explosive Clothes," CNN, September 23, 2014, www.cnn.com/2014/09/22/world/meast/al-qaeda-syria-khorasan.

241   as one rebel media activist put it: Fidaa Itani, "Opposition Fighters Are Rejecting US-Led Strikes in Syria," *NOW Lebanon*, September 9, 2014, now.mmedia.me/lb/en/reportsfeatures/564118-opposition-fighters-are-rejecting-us-led-strikes-in-syria.

241   ISIS has pledged rhetorical solidarity: Tim Lister and Raja Razek, "Islamist Rivals in Syria Find a Common Enemy in 'Crusaders' Coalition," October 6, 2014, www.cnn. com/2014/10/06/world/meast/isis-al-nusra-syria.

242   Chérif was arrested before he could join: Rukmini Callimachi and Jim Yardley, "From Amateur to Ruthless Jihadist in France," *New York Times*, January 17, 2015, www.nytimes.com/2015/01/18/world/europe/paris-terrorism-brothers-said-cherif-kouachi-charlie-hebdo.html.

ACKNOWLEDGMENTS

The authors are profoundly grateful to those whose knowledge and experience helped to bring an awful story to life.

Our discussion of the early years of the Iraq insurgency and then the Sahwa owes enormously to our very own "Council of Colonels." Derek Harvey, Rick Welch, Jim Hickey, and Joel Rayburn, whose friendship is already a nice return on this investment—all gave hours of themselves to be interviewed and in some cases re-interviewed via frantic emails dispatched at 3:00 in the morning.

Major General Doug Stone ran the Sing-Sing for al-Qaeda in Iraq for a little more than a year, which was long enough for him to surmise that there were jihadists trying to *break into* Camp Bucca. Ali Khedery and Emma Sky explained how decisions taken in Washington, particularly toward the end of the Iraq War, affected fortunes in Baghdad (and Ninewah and Anbar and Salah ad-Din). Laith Alkhouri, whose job it is to listen daily to what terrorists are saying to one another, proved an excellent and humorous dragoman in what is no doubt a still-terrified Starbucks in midtown Manhattan. Shiraz Maher took time out of finishing his dissertation on jihadism to explain the various categories of foreign fighters flocking to join ISIS. Martin Chulov and Christoph Reuter, two of the finest Middle East correspondents in print, generously shared their own fieldwork with us to help us ferret out some of the more obscure details from the Syria conflict.

NOW Lebanon's Hanin Ghaddar, apart from being the bravest and most principled editor we know, allowed work originally written for her magazine to be reproduced in this book. Alex Rowell read our drafts in their early stages and, as ever, offered insights, which ended up in the final manuscript. Tony Badran, who has made a life's work of studying the House of Assad, illuminated Syria's collusion with the very terrorism it now claims to be fighting.

The *Guardian's* Paul Webster, *Foreign Affairs's* David Mikhail and Kathryn Allawala, and *Foreign Policy's* David Kenner commissioned essays from the authors that led to research about ISIS before there was a book. (*Foreign Policy's* Ben Pauker generously allowed a leave of absence from his pages that was only intermittently interrupted with passive-aggressive reminders that we were due back at work.)

Lidiya Dukhovich, Olga Khvostunova, Boris Bruk, Grace Lee, Dmitry Pospelov, James Miller, Catherine Fitzpatrick, and Pierre Vaux at the Institute of Modern Russia and the *Interpreter* were already accustomed to fielding menacing or bewildering phone calls from another part of the world before being treated to few award-winning examples of these from the Middle East.

Colleagues, friends, and family who were similarly indulgent, patient, or helpful in seeing this project to completion include Linda Weiss, Leslie Wilson, Augie Weiss, Michael Pregent, Chris Harmer, Jessica Lewis McFate, Farha Barazi, Mariam Hamou, Bayan Khatib, Nada Kiwan, Qusai Zakarya, Ammar Abdulhamid, Lina Sergie, Phillip Smyth, Mubin Shaikh, Mike Giglio, Borzou Daragahi, Hamdi Rifai, Mishaal al-Gergawi, Mahmoud Habboush, Craig Larkin, Abdulsalam Haykal, Ahmed Hassan and Abdulhamid Hassan, Kareem Shaheen, Sultan Al Qassemi, Iyad al-Baghdadi, Abdullah al-Ghadawi, Elizabeth Dickinson, Faisal al-Yafai, Nick March, Hussain Abdullatif, Ghazi Jeiroudi, Abdulnaser Ayd, Abdulrahman Aljamous, Mousab al-Hammadi, and everyone at the *National* and Delma Institute.

And the team at Regan Arts who put this book together in record time: Lucas Wittmann, Lynne Ciccaglione, and Michael Moynihan, along with Laine Morreau, and Danielle Dowling

Finally, Mustafa L. and John Bundock started out as fact-checkers on this book and gradually became research assistants. Any errors of fact or interpretation remain our own.